MEDIEVALIST COMICS AND THE AMERICAN CENTURY

MEDIEVALIST COMICS AND THE AMERICAN CENTURY

Chris Bishop

UNIVERSITY PRESS OF MISSISSIPPI • JACKSON

www.upress.state.ms.us

Designed by Peter D. Halverson

The University Press of Mississippi is a member of the Association of American University Presses.

Portions of chapter 6 previously appeared in "Beowulf: The Monsters and the Comics" in the *Journal of the Australian Early Medieval Association* 7 (2011): 73–93.

Copyright © 2016 by University Press of Mississippi
All rights reserved

First printing 2016
∞
Library of Congress Cataloging-in-Publication Data

Names: Bishop, Chris, 1965– author.
Title: Medievalist comics and the American century /
    Chris Bishop.
Description: Jackson : University Press of Mississippi, [2016] | Includes bibliographical references and index. | Description based on print version record and CIP data provided by publisher; resource not viewed.
Identifiers: LCCN 2016019880 (print) | LCCN 2016005810 (ebook) | ISBN 9781496808516 (ebook) | ISBN 9781496808509 (hardback : alk. paper)
Subjects: LCSH: Comic books, strips, etc.—United States—History. | Fantasy comic books, strips, etc.—History and criticism.
Classification: LCC PN6725 (print) | LCC PN6725 .B49 2016 (ebook) | DDC 741.5/973—dc23
LC record available at https://lccn.loc.gov/2016019880

British Library Cataloging-in-Publication Data available

To Jen, who brings joy and love and light into my life

Jenny kiss'd me when we met, jumping from the chair she sat in;
Time, you thief, who love to get sweets into your list, put that in!
Say I'm weary, say I'm sad, say that health and wealth have miss'd me,
Say I'm growing old, but add …
Jenny kiss'd me.
    —Leigh Hunt (1784–1859)

CONTENTS

ACKNOWLEDGMENTS ix

INTRODUCTION: Medievalist Comics and the American Century 3

CHAPTER 1. *Prince Valiant* (1937) 27

CHAPTER 2. *The Green Arrow* (1941) 49

CHAPTER 3. *The Mighty Thor* (1962) 73

CHAPTER 4. *Conan the Barbarian* (1970) 97

CHAPTER 5. *Red Sonja* (1973) 121

CHAPTER 6. *Beowulf: Dragon Slayer* (1975) 145

CHAPTER 7. *Northlanders* (2007) 162

CONCLUSION: The Stories Upon Which We Agree 176

NOTES 195

BIBLIOGRAPHY 215

INDEX 228

ACKNOWLEDGMENTS

This book started life as a research project sponsored by the John W. Kluge Center in the Library of Congress. The Kluge Center is a relatively new establishment (2000), but the library itself is the oldest federal cultural institution in the United States, and it houses the largest collection of books ever assembled in human history. It is also the single largest repository of comics. I am not an American, and so the fact that the Kluge Center would provide me with a fellowship in order to further my research stands as an act of particular generosity and extreme civility. I am very grateful to Carolyn Brown, who was director of the library's Office of Scholarly Programs during my fellowship; to Mary Lou Reker, who was so helpful in acclimatizing me to the library; to Jason Steinhauer, for his tireless coordination of academic life at the center; and, especially, to Travis Hensley, for taking such good care of us all.

The E. S. Bird Library at Syracuse University houses an extensive collection of Harold (Hal) Foster's original artwork, together with numerous boxes of his correspondence. I was very fortunate to have access to this collection during my fellowship with the Library of Congress and wish to thank Syracuse for all their help.

When I left the Kluge Center in 2013 this book was far from finished, and so I would like also to extend my thanks to the Australian National University, who, upon my return to Australia, provided me with a base from which to complete my work. The College of Arts and Social Sciences, the School of Literature, Languages and Linguistics, and the Centre for Classical Studies at the ANU have all proffered their gracious support toward me over the past two years, and for this I am very grateful.

I would like to thank my colleagues Bruce Moore, Rosemary Huisman, and Louise D'Arcens for their support of this project from the outset, for their many kind words, and for their thoughtful encouragement.

Finally, I would like to thank Gemma Betros, Tania Colwell, Simon Westgarth, Dave Jacquier, Callan O'Donohoe, and Wen Huang, who all volunteered to proofread drafts of this text at various stages of its incarnation. I apologize for my atrocious typing skills and stand in awe of your patient forbearance.

MEDIEVALIST COMICS AND THE AMERICAN CENTURY

INTRODUCTION

Medievalist Comics and the American Century

So we beat on, boats against the current, borne back ceaselessly into the past.
—F. SCOTT FITZGERALD, *THE GREAT GATSBY* (1925)

The paradox that lies at the heart of this study lies also at the heart of *The Great Gatsby*. Fitzgerald's most famous novel is both an exploration of the American Dream as it unravels in the skyscrapers and country estates of jazz-age New York, and a desperately nostalgic romance about an unworthy knight-errant and his futile pursuit of an imperfect grail. Today, almost a century later, we still find ourselves, like the novel's narrator, caught between the "dark fields of the republic" and an "old, unknown world."

The republic stretches before us. It is modern and modernist. It offers the promise of democracy and the freedom from superstition that only science can bring. And yet, with so much before us, still we stare back at the past, are drawn inexorably into it, borne back like Fitzgerald's characters, like King Arthur crossing over to Avalon.

Modernity would seem to be the essence of the United States: skyscrapers; superhighways; space flight; jazz. If anything stands as the antithesis of the modern, it must be the medieval, and yet, during the course of the past century, the American Century, American popular culture has continued to engage deeply and consistently with the art, music, and literature of the European Middle Ages. This engagement has been particularly pervasive in the creation of comics, those intrinsically modernist and undeniably American icons of pop-culture ephemera.

The principal purpose of the following chapters is to survey the history of the medievalist comic from its genesis in the 1930s through to the present, and to contextualize that survey within a broader American narrative. I will be arguing that these comics are not merely happenchance artifacts, but that each individual success or failure was both a result and an indicator of the centrality of certain American preoccupations within a broader cultural context. Moreover, I will be arguing that medievalist resonances, like those found in these comics, rather than generating cultural anomalies, work instead to integrate transnational and transtemporal realities into our contemporary experience, while challenging the inherent limitations of problematic schema such as "the medieval" and "the Middle Ages."

MEDIEVALISM AND MEDIEVALIST COMICS

Historians work with artifacts. They study landform and geography, archaeological remains, cultural institutions, social interactions, art, architecture—anything that might offer an insight into the stories of our species. Above all else, though, they read texts, and these texts are never straightforward.

Objectivity in history became an academic aspiration only in the nineteenth century, it was almost nonexistent before that point, so the great bulk of the texts we study lie like unexploded ordinance in the landscapes of our consciousness. We scrutinize them for bias, for distortions of the truth, for hidden agenda, for anything that might undermine their utility. We differentiate the biography from the hagiography, the private letter from the public communiqué, the chronicle from the romance, and we assign to each a relative, intrinsic worth. Our task is to weigh the evidence, rather than dismiss it, and to locate it within a greater, contextualized body of knowledge. For me, this labor of assessment is never more rewarding than when surveying the historical relevance of literature.

It is expected, now, that historians interpret literature in order to illuminate the complexities of the cultures with which they engage. It would be unimaginable, for example, to produce a social history of the interwar United States without also looking at the literary contributions of John Steinbeck, or Ernest Hemingway, or F. Scott Fitzgerald. Fitzgerald's magnum opus, quoted above, is now ranked among the greatest modern novels, yet when Fitzgerald died in 1940, fewer than 25,000 copies of the book had been sold. That same year, *Superman* comics were selling more than a million copies every month.

If historians study literature in order to understand culture, why then would we limit our inquiry to those texts that were least accessed by the majority of people? If so many Americans were reading comic books during the 1930s, 1940s, and 1950s, then we need to ask just how important those mass-produced pieces of disposable literature were. Do they reflect any greater truths about the society that created them? What factors contributed to their popularity? What effect did their mass consumption manifest? These questions lie at the heart of this book.

The comic book itself has become an essential icon of the "American Century," a term coined by *Time* publisher Henry Luce in early 1941. In that year, Luce's *Life* editorial urged America to leave behind isolationism, to embrace with missionary zeal the task of global democratization, "the triumphal purpose of freedom" as he put it.[1] Before the year was out, America's hand was forced, and millions of United States personnel began pouring into European and Asian theaters of operation. In their kits they carried comics, and these unpretentious, disposable magazines quickly became an integral component in the worldwide Americanization of popular culture.

As such, these comics are intrinsically modern, an essential "apparatus of modern culture," as Aldo Regalado has called them, and yet Regalado has also rightly elucidated the challenges to modernity posited by these same comic books.[2] The ambiguity of this comic book engagement with modernity becomes even more pronounced when we turn our attention toward medievalist comics—comics that utilize stories, characters, settings, and themes taken from the European Middle Ages. Furthermore, the use of terms such as these—the Middle Ages, medieval, medievalist—brings us immediately into an arena of academic debate, a debate presently preoccupied with the intrinsically problematic theory of medievalism.

My research has always played in the slipstream between history and literature, particularly popular literature. The corpus on which I began my earlier research was drawn from the vernacular texts of the Anglo-Saxons, composed and compiled in that long morning between the waning of Imperial Rome and the waxing of European modernity. The significance of this literature is not at all apparent in the original manuscripts in which it survives, nor in the commentaries contemporary with its production, and so my attention was drawn inextricably toward the Victorian scholarship that made of these early poems a national legacy and exploited them to further entirely political, usually Imperial, ends. While it is my intention now to bring that same methodology to a study of medievalist comics, it is important to state also that a focus on medievalist artifacts does not make this a work of medievalism per se. Medievalism will inform the discourse, naturally, but reception history is the primary objective of this study, a reception history heavily informed by modern historicism.

Medievalism, in its simplest sense, is a devotion to, or an acceptance of, the ideas, beliefs, customs, or practices of the medieval period. As such, the term itself would appear to be a simple noun constructed from a common adjective—were it not for the inherent difficulties of defining the word *medieval*. The temporal demarcation of the Middle Ages is far from straightforward, and the ontological preconceptions upon which the concept is constructed are intensely problematic. Little wonder, then, that medievalism should enter the English language with a similarly contested association.[3]

The term itself first appeared in print in the middle of the nineteenth century. An article in the August 1844 edition of the *British Churchman* urged the thorough denunciation of "mediævalism," along with its "monastic or antisocial poison."[4] Another reference to medievalism in the *Southern Literary Messenger* of 1849 was correspondingly derogatory, equating the term with "Toryism, feudalism . . . all manners of retrogradism and rottenness in opinion."[5] Paradoxically, we know that the artist and poet Dante Gabriel Rossetti was using the term in a positive sense by 1851 and that, by 1853, the English scholar John Ruskin was extolling the virtues of medievalism in his public lectures.[6]

It would seem, then, that churchmen and politicians originally employed the term as a pejorative, and that nostalgic artists and intellectuals quickly rehabilitated it. It may be, however, that the word's entry into the written record as a negative was merely an accident of history and that medievalism had always carried with it an essentially contested interpretation. Certainly, that is the case today.

For some, medievalism necessarily implies an adherence to obsolete philosophies and the perpetuation of a cruel, uncivilized, or primitive past. This dystopian view of medievalism is most evident in analyses that embrace a narrative of human progress and emphasize the "March of History." Self-consciously "modern" and "scientific," dystopian medievalism impacts powerfully on the creative arts as well—it is the genius behind the lurid tales of the dungeon, the torture chamber, the immured nun, and the rat-borne plague. Although the creative capacity of this interpretation is seldom acknowledged, the Black Legend of the Inquisition, the Pied Piper of Hamelin, and the Man in the Iron Mask all come from the dark recesses of dystopian medievalism.

This rejection of the Middle Ages as a lesser time shares the same inspirational aesthetic that fueled the Reformation, and this means that dystopian medievalism has at its heart an essentially anti-Catholic bias, but this is not to say that all proponents of dystopian medievalism are Protestant, or even Christian. When political scientists discuss "neo-medievalism," for example, they typically promote a dystopian definition, but their dialogue is divorced from religion and the underlying principles of conjecture are essentially atheistic.[7] In these debates the point of comparison revolves around systems of sovereignty, with the transnational neo-medieval model serving as antithesis to the modern nation state.

Nevertheless, dystopian medievalism still operates within an essentially Protestant culture, no matter the espoused religion of the proponent (or lack thereof). By adopting a periodization of time that projects the Reformation as the end of a dark age, by separating the scientific, philosophical, and architectural achievements of medieval Europeans from the religiosity of their era, and by refusing to acknowledge the interconnectedness of the modern, medieval, and classical worlds, dystopian medievalism promotes a distinctive and singular construction of history—a construction that will be dealt with in greater detail in the final chapter of this work—but it is not the only medievalism available.

For many Catholics, their church embodies an unbroken apostolic lineage stretching back to Christ's first disciples. For these people, Luther's protest was not a defining moment in history. Nor for them is the time before the Reformation, when the authority of the church was accepted more universally in Europe, seen as inferior to the modern epoch. For some, this "Age of Faith," as Will Durant famously came to call it,[8] was an era of considerable philosophical and moral integrity.

Moreover, just as many proponents of dystopian medievalism are not Protestant, utopian medievalism finds many advocates outside the Catholic Church. Many people, Catholic and non-Catholic, imagine the Middle Ages to be a time of simplicity, spirituality, and positive authenticity. Less attractive to academia, it would seem, this utopian medievalism finds its strongest representation in architecture, literature, music, and the visual arts.

The persecution of Catholics in England began to ease with the passage of the *Papists Act* in 1778, which lifted from them the ban on inheriting or purchasing land, and removed from priests the threat of automatic arrest. The setbacks of the anti-Catholic Gordon riots notwithstanding, Catholic emancipation continued over the next few decades. Their numbers swelled with refugees from the French Revolution and, with the passage of the

Roman Catholic Relief Act of 1791, Catholics were finally permitted to operate schools and to worship openly. The following year, Dr. John Milner built a new church at Winchester in a style that was eventually to be termed the "Gothic Revival."

Milner publicized his new interpretation of a traditional style in 1798 with the first volume of his *History, Civil and Ecclesiastical, and a Survey of the Antiquities of Winchester*. The second volume of Milner's thesis found publication in 1801 and was followed shortly thereafter, in 1809, by G. D. Whittington's *An Historical Survey of the Ecclesiastical Antiquities of France with a View to Illustrate the Rise and Progress of Gothic Architecture in Europe*. The architect Thomas Rickman published his *Attempts to Discriminate the Styles of English Architecture* in 1817.[9]

This Gothic Revival offered English architects an alternative to the neoclassical forms that had dominated the local landscape since the Restoration. At a time when the new British Empire was establishing itself in opposition to France and America, polities whose art and architecture were self-consciously Greco-Roman in their reference, the Gothic Revival provided the British with an aesthetic that seemed if not more indigenous, then at least less foreign. Significantly, when fire destroyed the Houses of Parliament in 1834, the brief for their rebuilding stipulated that any proposal must be either Gothic or Elizabethan in its orientation.[10]

The contract to rebuild the Parliamentary buildings was won by the young Augustus Welby Pugin, and his 1836 publication of *Contrasts: or a Parallel Between the Noble Edifices of the Fourteenth and Fifteenth Centuries, and Similar Buildings of the Present Day* established both his own reputation and the preeminence of the Gothic Revival in England. When Pugin's ideas eventually began to filter across the channel, they found a ready audience.

Auguste le Prévost had translated Whittington's study into French more than a decade earlier, and when the newly appointed inspector-general of historical monuments, Prosper Merimeé, sought an architect to begin the restoration of France's medieval heritage, he encountered Eugène-Emmanuel Viollet-le-Duc. Viollet-le-Duc was heavily inspired by Pugin, although it would be true to say that his style embraced as much innovation as it did restoration, a fact that earned him the enmity of commentators such as John Ruskin.[11]

In England, the Gothic Revival was also inextricably linked to the Tractarian conversions of the 1840s. A similar controversy was never a possibility in France, still strongly Catholic despite the privations of both the

Revolution and the First Empire. In Germany, too, work on the cathedral at Köln was resumed about this time, partly inspired by the Gothic Revivalism of Christian Ludwig Stieglitz and his *Von Altdeutscher Baukunst* (On Old German Architecture), which had been published in 1820. Stieglitz had been commissioned to renovate the cathedral of St. Mary in Wurzen in 1817, but his interest in utopian medievalism was evident as early as 1787, when he published his *Erzehlungen aus den Ritterzeiten* (Tales of Chivalry). Nor was the Gothic Revival restricted to Europe.

Catholics had initially represented a sizable minority in the Australian colonies, but, by the mid-nineteenth century, their numbers were being swollen by emancipists and free settlers, especially those from Ireland. In 1845, work began in Sydney on St. Benedict's church. Designed by Pugin, the church was finished in 1852. Just as in England, however, Pugin's designs were also being adopted in a number of Anglican dioceses.

The widespread acceptance of the Gothic Revival by English Protestants facilitated its passage into even the most anti-Catholic communities. The American Richard Upjohn saw nothing acceptable in Catholicism, but this did not prevent him from building Episcopalian churches in the style of the Gothic Revival.[12] Upjohn's work on projects such as the Trinity Church in New York became, in turn, instrumental in the establishment of both the Carpenter Gothic churches of the later nineteenth century and the distinct American Gothic style of the post–Civil War period.[13]

All these innovations in architecture were accompanied by concurrent developments in the visual arts. William Holman Hunt, John Everett Millais, and Dante Gabriel Rossetti formed their "Pre-Raphaelite Brotherhood" in 1848 with the intention of reforming art. The Brotherhood denounced the mechanical reproduction of the Mannerists and rejected Raphael's classicism, advocating a return to the intensity and detail of the Italian and Flemish art of the fifteenth century.

William Morris was part of the Pre-Raphaelite circle, and had been an apprentice to the Gothic Revivalist architect George Street, but his interests lay not in the high art of the Middle Ages, but rather in the everyday crafts of textile manufacturing, metalwork, and wood carving. With the help of Ruskin, who was also a patron of the Pre-Raphaelite Brotherhood, Morris established the "Arts and Crafts Movement" in the second half of the nineteenth century. His "Morris, Marshall, Faulkner & Company," founded in 1861, popularized medievalist furnishings and decorative arts among the emerging middle classes of both the British Empire and the United States.

The utopian medievalism of John Ruskin, the Pre-Raphaelite Brotherhood, and the Arts and Crafts Movement, however, was strongly Protestant, and Ruskin himself stood in solid opposition to architects like Pugin and Viollet-le-Duc who sought to restore ancient buildings. This brings us to an important point. Neither utopian medievalism nor dystopian medievalism are consistent philosophies. These terms are usually applied retrospectively to the products of people who are, in themselves, often trying to satisfy quite different agenda. Nor do either strains of medievalism necessarily seek fundamentally different things.

Dystopian medievalism ultimately seeks a way forward by rejecting a maladaptive historical past. Utopian medievalism, however, often claims, perhaps somewhat paradoxically, that the way forward can only be navigated successfully by returning to the past, albeit a nostalgic and often idealized past. This essential confusion that lies at the heart of medievalism is even more pronounced when we look at the literature that accompanied the nineteenth-century innovation, or preservation, in medievalist art and architecture.

Medievalism, either utopian or dystopian, was quickly adopted by nationalists throughout Europe. This is a perplexing phenomenon in itself. The politics of medieval Europe were essentially transnational. Rulers were forced to negotiate a complex path between a range of interrelated, and often conflicting, sovereignties. It was only with the waning of the church as the central authority that nations began to awaken to self-awareness, and yet medievalism was, from its outset, used as a refutation of transnational neoclassicism and as an expression of an anachronistic national identity.

Romanticism developed out of nineteenth-century neoclassicism, or possibly as a reaction against it, and quickly began rejecting transnational epics like the *Iliad* and the *Aeneid* in favor of more parochial, medieval works composed in the vernacular. These medieval languages were no longer spoken, of course, and so the antiquarians began to publish their translations into contemporary national languages. James Macpherson published his creative retelling of the "Scottish" Ossian cycle in 1762. It was followed by a German version of the *Nibelungenlied* in 1782, a Spanish version of *El Cantar de Myo Çid* in 1799, an English version of *Beowulf* in 1814, and a French version of *La Chanson de Roland* in 1837.

This utopian medievalism was then met by a second wave of dystopian medievalism as popular novelists began to use the Middle Ages as a virtual accomplice in tales of cruelty and perversion. It was at this time that works like Walter Scott's *Ivanhoe* (1820), Alessandro Manzoni's *Adelchi* (1822), and Victor Hugo's *Notre-Dame de Paris* (1831) established medievalism as a genre in its own right. To delineate the intentions, or even inspirations, of writers who, by the middle of the nineteenth century, had adopted facets of utopian or dystopian medievalism to inform their writing, would be pointless here. It is being done too well elsewhere, and it is not necessary to the purpose of this book.

Suffice it to say that once it had entered the realm of popular consciousness, medievalism never departed, and for every *Idylls of the King* (1842) composed by utopians like Tennyson, there was a contradictory *Connecticut Yankee in King Arthur's Court* (1889) by dystopians like Mark Twain—and these two works are as good a juxtaposition as any on which to end this section. Both works were important in their day and have remained so. Both works have influenced generations of writers who followed in their wake. Both works are intensely perplexing.

Tennyson's *Idylls* is a powerfully destructive piece of poetry. In illuminating his vision of this utopian past, Tennyson was guilty of engendering the same paralyzing nostalgia that has led commentators such as Isaiah Berlin and Umberto Eco to condemn medievalism in general.[14] And yet, as an audience, we do not know what to do with Tennyson's utopia. There seems to be an evil at the heart of it, and more than a passing acknowledgment that utopias are not for this world. In the end, we are left like Sir Bedivere, grasping an artifact we fear, and charged with an impossible task. Perhaps Tennyson meant for us to let Arthur go. If so, he was spectacularly unsuccessful—but no less so than Twain.

Twain's *Connecticut Yankee* was intended as an attack against exactly the sort of sentimentalism that Tennyson's *Idylls* espoused, but, in attacking the pomposity and backwardness of King Arthur's Camelot, Twain, possibly more than any other author, fixed Arthur in the cultural psyche of the United States. Twain turned his compatriots toward Camelot, rather than away from it, and, as we shall see in the next chapter, Camelot was to become an integral part of the American mythos.

Finally, even though the utopian medievalism of Tennyson and the dystopian medievalism of Twain would appear to be diametrically opposed, it must also be stated that both men admired the other. Twain read Tennyson, of course, and loved Malory, and we know that Tennyson "longed to hear" Twain lecture.[15]

More recent contributions to the scholarship of medievalism will become obvious through the footnotes of the following chapters, although it should be stated at this point that, for the purpose of this study, the term medievalism will be used in preference to neo-medievalism. Neo-medievalism is a neologism that was popularized by Umberto Eco in his 1973 essay "Dreaming in the Middle Ages" and has since become popular with some European scholars.[16] The term has been used derivatively to describe the intersection between popular fantasy and medieval history, as well as Postmodern engagement with medieval history in general.[17]

Hedley Bull also capitalized on the term in his 1977 publication *The Anarchical Society* in which he suggested that society was moving toward a form of "neo-medievalism" in which the individual's notion of liberty and a growing sense of a "world common good" would undermine national sovereignty. Bull predicted a multifaceted layering of transnational, national, and subnational organizations that might help "avoid the classic dangers of the system of sovereign states by a structure of overlapping structures and cross-cutting loyalties that hold all peoples together in a universal society while at the same time avoiding the concentration inherent in a world government."[18] More recently, Stephen Kobrin has also utilized neo-medievalism in formulating and describing his political theory about modern international relations.[19]

Ultimately, the differences between medievalist and neo-medievalist theories are relatively semantic. All commentators in this field, whether medievalist or neo-medievalist, have discussed why medieval themes continue to fascinate audiences in a modern, technological world and why romanticized historical narrative is still so widely used to clarify the confusing panorama of current political and cultural events. Competing medievalisms that concur, complimentary medievalisms that disagree—little wonder, then, that we end up in a situation where the premier academic journal dealing with medievalism today must devote four consecutive years of scholarship to its very definition.[20]

For the purpose at hand, though, it is important to note that the medievalism that has shaped American culture, that shapes it still, does not exist outside the medievalism of other nations. Rather, American medievalism has both been inspired by, and served as inspiration for, the medievalism of allied cultures—those of Great Britain and France in particular. Any discussion of American medievalism must, therefore, take the cultural history of these allies into account. Moreover, there is a demonstrable link between the medievalism of the nineteenth century—the nation-defining, self-legitimizing medievalism of Europe—and modern comic book representations of the "Middle Ages," but the transmission history subsumed within that link is circuitous, complex, and multidirectional.

Comic book medievalism is not a received ontology. It is not the simple product of a parental ideology transferred to an infantile and uncivilized recipient. It is a series of sustained and intricate evaluations, emendations, and transformations that have both borrowed from and informed the cultures from which they were retrieved.

For the purposes of the present work, therefore, we can agree at least on the lesser category of medievalist comics—comics that utilize components ascribed to the European Middle Ages by the popular culture that created them. Whatever the truth might be of knights or Vikings or Sherwood bandits, the creators of the comics at which we shall be looking believed them to be representations of the Middle Ages, and the intended audiences for these comics believed that too.

THE MODERN COMIC BOOK

The principal artifact with which this study engages is the comic book. The modern comic book is a quintessentially transnational and transtemporal phenomenon. In Europe, illustrations have been an integral component of high-status codices for more than a millennium, and some texts, such as the early twelfth-century *Bible of St. Stephen Harding* now held in the Bibliothèque Municipale at Dijon, feature multiple pages of sequential, storytelling art.[21] In Asia, scholars have traced the continuity of the Japanese *manga* tradition from the twelfth- and thirteenth-century *Chōjū-jinbutsu-giga* (Animal-person Caricature scrolls), through the sublime talent of such luminaries as Katsushika Hokusai (1769–1849) and Kyokutei Bakin (1767–1848), and into the modern era.[22] For centuries these traditions developed in isolation from each other.

The sequential art forms pioneered by illustrators of prestige texts in early Europe devolved steadily into elliptical, clandestine sketches executed furtively in the margins of the great books. These marginalia, in turn, were appropriated by Renaissance pamphleteers and solidified into a recognizable "comic" art form—salacious, often antiauthoritarian, broadsheets that became stock-in-trade for European printers and that were used to balance ledgers against the more costly adventure of "serious" book production. The production quality of such *centsprenten*, combined with their content-matter, ensured that they remained undervalued by the "better classes." Undervalued, perhaps, but not unused.

European comics continued to be the weapon of choice for political satirists and social commentators throughout the eighteenth and nineteenth centuries. William Hogarth (1697–1764) not only reproduced prints of his most famous paintings for popular consumption, but also utilized simple etchings for public moralizing—*Gin Lane* and *The Four Stages of Cruelty*, for example, in 1751. In the years following Hogarth, this artistic form became so ubiquitous to British politics that magazines such as *Punch*, established in 1841, sold themselves on the reputations of their cartoonists, while continental illustrators such as Rodolphe Töpffer (1799–1846) transformed the medium through the lens of Continental artistic sensibilities.

Meanwhile, the introduction of Western lithographic techniques into China during the nineteenth century also facilitated the advent of the *manhua* comic book tradition there,[23] and European contact with the visual arts of Imperial China and Meiji Japan shifted the focus of some European artists even further. The engagement of Impressionists such as Claude Monet (1840–1926) and Edgar Degas (1834–1917) with Japanese Ukiyo-E saw them embrace a stronger linear aesthetic. As *Japonisme* bled from the salons of the Rue de Rivoli into the posters of the *Moulin Rouge*, and transformed itself into the sumptuous lines of the Art Nouveau, comic art began to temper its popularity with a newfound respectability.

A worsening economic climate in the later nineteenth century combined with limited prospects of social advancement to drive millions of Europeans into the arms of the United States. Artists of this continental diaspora began to ink popular cartoons for newspapermen like Joseph Pulitzer and William Randolph Hearst—men who saw new markets for popular entertainment in the burgeoning immigrant slums. Richard Outcault's *The Yellow Kid* debuted in Pulitzer's *New York World* in 1895, before moving to Hearst's *New York Journal* two years later. Hearst had been an avid collector of comic art since childhood and it was his particular vision that financed comic-strip pioneers such as Rudolph Dirks (*The Katzenjammer Kids*, from 1897), Winsor McCay (*Little Nemo in Slumberland*, from 1905), George Herriman (*Krazy Kat*, from 1913) and, eventually, Hal Foster (*Prince Valiant*, from 1937).

Cartoons evolved into regular comic strips and these, in turn, evolved into discrete compendia within the newspapers—the funny pages, or just *Funnies*, as they came to be called. In 1931, San Francisco immigrant Yoshitaka (Henry) Kiyama took a series of episodic comics that he had written for the papers and published them in a single volume. Kiyama's *Four Students Manga* was the first comic book ever produced—written in California, printed in Japan, sold in America, and featuring characters speaking English, Japanese, and Cantonese.[24] *Four Students Manga* was to become a blueprint for a publishing phenomenon, as newspapers began to republish their comic strips in separate magazine collections beginning with *Famous Funnies* in 1933.

The flamboyant Malcolm Wheeler-Nicholson founded National Allied Publications in 1934 in an attempt to exploit this new market, but Wheeler-Nicholson found himself shut out by the established newspapers who retained absolute copyright on the work of their staff artists. His solution was to produce a magazine featuring all-original content, and in 1935 he published *New Fun: The Big Comic Magazine*. National Allied Publications, which was to become the corporate predecessor of DC Comics, launched a second title *New Comics*, later that same year.

In 1937 *New Comics* became *Adventure Comics* and a third title, *Detective Comics*, was added to their inventory. Soon after, National Allied passed into the control of Harry Donenfeld and Jack Liebowitz, and, in 1938, the first edition of *Action Comics* appeared. It was the first issue of *Action Comics* that famously introduced the world to Superman, and, by 1940, America was going superhero crazy.[25]

By this stage *Action Comics* were selling one million copies per month. *Detective Comics*, the home of Batman since 1939, was selling almost as many. New comic book companies were springing up across the United States and pandering to an ever-increasing market. When America entered the Second World War in 1941, superheroes were suborned into the war effort selling bonds, pushing propaganda, and entertaining the troops. The United States Army purchased bulk orders of comic books for their servicemen and women, and both Europe and Asia were flooded with these cheap, patriotic publications. By 1945 more than a third of comic book readers were over the age of twenty-one.

Bill Gaines spent most of the war peeling potatoes stateside for the United States Air Force. Like a lot of GIs, he opted for a government-sponsored enrollment at college after the war, but his father's death in 1947 saw him drop out to take over the family business. Gaines's father, Max (born Max Ginzberg), had started up Educational Comics in the 1930s. Max Gaines published illustrated Bible stories, but he had changed the name of his company to Entertaining Comics once they had broadened their portfolio to include superheroes. It was Max who gave the Harvard-trained psychologist William Moulton Marston an outlet for his "feminist" vision of Wonder Woman.

Marston, more famous for his contested role in the invention of the systolic blood pressure (or *polygraph*) test,[26] envisaged his Amazonian crime fighter as a woman of superior intellect and superhuman strength, and armed her with a magic lasso that forced those encircled by it to tell the truth. Marketed originally to Allied service women, Wonder Woman proved incredibly popular with GIs as well, so popular that the comics giant National purchased her (along with the other EC superheroes Flash, Green Lantern, and Hawkman) to team up with their own best-sellers Batman and Superman. By 1947 the only copyrights that National had left EC with were its Bible stories.

When Bill inherited his father's company, he set about building it up from scratch again, and he did so by playing to a market that he understood all too well—returned servicemen. The proliferation of "pulp" crime novels and sordid gangster magazines found resonance in the unspoken world of the demobilized veteran. It was the same dark vein of resentment and denial that ran through contemporary novels like Nelson Algren's *The Man with the Golden Arm* (1949), James Jones's *From Here to Eternity* (1951), and Sloan Wilson's *Man in the Gray Flannel Suit* (1955). Gaines knew what sold—horror, gore, misanthropy, and nihilism. By 1948 the American public was purchasing between 80 and 100 million comic books every month, compared to about 100,000 books. Gaines made a killing with sell-out series like *Vault of Horror* and *Tales from the Crypt*, but not everyone was happy.

Fredric Wertheimer was born into the prosperity of the Jewish-quarter in Munich, in 1895. As a young man he had corresponded with Freud, been converted to psychoanalysis, and immigrated to America. By 1934, when he appeared as an expert witness in a murder trial, he had changed his name to Wertham and become an American citizen. In 1954 Wertham was asked by the New York District Court if Brooklyn "Thrill Killer" Jack Koslow was sufficiently sane to stand trial. That same year Wertham published *Seduction of the Innocent* in which he described television as "a school for violence" and labeled comics as the source of delinquent behavior in adolescents.[27] Nineteen fifty-four was also the year of the Senate Subcommittee on Juvenile Delinquency hearings that focused specifically on comic books.

Nervous about the outcome of the Subcommittee hearings and the possibility of subsequent government regulation, a number of comic book publishers decided to form a self-regulatory body in order to circumvent the possibility of outright censorship. This body, the ACMP (Association of Comics Magazine Publishers), then created the CCA (Comics Code Authority), which remains in force today, but is now rarely consulted. The

CCA code was based on a seldom-enforced antecedent from the ACMP that had been drafted in 1948, a code that was itself modeled loosely on the 1930 Hollywood Production Code. The CCA, however, imposed many more restrictions than the ACMP predecessor.

The CCA of 1954 prohibited the comic book presentation of "policemen, judges, government officials, and respected institutions . . . in such a way as to create disrespect for established authority." Moreover, it added the requirements that "in every instance good shall triumph over evil" and discouraged "instances of law enforcement officers dying as a result of a criminal's activities." Specific restrictions were placed on the portrayal of kidnapping and concealed weapons.

Depictions of "excessive violence" were forbidden, as were "lurid, unsavory, gruesome illustrations." Vampires, werewolves, ghouls, and zombies could no longer be portrayed, and comic books could not use the words "horror" or "terror" in their titles. Even the use of the word "crime" became subject to numerous restrictions.

Where the previous code had condemned the publication of "sexy, wanton comics," the CCA was much more precise—there were to be no depictions of "sex perversion," "sexual abnormalities," and "illicit sex relations." Seduction, rape, sadism, and masochism were also specifically forbidden. Love stories were henceforth to emphasize the "sanctity of marriage" and those portraying scenes of passion were advised to avoid stimulating the "lower and baser emotions."[28]

There was one "base" emotion, however, that the CCA did not seek to curb, a desire that lay at the heart of the ACMP's rush to self-regulation, and that was simple materialism. The pittance charged for comic books at the newsstand went nowhere near paying for their production, let alone the salaries of the scriptwriters, artists, and editors involved. Comic book revenue came from advertising, and Wertham's most vociferous criticisms were reserved for the objects offered by mail-order companies in the pages of these superhero fantasies—guns, knives, skeleton keys, lock-picking courses, handcuffs, batons, martial-arts manuals—all manner of antisocial paraphernalia. The ACMP agreed to crack down on perversion, as long as they could continue to advertise these items.

Following the Senate Subcommittee hearings and the introduction of the revised CCA, the comic book industry went into decline, a decline not counteracted until the advent of the new-look Marvel Comics material in the early 1960s. Although Marvel Comics had been in business since 1939, trading first as Timely Publications and then as Atlas Comics, their genesis as a publishing superpower began in 1961 when editor Stan Lee changed the company name and launched the first of their superhero titles *The Fantastic Four*.[29]

Marvel soon began to set the pace for comic books by introducing darker storylines and morally ambiguous superheroes. Lee introduced characters from Greek and Norse mythology who morphed subtly from humans with godlike powers into actual pagan gods. The popular *Silver Surfer* series chronicled the plight of a world-weary intergalactic traveler enslaved by a demigod who forces the Surfer to scout out planets that can then be devoured. Superheroes like Iron Man began to doubt themselves and plunge into an abyss of alcoholism and despair.

The self-censorship of the CCA did not destroy public appetites for even darker themed comic books, though, and by the time Marvel was moving toward its ascendency, independent publishers were busily producing limited runs of "underground comix." Although these comix were not commercially successful at the time, they were influential in the minds of writers, artists, and editors of more mainstream publications.

By the mid-1970s, Marvel was producing horror comics (*Dracula, Werewolf by Night, Man-Thing*) and heroes who were demonstrably satanic (*Ghostrider, Son of Satan*), while still managing to stay (just) within the CCA guidelines. Sales had never been better. DC, unable to cope with the competition, collapsed in on itself, canceling more than two dozen of its own series in an attempt to reduce staff and publication costs—an event that came to be known as the "DC Implosion." Faced with imminent insolvency, DC looked to the pre-CCA past for inspiration.

DC was soon to recruit two new prophets of the dark (visual) arts. Alan Moore, self-styled anarchist and practicing warlock, took *Saga of the Swamp Thing* back to its roots in the pulp fiction of the 1950s, both in terms of artwork and storyline. Sales increased. By issue 31 (December 1984), the *Saga of the Swamp Thing* no longer appeared with the CCA imprimatur on its cover. Sales increased even more.

Soon after, Frank Miller resurrected Batman in *The Dark Knight Returns* (1986). The Boy Wonder was gone, and so was Bruce Wayne's philanthropy. In its place, Miller gave his audiences a vigilante fueled by hate, and mistrustful of the efficacy of the legal system—so mistrustful, in fact, that he opted for his own "rough justice" instead of the "rule of law."

DC encouraged Moore to publish new series. He produced *Watchmen* in 1986, a savage attack on suppression and heroism. "Who watches the watchmen?" he asked. The sales department must have said "just about everybody." *V for Vendetta* was resurrected from Moore's earlier independent days and, although the central protagonist was no longer a transsexual anarchist, there was still plenty of bile to be poured out on censorship, mass media, and the state—an inherently fascist institution in Moore's imagining. By 1989 the CCA was more ignored than consulted, and academics were arguing about the artistic merit of material that had been considered comic pornography only scant years previous.

Hollywood, unlike academia, had no doubt as to the value of the comic book, just reservations as to how best they might exploit the market. *Superman* (1978) was the first comic book movie to enter a top-ten grossing list. The 1980s saw another two superheroes manage the same feat—*Superman II* in 1981 and *Batman* in 1989. In the 1990s six comic book films featured in the top-ten lists. Since 2002, the lists of top-ten highest grossing films for each year have included at least one title drawn from a comic book franchise. Of the ten highest grossing films to date, four have been based on comic books—*The Avengers*, *Iron Man 3*, *Transformers: Dark of the Moon*, and *Transformers: Age of Extinction* have generated almost five billion dollars of revenue between them. Nor has Hollywood been content to limit itself to standard superhero comics.

The comic books that have been rendered into film have featured heroes taken from literature, Alan Moore's *The League of Extraordinary Gentlemen* (2003) for example, or heroes transposed into an imagined past, as with *The Rocketeer* (1991). Movies based on comic books have been used as a means by which to critique the very society that produces them—*Mystery Men* (1999), *Watchmen* (2009), *Kick-Ass* (2010), *Kick-Ass 2* (2013)—or to warn of dystopian futures—*Judge Dredd* (1995), *V for Vendetta* (2005), and *Dredd* (2012). They have portrayed gangsters as one-dimensional cartoon-noire characters—*Dick Tracy* (1990) and *Sin City* (2005)—and as complex characters in search of redemption—*Road to Perdition* (2002) and *A History of Violence* (2005). There have been comedy action heroes who operate under more or less "real-world" conditions—*Bulletproof Monk* (2003), *The Losers* (2010), and *Red* (2010). There have been historical comic book movies—*300* (2006); horror comic book movies—*30 Days of Night* (2007), *Blade* (1998), *Constantine* (2005), *From Hell* (2001); quirky comic book movies—*Weird Science* (1985), *Scott Pilgrim vs. the World* (2010); and even thoughtful, literate comic book movies such as *Ghost World* (2001).

With such a bewildering array of interrelated texts, modern commentators find themselves embarrassed for choice. In order, then, to narrow the focus, this particular study will concentrate on a single aspect of comic book analysis that offers a wealth of potential intersections between social history, popular culture, high art, and subversive literature.

MEDIEVALIST COMICS AND THE AMERICAN CENTURY

Central to this thesis, then, is the establishment of a reception history—the ways in which stories from a European past were translated into an American present, and the ways in which that comic book medievalism was then reinjected into an increasingly transnational and mythopoeic superstructure. Establishing that history is the principal purpose of this book.

Each of the subsequent chapters, therefore, takes as its starting point a particular medievalist comic. These comics have been chosen because each of them demonstrates a crucial development in the reception history of the Middle Ages, a significant moment in which the imagined Pre-Modern past of European America was transmitted, interpreted or, at times, created.

These three terms—transmission, interpretation, creation—will be encountered frequently in the following pages. In an ideal sense they represent three separate functions of a receptive equation, but such discrete divisions are seldom discernable. Medievalist comics certainly contain transmitted elements—stories, characters, settings, and themes transmitted from European antecedents. These elements, however, are often transmitted from a variety of sources, and this complex transmission history complicates, perhaps even obfuscates, any discernable authorial intention.

Moreover, although the intention of the medievalist comic producers (the writers, the artists, the editors) is to interpret these transmissions and to transform them into a product both recognizable and salable to a new intended audience, these transmissions rarely arrive unadulterated, they are invariably subject to transformative interpretations in the long process of transmission. It may be, at times, that we are witness to actual creation, to the invention of totally new elements, but, for the most part, medievalist comics are largely the product of processes such as polyvalent interpretation, redaction, and recension. At times, these process might be so drawn out, and the product so tangential to its original form, that the distinction between creation, interpretation, and even transmission becomes a semantic one.

Title multiplicity is, of course, the hallmark of the comics industry, and so, while each chapter bears the title of a single medievalist comic, the reception history detailed therein will, by necessity, encompass a number of other titles as well. Most of the comics discussed in each chapter will be of a similar nature—Arthurian comics in the chapter entitled *Prince Valiant*, for example—but sometimes quite different comics will be used to demonstrate antithesis. Although a great many comics will be discussed, it will not be necessary (perhaps not even possible) to discuss every medievalist comic ever produced, but every *major* medievalist title produced since 1937 will find representation within this work.

The chapters are ordered chronologically according to the year in which each of the title comics first came into production. This serves to create a linear framework with which to scaffold this history, although the greater narrative and subsequent analysis will range widely. Some reception histories dealt with here—those of Arthur and those of Robin Hood, for example—are inextricably intertwined, and so it will be necessary to move backward and forward temporally in order to elucidate this interconnectedness. Others will stand alone as products of their particular time.

The fact that I have chosen to focus my discussion on particular titles, however, and the fact that I have included a year in the title of each of my chapters, is far more than authorial expedience. These dates are important. The comics that serve as chapter titles are products of their time. Any commercial success enjoyed by each comic, each failure they suffered, was directly a product of their time. *Prince Valiant* emerged from a long Arthurian and medievalist dialogue that reached its peak in the 1930s. *Green Arrow* had its origins in the same dialogue, but developed in a separate way. *The Mighty Thor* was a sustained response to Germanic immigration. *Red Sonja* was a product of the feminist revolution. The purpose of this book is to demonstrate the ways in which a multitude of historical realities coalesced so that these comic book stories might bleed into the American consciousness.

That such an approach might sound unrelentingly historicist should be no cause for concern. This work does not propose an interpretation for the texts to be studied, but rather a contextualization for them. There are lessons to be learned from close analysis of the interplay of image and script, and many of these interpretations will remain valid even once removed from the time in which they are made, but the artifacts to be studied here are not on trial for their artistic or literary merit, they are sources for contextualizing a greater cultural history and it remains axiomatic to this thesis that they are inextricably bound to the times in which they were produced. It is precisely their incarnation as a time relevant artifact that makes these medievalist comics so integrally useful as historiocultural indicators.

The first chapter takes as its entry point the publication of Hal Foster's syndicated comic strip *Prince Valiant* in 1937. Foster's creation, ostensibly Arthurian, is neither an isolated nor an unprecedented manifestation of that strain of medievalism, but remains a significant locus on a vast spectrum of possibilities that ties together such disparate characters as Thomas Malory, Lord Tennyson, T. H. White, William Randolph Hearst, and John F. Kennedy. Foster's contribution to an ongoing Arthurian dialogue owed much to the vision of the American Realist painter Howard Pyle and his live-in student Newell Convers Wyeth, and it engages us immediately in an exploration of an American medievalism that is paradoxically nostalgic and modernist in equal measure—a medievalism that was to become a driving force behind the works of F. Scott Fitzgerald, Ernest Hemingway, John Steinbeck, and William Faulkner.[30]

If the tales of Arthur represent a literary revenant of the medieval elite—the world of kings, knights, and maidens fair—then the stories of Robin Hood and his merry band constitute the collective memory of popular counterculture. It will come as no surprise to find that the focus of the chapter entitled *Green Arrow* posits the legends of the green wood as the antecedent for this successful comic book series, but readers might be interested in the directions in which such lines of inquiry lead. Any look at Robin Hood leads inevitably to the contested medievalisms of James Macpherson and Thomas Percy, but the relationship of these men with Samuel Johnson, and the democratization of their vision through the work of the American scholar Francis James Child is something of particular importance to this study. Child, in turn, brings into our gaze the Boston Brahmin Charles Eliot Norton and, through him, the poet Henry Wadsworth Longfellow, before we return once again to Howard Pyle, whose singular vision, perhaps more than any other person, has shaped so much of how the twentieth century sees the Middle Ages.

In exactly the same way that *Prince Valiant* permits an analysis of American Arthurianism, and *Green Arrow* illuminates the American engagement with Robin Hood, so too our analysis of *The Mighty Thor* will allow us to shift our focus to the German and Scandinavian immigrants of the American Midwest and the transmission of their folk heritage through the scholarship of men like Rasmus Rask and Jacob Grimm, and through the questionable partisanship of men like Richard Wagner. These immigrant traditions were amplified, in turn, by the pioneering works of established Yankees like Longfellow, Wyeth, and Pyle, but also through the efforts of first-generation Americans Rasmus Anderson, Lee Hollander, Arthur Brodeur, and James Baldwin.

The Mighty Thor shares an immigrant history with *Prince Valiant* and *Green Arrow*, but, unlike them, it bears witness to the translation of a foreign song-cycle into an American vision. Like the Robin Hood legends, the Norse tales that lay at the heart of *The Mighty Thor* were not artifacts of a cultural elite, nor were the people who transported those stories representative of any patriciate themselves, but against the history of all those stories that never took root in the new soil, the success of this particular tradition deserves careful consideration.

Prince Valiant, *Green Arrow*, and *The Mighty Thor* are all exceptionally successful products, and this success is even more remarkable when viewed against the disposable nature of their medium and the abject failure of so many of their competitors. The point being made in these three chapters, however, is that America was predisposed to embrace these particular comic books through continuous exposure to European medievalism in the decades preceding their initial publication. Moreover, what is truly extraordinary in this story is the means by which the nationalistic and aristocratic ontologies of nineteenth-century European medievalism were transformed into an essentially democratic and radically popular American alternative.

With the chapter on *Conan the Barbarian*, the focus of this study shifts away from the intertranslation of this earlier medievalism, toward the establishment of the mythopoeic visions that dominate medievalist discourse today. Robert E. Howard's pulp-fiction heroes were born out of his experiences in the flint-hard mining towns of Depression-era Texas and out of his desire, perhaps, to escape them. He carried on intense friendships by correspondence with a number of other writers, among them H. P. Lovecraft, and Conan, Howard's most enduring character, was elevated from obscurity to celebrity purely through comic books. This chapter will contextualize that success within a greater analysis of fantasy literature, focusing in particular on the interrelationship of Howard's creations with those of J. R. R. Tolkien, and with the genesis of new and immersive fan experiences that included comic conventions, costume play, and fantasy role-playing games.

As surely as the impact of European medievalism had paved the way for *Prince Valiant*, *Green Arrow*, and *The Mighty Thor*, and Robert E. Howard's bleak vision of an imagined past had breathed life into *Conan the Barbarian*, the women's liberation movement, with its demand for equality and respect, could not go unanswered in the comic book universe. Red Sonja sprang from much the same place as Conan. A reworked character from a Howard pulp-fiction adventure, she was equally a creation of the comic book industry, springing from the same traditions, but drawing impetus from the so-called gender wars of the later twentieth century. In the chapter on *Red Sonja*, we track the fortunes of the "she-devil with a sword" against the complex narrative of a renaissance in female superheroes during the 1970s, a disturbing backlash against them in the 1980s, and a gradual movement toward equilibrium in the years that have followed.

Each of the five chapters outlined so far seeks to explain the success of a particular comic book within a historical framework of creation, transmission, and interpretation. Failure, however, can be just as illuminating as success, and so the sixth chapter looks at the alarmingly short-lived *Beowulf: Dragon Slayer*. That the Norse legends of Thor could translate into one of comics' longest-lived series, while a similar treatment of an English analogue could not make it past issue six, elucidates the specific requirements of a successful comic book interpretation. By the mid-1970s, when the Anglo-Saxon hero appeared in his own title series, *Beowulf*, the Anglo-Saxon poem, was yet to transition from an academic to a popular *milieu*, and a continuous and steadfastly nationalist interpretation made it very difficult for the poem's eponymous hero to get the sort of traction enjoyed by folk heroes such as Robin Hood or Thor. Subsequently, *Beowulf: Dragon Slayer*, despite the innate worthiness of its subject and despite the efforts of DC heavyweights like Michael Uslan, was doomed before issue one hit the newsstands.

The final of the comic book chapters is a study of the twenty-first-century series *Northlanders*, which began publication in early 2008 and ceased in 2012. What makes this comic book so interesting for the purposes of this study is not its medievalism, but rather its lack thereof. The series is set entirely within the geographical and temporal borders of what some might call the "Viking Age"—the world inhabited or raided by Scandinavians during the dark centuries before Snorri Sturluson began inscribing his *Prose Edda*. The artwork and storylines of *Northlanders* prepares the viewer for a medieval experience not dissimilar to that of Prince Valiant, but we are soon made aware that rather than viewing a stylized interpretation of the Middle Ages (as we might in *Prince Valiant* or *Beowulf: Dragon Slayer*), or the transposition of an imagined medieval past onto modernity (as is the case with *Green Arrow* or *The Mighty Thor*), or even the creation of an entirely new and mythopoeic medievalism (*Conan the Barbarian* or *Red Sonja*) in *Northlanders* we are witness to modernity transposed onto the Middle Ages.

The characters in *Northlanders* think, behave, and speak like film-noir gangsters, as the blood feuds and conquests of the northern Dark Ages mutate into barrio-style turf wars and gangland vendettas. The writer of the series made no attempt to portray the ontology of his Norse subjects or to represent historically the multifaceted culture from which they sprang—his goal was to produce a crime series based on seminal Yakuza films from the 1970s. This is not meant as criticism, of course. The series is exceptional in many ways and, for the purposes of this study, a nonmedievalist series set in the Middle Ages makes for a perfect and final counterpoint to our consideration.

The conclusion of this monograph is subtitled "The Stories Upon Which We Agree." This chapter consists of an extended meditation upon the nature and historical expression of medievalism, and the historiographical links between medievalism and feudalism, a term more commonly encountered in European, especially French, commentary. Much of this concluding chapter had originally been integrated into this introduction, but, although valuable, this section became so protracted that it threatened to undermine, rather than expand, the central thesis here explored, and so it was excised from the beginning and remaindered to its end. You will want to dive straight into the comic books, of course, and so I am removing a barrier that might have prevented you from doing so sooner—but, after you have made your way through the next seven chapters, a *digestif* such as this should serve to further contextualize, and hopefully intensify, my *discursus*.

Finally, brief explanations for two terms that appear at length throughout this study. Each chapter takes its name from a comic book that was published over a period of time and the commercial nature of the comic book series is an analytical axiom that underlies this study. Because these series were ongoing, and because they were published over a period of time, they serve as registers of public opinion. Comic book series that did not excite the public imagination, series like *Beowulf: Dragon Slayer*, failed, but the ongoing success of franchises like *The Mighty Thor* must tell us something about the societies in which they thrive. Subsequently, I have employed the term "comic book" throughout this study to differentiate the story-based sequential art that I am studying, from other similar manifestations such as cartoons, comic strips, and graphic novels.

The difference between a comic strip and a comic book might seem like a purely semantic argument in regards to *Prince Valiant*, which appeared for decades in the Sunday supplements of various newspapers. I would argue, however, that Hal Foster's creation is a serialized comic book, rather than a comic strip, because each storyline invariably appeared across a number of sequential editions of a Sunday newspaper, never in a single issue. Comic strips like *Peanuts*, by comparison, typically consist of three or four panels in which is contained both the story set-up and the resolution. It helps to know the characters in the panels, and this knowledge augments the humor, but the strip is essentially a single, self-contained story. *Prince Valiant* is not.

Secondly, you will note that I eschew the term heroine and superheroine throughout this book. There are few other avenues of historical research where one gets to use the term hero, but, when writing on comic books, it is a very common word indeed. While heroine is a well attested, antique, and grammatically correct variant of the male counterpart, the tendency in recent years has been to turn away from nouns that have been uselessly gendered. Actors act, for instance, and so we see their gender as increasingly irrelevant in regards to their professional capacities. Subsequently, we hear less of "actresses" these days. So too with heroes, or superheroes, who are just heroic, or even superheroic, irrespective of their gender. With the steadily growing number of transgender and gender nonspecific heroes emerging in modern comic books today, terms such as hero and superhero will certainly only increase in utility, while terms such as heroine and superheroine must surely go the way of the aviatrix, the lady doctor, and the teacheress.

CHAPTER 1

Prince Valiant (1937)

Life was not "one damn thing after another" then. It was one wonderful adventure after another... There was delight in work, happiness in service, joy in life—for we were young.
—WILLIAM RANDOLPH HEARST (1863–1951)

It seems appropriate to begin this chapter with a quote from William Randolph Hearst, that powerhouse of American publishing without whom there would be no *Prince Valiant*. When Hearst wrote these lines in his regular column, a few years before his death in 1951, he was not, of course, referring to the comic which had, by that time, been syndicated through his newspapers for some two decades—he was referring to his years as a young journalist, when he practiced that "glad sport" with a sense of satisfaction that he could, in his later years, no longer muster.[1] At the heart of the statement, though, in its wistful and melancholic nostalgia, lay the same aesthetic that fueled both Hearst's personal obsession with the medieval and the American people's engagement with the promise of Camelot, a promise that interpreted the poetry of Tennyson through the art of Howard Pyle, refashioned that interpretation into comics and musicals, and finally divested itself into the brief tenure of an assassinated president.

HAL FOSTER AND WILLIAM RANDOLPH HEARST

Few authors have been as influential on modern comic books as Hal Foster. Foster had never planned to make comic art his career and treated the industry with a certain level of equanimity his entire life. Even in his later years, Foster seemed unimpressed by both the world of comics and by his contribution to that world. "I'm not doing the kind of work that lasts for generations," he told Arn Saba (now Katherine Collins) in an interview recorded just three years before his passing in 1982, "(m)ine is a comic, during this decade or this century, and what people like this century might not be popular in the next one, and paper doesn't wear well."[2]

Foster had come to comic art via a most circuitous route. Born in 1892, he spent much of his childhood on the harbor of his hometown of Halifax, Nova Scotia. When his stepfather moved the family to Winnipeg in 1906, Foster left school in order to help support the family, but at nights he taught himself from books he had borrowed from the public library and practiced his drawing. His diligence was rewarded with a job drawing merchandise for a Hudson's Bay Trading catalogue. He turned his hand to gold prospecting and, together with his wife, Helen, whom he married in 1915, worked as a hunting guide in Ontario and Manitoba. In 1921, fed up with the opportunities offered in Canada, Foster moved to Chicago, where he began work for the Jahn and Ollier Engraving Company while taking evening classes at the Chicago Art Institute.[3]

Early in 1929, Foster was asked to illustrate a newspaper adaptation of Edgar Rice Burroughs's *Tarzan of the Apes*. By Foster's own admission the artwork wasn't particularly good, but it impressed Burroughs, who, in 1931, asked Foster to illustrate a Tarzan comic strip for the Sunday papers. Foster never thought much of Burroughs's writing and quickly realized that he could earn much more writing and illustrating his own strip. He began working on a medievalist comic he called *Derek, Son of Thane*. In the process of refining the strip he changed Derek to Prince Arn and, when the King Features Syndicate finally took up the strip, Joseph Connelly, the syndicate's general manager, suggested a further change to *Prince Valiant*.[4] The strip began publication on February 13, 1937.

The United Features Syndicate, which published *Tarzan*, had rejected Foster's pitch, but the project had personally excited William Randolph Hearst, whose publishing corporation owned King Features. Foster had pitched the strip to United out of courtesy, but Hearst had promised syndication of the comic more than a year before it was finished and, in order to assure himself of the acquisition, Hearst had offered Foster 50 percent ownership of the finished product, an exceedingly rare opportunity in the world of comics.

That Hearst should be so excited by Foster's new comic, and that he would offer such a good deal to obtain it, is explicable in more than just business terms. True, Hearst had lost the opportunity (via one of his subordinates) to buy the *Tarzan* series when it had been offered to King Features and the strip had turned out to be wildly successful, but there was more than just finance motivating Hearst's acquisition of the new Arthurian strip. Hearst was himself obsessed with the medieval world.

By the time Hearst had acquired the rights to publish *Prince Valiant*, he could already lay claim to a sizable collection of medieval objects. Hearst reputedly possessed the world's largest private collection of medieval armor, far outstripping his nearest rivals the industrialist Henry Ford and the banker Andrew Mellon.[5] In the early 1920s, Hearst had begun work on his 240,000-acre property at San Simeon, California, constructing a castle, which he filled with medieval furniture and artworks purchased in Europe.[6] In 1925 he bought an actual medieval castle in St. Donat's, Wales, renovated it and stocked it with even more antiques.[7] In 1927 Hearst purchased a third castle, Sands Point on Long Island, from Alva Vanderbilt Belmont. It was this property that served as the inspiration for the mansion in F. Scott Fitzgerald's *The Great Gatsby*.[8] *Prince Valiant*, therefore, appealed to Hearst's passion for the medieval, but it also appealed to his taste for comics.

Hearst was a fan of the comics. He maintained a collection of German comic books he had begun as a boy[9] and he was "deeply involved in choosing the contents of the ... comic supplements of his own papers."[10] Hearst's own King Features Syndicate owned the rights to a great many comic strips that appeared in Hearst's publications, and Hearst was known for his promotion of these strips. In 1896, Hearst famously acquired the popular *Hogan's Alley* strip from his longtime rival and publishing tycoon Joseph Pulitzer.

Pulitzer's *New York World* published Richard Outcault's *Hogan's Alley*, featuring the famous "Yellow Kid," from 1895 until 1896, when Outcault was offered a substantially higher salary to work for Hearst's *New York Journal*. Pulitzer, who retained the rights to the name *Hogan's Alley*, hired another artist (George Luks) to continue the strip and so, for a while, the Yellow Kid could be seen in both publications.[11] Indeed, the phrase "Yellow Journalism," the pursuit of sensationalism and profit at the cost of investigative integrity, came to be synonymous with both Pulitzer and Hearst through their association with the Yellow Kid.[12]

The Yellow Kid also became one of the first examples of successful cross-promotional merchandising. At the same time he was appearing in the funny pages of the *New York Journal* and the *New York World*, his image was gracing billboards, advertising pamphlets, and posters. Children were being encouraged to buy Yellow Kid sheet music, buttons, trading cards, chewing gum, and toys. Adults could buy Yellow Kid whisky and cigarettes.

Merchandising is a key element of the modern comic book industry, but the business today is typically orientated toward a younger market. To target adults with cartoon merchandising might seem odd, but this phenomenon needs to be contextualized within a more general appreciation of late nineteenth-century print culture.

Newspapers and magazines of the 1890s, publications like Pulitzer's *World* and Hearst's *Journal*, relied upon artists such as Hal Foster to sell their stock, in every sense. George Eastman's "Kodak" camera had only come onto the market in 1888, the year before Eastman started marketing celluloid film, so most photography still involved the use of photographic plates and unwieldy apparatus. As a result, newspapers relied on artists to illustrate their stories and an audience acclimatized to their use saw these illustrations as authentic. When a newspaper reader saw a drawing like Frederic Remington's infamous *Spaniards Search Women on American Steamers*, they were viewing a type of image they had become accustomed to seeing in schoolbooks, popular novels, and university texts.

Hearst had understood the power of these images even before he had ventured into the newspaper industry. In a letter to his father, mining tycoon George Hearst, the young William outlined his plans to reinvigorate the *San Francisco Examiner*, should his father allow it. Hearst saw "illustration" as being key to success in both circulation and advertising:

> The illustrations are a detail, though a very important one. Illustrations embellish a page; illustrations attract the eye and stimulate the imagination of the lower classes and materially aid the comprehension of an unaccustomed reader and thus are of particular importance to that class of people which the Examiner claims to address.[13]

The authenticity loaned to such illustrations by their constant use in instructive media, meant that audiences believed what they saw (like the monstrous liberties of the Spanish soldiers in Remington's sketch), but it also meant that the line between advertisement and information was extremely permeable.

This permeability was then augmented by the tendency for advertisements to use the same artists that illustrated news stories, so a detailed representation of a group of Roughriders, for example, might be interpreting a feature on the war in Cuba, or it might be selling toothpaste. Readers picking up a copy of the Sunday pages would drift from the Yellow Kid's strip straight into an ad featuring the same characters before they had realized what they were reading. Breaking down the barriers that separated news, advertisements, and comics was clever, and it was very good business.

The turn of the twentieth century was a critical watershed in the economy of the American newspapers. Before 1900, revenue had been generated primarily by circulation, but with advertising income climbing from $39 million in 1880 to $150 million in 1900, that balance was starting to tip—"circulation means advertising" said Pulitzer, "and advertising means money."[14] Hearst knew that the Sunday supplements were central to this equation. Daily newspapers were just that, daily. They were read one morning and then used to line garbage cans the next. Sunday supplements, on the other hand, had much longer shelf lives. They were miniature magazines that might be kept in circulation for weeks, they were passed around extended families and articles were clipped from them to be stored away. This meant that advertising in a Sunday supplement could be sold at a much higher premium.

Three months after taking over the *Journal*, Hearst had increased the daily circulation from 30,000 to 130,000, but his Sunday edition had not fared as well, so he head-hunted Morrill Goddard, editor of the Sunday *World*, and risked financial ruin by buying a full-color printing press.[15] This machine furnished Hearst with a considerable edge on his rival, and he began assembling a cadre of artists who could best exploit the new technology. Outcault was lured away from the *World*, and Hearst used his own *Bilder Bücher* (comic books gleaned on an earlier trip to Germany) to develop the *Katzenjammer Kids* with Rudolph Dirks.[16] In developing his funny pages, though, Hearst was interested in more than just the money, he seems to have been interested in the comics themselves, as demonstrated by his lifetime support of George Herriman.

George Herriman started drawing his *Dingbat Family* for Hearst's *New York Journal* in 1910. The comic often included an additional "basement" strip beneath the main work that chronicled the life and unconventional love of the Dingbat's cat, Krazy. By 1913, Krazy had a daily of his/her own (the gender of the cat was never resolved) and by 1916, *Krazy Kat* was a full-page comic.[17]

Krazy Kat was popular with the American intelligentsia. In 1924, Gilbert Seldes described it as "the most amusing and fantastic and satisfactory work of art produced in America today"[18] and e. e. cummings agreed to write the introduction to the first *Krazy Kat* compendium,[19] but the strip seems to have eluded the tastes of the general public and it became less popular over the years. By the time of Herriman's death in 1944, *Krazy Kat* was being published in only thirty-five newspapers. *Blondie*, by comparison, was being published in more than one thousand.[20] Nevertheless, Hearst remained an ardent fan of Herriman's strip and gave him a lifetime contract to produce the comic.[21] Hearst, it seems, loved the strip and was willing to continue its publication no matter what the public thought.

HAL FOSTER AND THE BRANDYWINE SCHOOL

For the most part, though, Hearst's tastes in cartoon art coincided with his readership. He knew, also, what popular comics could mean for his circulation numbers, and Foster's *Tarzan* had been very popular. Moreover, Foster's style was consistent with the advertising draftsmanship that Hearst had employed elsewhere in his publications, so the venture promised to keep liquid the border between the two disciplines. Even so, it must have come as a relief when *Prince Valiant* proved as well received with the general public as it had been with Hearst himself.

Foster was determined to reward both Hearst and his own readership. Whereas his *Tarzan* strip had been little more than "scratching" to illustrate a "tiresome," "ridiculous" script that he "despised,"[22] Foster now endeavored to bring to his comic art the same sort of veracity and attention to detail that he had demonstrated in his advertising layouts. As a young artist, Foster had been heavily influenced by the contemporary giants of advertising art—Maxfield Parrish, Joseph Leyendecker, James Montgomery Flagg, and, most importantly, Newell Convers Wyeth.[23] His appreciation of Wyeth's work, in turn, was to bring him into the artistic orbit of the Brandywine School.

Wyeth and Foster had a lot in common. Both grew up with an intense appreciation of the outdoors—hunting, fishing, and camping. In 1904, at the age of twenty-two, Wyeth determined to set out west in order to experience frontier life firsthand. Scribner's, the New York–based publishing company, agreed to commission some illustrated stories from Wyeth, thus funding a trip that ultimately saw Wyeth attending rodeos, witnessing Ute and Navajo festivals, and even, for a while, working as a "cowpuncher."[24] Subsequently, Wyeth's singular interpretation of American *realism* was an important force in the popular culture of his homeland during the early years of the twentieth century. He produced advertising as well as illustrations, and his work was well known to the American public through publication in magazines such as the *Post* and *Harper's Monthly*, although, by 1914, Wyeth had grown to hate the commercial aspects of the art he was asked to produce.²⁵ Wyeth's interests, however, were not only focused on the dawning of the American Century. His view could be directed backward as well.

Wyeth appreciated fine art and maintained an unfashionable chauvinism for Romanticism and Realism.²⁶ He was acquainted, through his mother, with such American luminaries as Henry David Thoreau and Henry Wadsworth Longfellow. Later on, F. Scott Fitzgerald would become a frequent visitor to the Wyeth household.²⁷ Wyeth's particular engagement with the Middle Ages is witnessed by his illustration of an edition of *Robin Hood* in 1917, Arthur Conan Doyle's *The White Company* in 1922 and, in the same year, a reprint of Sidney Lanier's *The Boy's King Arthur*. This engagement, of course, can hardly be a surprise given Wyeth's mentorship by Howard Pyle.

Pyle, perhaps more than any other American, had worked fastidiously to transplant the stock of medievalist art into the soil of the New World and Wyeth had been a live-in student of Pyle from 1902. Pyle, who sustained a lifelong focus on illustration, produced work for magazines like *Harper's Weekly*, but it would be his dark, heavily lined, Düreresque images of pirates and knights that would secure for Pyle his place in the hearts and minds of middle America. The beginning of this new American aesthetic can be seen in Pyle's illustrations for James Baldwin's *Story of Siegfried*, first published in 1882, but by the following year, Pyle's own reworking of the Robin Hood legends was to make his career.

The Merry Adventures of Robin Hood (1883) was followed by the original (and medievalist) novels *Otto of the Silver Hand* (1888) and *Men of Iron* (1891). The success of these ventures meant that by 1894 Pyle had become "one of America's premier authors and illustrators."²⁸ In November 1902, Pyle began his serialization of the Arthurian legends in Scribner's children's magazine *St. Nicholas*. The success of the serial, coupled with Pyle's own celebrity, allowed him, in turn, to petition Scribner's for a considerable advance in order to finance a multivolume retelling of the Arthurian cycle, in substance much like his earlier *Robin Hood*, but more elaborate in its scope.

By this time, Pyle's own library of medieval sources was extensive. We know, for example, that he possessed Samuel Rush Meyrick's *Critical Inquiry into Ancient Armour*, Henry Shaw's *Dresses and Decorations of the Middle Ages*, Hugh Clark's *Concise History of Knighthood*, and Madame de La Curne de Saint-Palaye's *Memoirs of Ancient Chivalry*.²⁹ These last two editions were both published in 1784 and could not have been easy to obtain. Armed with his library, Pyle produced *The Story of King Arthur and His Knights* (1903), *The Story of the Champions of the Round Table* (1905), *The*

Story of Sir Launcelot and His Companions (1907), and *The Story of the Grail and the Passing of Arthur* (1910). These four volumes of Arthuriana quickly became the "classic" retelling for children and remain in print even today, more than a century later.[30]

Tennyson's *Idylls of the King* (1856–1885) had been intensely well received in the United States, of course, but it was the work of authors such as Sidney Lanier and, more especially, Howard Pyle who, by adapting the Arthurian stories for a younger audience, cemented the primacy of these legends into the emergent American culture. With parents reading aloud to their children, families shared the experience of this medievalist literature and, by adapting it for American tastes, writers like Pyle made that experience uniquely and intensely American. As a young man growing up in Canada at the turn of the twentieth century, it would seem impossible to imagine that Foster had not been exposed to Pyle's medievalism. It comes as no surprise then, that Foster's Gawain should be modeled so closely on Pyle's, or that panels and storylines from *Prince Valiant* should mirror those from Pyle's *Otto of the Silver Hand*.[31] While Foster was open about his admiration for the work of Pyle's protégé, Wyeth, he was no less indebted to the master himself.

To this legacy of Wyeth and Pyle and, to some extent, Tennyson, was added Foster's own meticulousness. Like Pyle, Foster had developed an obsessive attention to detail and, like Pyle, Foster fed that obsession with laborious research. It was this preoccupation that drove Foster to research his subject for some eighteen months before launching the strip. In fact, Hearst had offered the job to Foster in 1935, but the artist had delayed taking up the position until he had sufficiently researched his topic and come up with a look and a series of storylines with which he was happy.[32]

The art available to Foster at that time was largely from what historians of the day referred to as the "High Middle Ages," the twelfth and thirteenth centuries, and Foster's research into weapons, armor, and architecture was largely restricted to that of the Crusades. Indeed, Foster had originally intended his work to be set during the Crusades, but decided against this in favor of storyline longevity—"it suddenly occurred to me, after the Crusades were over, what? Then I'd have to change the whole character of the story."[33] *Prince Valiant* maintained a high-medieval sensibility, of course—Foster argued that there was just not enough information available for him to illustrate a historically accurate fifth-century setting[34]—and it would it be this anachronistic depiction that became the model for the American imagining of Arthurian Britain in the decades to come.

During the Second World War, Foster was able to channel his previous research into a more historically accurate comic strip called *The Medieval Castle*. Wartime rationing meant that newspapers were asked to reduce their paper consumption. One way to achieve this was to reduce the size of the Sunday comics. *Prince Valiant* was to be rationed back from its full-page spread, but Foster circumvented this by producing a second strip to replace the missing panels of *Prince Valiant*. *Medieval Castle* followed the adventures of two young squires, Arn and Guy, at the turn of the twelfth century. The strip allowed Foster to execute his, by then, famous style in a completely historical setting, but it proved less popular that *Prince Valiant*, and finished late in 1945, less than two years after it began.

Prince Valiant, on the other hand, became one of the best-loved and longest-running comics of all time. Foster continued to draw *Prince Valiant* until his partial retirement in 1971 and continued to write the scripts until his complete retirement in 1980. Other authors and artists took over from Foster at that point, and *Prince Valiant* remains in syndication today.

HAL FOSTER AND CAMELOT

Influence is a difficult property to quantitate. We know that *Prince Valiant* was popular with Hearst's readership, and we know that his readership was huge. Full-color comics were a conspicuous feature of the Sunday lift-out sections of Hearst's *New York Journal*, and central to Hearst's strategy for growing his readership. So successful had this strategy become that, within a year of taking over the *Journal*, Hearst had boosted his Sunday readership from 54,308 to 408,779.[35] By 1935, when Hearst first asked Foster to come onto his staff, the *Sunday Funnies* boasted a paid circulation of more than 5,000,000,[36] although the actual readership may have been ten times that number. That would mean that almost one American in every two read Hearst's funnies. Hearst knew what people liked to read, and Americans, it seems, liked to read about knights in shining armor.

Hearst's own interest in the medieval was constant and abiding. His redevelopment of San Simeon and his acquisition of St. Donat's were themselves the product of a fascination he had developed during his first tour of Europe as a child, and then augmented during a second trip undertaken in his very early twenties.[37] During subsequent trips to the continent in the decades that followed, Hearst "ravaged" European collections in order to amass the "loot" that he would later use to furnish his castles.[38] In Hearst's fascination with all things old, however, we can easily discern certain traits that typify American medievalism.

During his first tour of Europe, Hearst developed a profound respect for both Charlemagne and Napoleon. Charlemagne's father, Pepin the Short, was the first of the post-Merovingian rulers of Frankia to replace the *de facto* power of the *dux* with the *de jure* power of a king. Charlemagne inherited the title of a king and, through a lifetime of struggle, transformed himself from a king into an emperor. Napoleon, of course, was a junior artillery officer from a newly conquered province who dismantled kingdoms and who made himself an emperor. These self-made men were perfect heroes for an emergent and egalitarian United States.

We know also that Hearst, during this first tour, was strongly drawn toward antiauthoritarian heroes as well (he was instantly taken with the story of Rob Roy, for example) and that, despite his interest in the ancient traditions of Europe, he was not impressed with what he saw in the Europe of his own time. He enjoyed traveling through Ireland, we are told, but he was distressed by the poverty of the people there and by the way that Irish men treated their "women and horses."[39]

It was, of course, this lack of equality and opportunity for women in Ireland that led to their large-scale migration to the United States during the nineteenth century. Irish women "were the only significant group of foreign-born women who outnumbered men" in nineteenth-century America and "the only significant group of women who chose to migrate in primarily female cliques."[40] Irish men also migrated in huge numbers, of course, and after the tribulations of the *Gorta Mór* (the "Great Hunger") from 1845, Irish immigrants became a major force in the American landscape. Hearst's governess, Eliza Pike, his "second mother," was Irish and had even taken upon herself the liberty of having Hearst baptized by her own (Catholic) priest.[41] From his earliest foray into politics, as candidate for the governor of California in 1882, Hearst had openly championed the Irish vote.[42]

Hearst's own migration from his Californian base during the closing years of the nineteenth century bought him into closer contact with the Irish power brokers of the eastern seaboard. Certainly by the 1930s he was in close correspondence with Joseph Kennedy. During the 1932 presidential elections, Hearst had funneled his contributions for Franklin Delano Roosevelt's campaign through Joe, and Joe, in turn, had promised to remain Hearst's "ally, defender and liaison."[43]

Released from active duty in late 1944 and then honorably discharged a few months later, Joe's famous son John F. (Jack) Kennedy began working as a correspondent for the Hearst newspapers in April 1945.[44] Upon marrying Jacqueline Bouvier in 1953, "Jack and Jackie," as they came to be known, spent one week of their honeymoon in the Beverley Hill's mansion of Marion Davies, Hearst's long-term mistress.[45] Jack was also close to Hearst's son, William Randolph Junior. Writing to thank Jack for sending him a copy of his book *Profiles in Courage*, "Bill" Hearst wrote that both he and his wife "think it's a swell piece of work, and are proud to know the author."[46]

Interestingly, Jack stayed at Hearst's castle in Wales as a young man. In 1938 Joe, American ambassador to London at that time, took Jack to the National Eisteddfod in Cardiff, and the two stayed at St. Donat's during the trip.[47] It is impossible to know, of course, how deeply such a visit might have impacted on the young Kennedy, but it must have reminded him, at the very least, of his boyhood fascination with Arthuriana.

We know from Jack's mother that he spent a considerable part of his youth reading and rereading his copy of *King Arthur and the Round Table*.[48] The association of John F. Kennedy with this palpable symbol of American medievalism becomes all the more poignant when read in the context of Jackie's comments following the assassination of her husband on November 22, 1963. Speaking on the phone just a week after his death, Jackie Kennedy famously told *Life* reporter Theodore H. White that the Kennedy administration "was Camelot" and implored the journalist to impress upon his readers that they should not "forget the time of Camelot."[49]

White's article achieved exactly that, and the association in the minds of most Americans today between Kennedy and Camelot is inextricable. That this should be so must speak to more than just the popularity of the man. It speaks about the collective desire of a nation to build its own mythos and to embody that mythos in a time and a place.

This desire to build Camelot in America had been building throughout the twentieth century. In the interview with White, Jackie Kennedy had said that "when Jack quoted lyrics they were usually classical," but that, at night, "before we'd go to sleep, Jack liked to play records, and the song he loved most came at the end of this record (the soundtrack to the musical *Camelot*), and the lines he loved to hear were *don't let it be forgot, that once there was a spot, for one brief shining moment, that was known as Camelot*."[50]

Camelot, with lyrics by Alan Jay Lerner and music by Frederick Loewe, was a loose adaptation of Terence Hanbury (T. H.) White's *Once and Future King*. White's tetralogy was finished in 1958 when the final installment of the series, *The Candle in the Wind*, was published in a composite edition with the preceding works *The Sword in the Stone* (1938), *The Queen of Air and*

Darkness (published in a different form in 1939 as *The Witch in the Wood*), and *The Ill-Made Knight* (1940). Lerner augmented White's scope by focusing on the tripartite relationship of Arthur, Guenevere, and Lancelot—a narrative tradition that had a long history in Arthurian romance, tracing its origins back to Chretien de Troyes and the conventions that emerged from his recension.

The new musical enjoyed immediate success upon its opening in 1960. After two years on Broadway, the show went on to tour the United States, Britain, and Australia. The original Broadway run won four Tony awards and the original cast soundtrack topped the American charts for sixty weeks. When Jackie Kennedy recited those lines, she knew she was going to be understood.

The success of *Camelot*, however, was not just a matter of some well-written tunes and a touching story. White's foundational series had its genesis in a world that was descending into war and voiced his confusion about the legitimacy of power and violence. Violence is an evil, and yet how can violence be opposed except by violence? The proposition of the *bellum iustum* (the "Just War") was a concept that had occupied both Augustine of Hippo and Thomas Aquinas. White's meditation upon the question revolved around concepts of nobility and chivalry as limitations to violence, all the time acknowledging the fragility of those concepts. The question, and White's tentative answer, struck a chord in the reading public, falling as it did on fields made fertile but earlier utopian medievalism.

Foster certainly took some of his leads from White. The character of Morgause did not appear in *Prince Valiant* until section number 763, published on September 23, 1951, by which time the first three of White's Arthurian novels had been in publication for more than a decade. Morgause, a relatively innocuous character in earlier versions of the Arthurian cycle, was introduced into *Prince Valiant* as a sorceress. White's interpretation of the character, based on his own conflicted feelings for his mother, Constance, was to become the dominant interpretation for the latter twentieth century and Foster's take is clearly influenced by White. A much earlier comic duel between "Sir Avoirdupois" and "Sir Malnutrition" was also likely based on White's depiction of the combat between King Pellinore and Sir Grummore Grummorson.[51]

Foster's comic, therefore, continued to stay in tune with the popular culture of contemporary America, as it gravitated toward White's vision and reinterpreted it. White himself was frequently engaged in lecture tours in the United States and, after he died in 1964, the University of Texas at

Austin acquired his archives. Ironically, the author of *England Have My Bones* (1936) was buried in Greece while his literary remains were shipped to America.

That White's vision found such easy purchase in America was itself due to the groundwork laid by the great American authors who preceded him, the so-called Lost Generation. The centrality of medievalism in the works of these writers is sometimes overlooked today,[52] and yet it seems hard to imagine an understanding of the works of Eliot, Fitzgerald, Hemingway, Faulkner, or Steinbeck that does not begin with the legends of Arthur.

In the wake of the Great War, Eliot saw the wasteland of Malory's King Pellam devouring the future, as if an entire generation had suffered the "dolorous stroke" Sir Balin had dealt the Fisher King: "I sat upon the shore fishing, with the arid plain behind me. Shall I at least set my lands in order?"[53] Francis Scott Fitzgerald's long-term fascination with medievalism led him to reinterpret the Grail quest in *The Great Gatsby* (1925), with Gatsby as the unworthy Percival and Daisy as the unobtainable grail. The legend of the Fisher King is also the basis for Ernest Hemingway's first novel *The Sun Also Rises* (1926). The Arthurian legends suffuse all the works of William Faulkner, although perhaps nowhere more so than in *Absalom, Absalom!* (1936), where the central character, Thomas Sutpen, "creates within his very coffin walls . . . fabulous immeasurable Camelots."[54] John Steinbeck never managed to complete his version of Malory's *Le Morte D'Arthur*, although *The Acts of King Arthur and His Noble Knights* was published posthumously in 1976. Even so, Steinbeck's work, beginning with his first novel *Cup of Gold* (1929), "drew extensively on Arthurian themes and images."[55]

White's tetralogy began to be published at the end of this wave of reinterpreted Arthuriana, but where the Lost Generation had modernized old story cycles to elucidate a truth about their experience of the world, White medievalized his anxieties about the future in order to create an inclusive, universal narrative. It should be pointed out, however, that *The Once and Future King* did not end America's engagement with modernized Arthuriana. In 1952, for example, Bernard Malamud published *The Natural* allowing readers to experience Perceval as that most iconic of all American heroes, the baseball player.

So it was that during the second half of the twentieth century, generations of Americans who had learnt to read from Lanier and Pyle embraced the medieval as never before. In Hollywood, medieval movies were being churned out by the dozen. Although there had been a few movies dealing with medievalist themes produced in America before the war, the 1950s, more than any other decade, was dominated by "knight" films. Starting with *The Flame and the Arrow*, *The Black Rose*, and *Rogues of Sherwood Forest*, Hollywood went on to produce some three dozen major motion pictures set in the Middle Ages during the decade from 1950 through to 1959, more than all the medievalist movies produced in all the other decades added together. Pyle's *Men of Iron* was filmed as *The Black Shield of Falworth* and released the same year as a live-action *Prince Valiant* movie (1954). In 1954, seven major motion pictures set in the Middle Ages were released. This happened again in 1957.

Jackie Kennedy's call to remember Camelot, then, could hardly have gone unheeded. It would seem that all America wanted to read, watch, or listen to in the decade leading up to her husband's inauguration was tales of knights and derring-do.

By the time that a cinematic version of *Camelot* found release, however, the bubble had burst and the motion picture fared poorly. Medievalist movies had become more intense and introspective during the 1960s. Movies like *The Agony and the Ecstasy* and *The Warlord* (both starring Charlton Heston and both released in 1965) had replaced Robin Hood and King Arthur. In fact, after watching *Camelot* fail so dismally at the box office, Hollywood would not revisit the Middle Ages with a major motion picture for more than two decades (*Robin Hood, Prince of Thieves* in 1991).

There is one final point to be made about the Kennedy association with *Camelot*. It seems particularly poignant that John F. Kennedy would be so inextricably linked with a musical that has, at its heart, a meditation upon adultery and betrayal. Teddy White, remembering his telephone conversation with Mrs. Kennedy years later, commented that she had told him "so many things that I realized should not be printed at that time."[56] Given the president's connection with Marilyn Monroe, it only adds to the poignancy to think that T. H. White's final Arthurian tome should be called *The Candle in the Wind*, a title now synonymous with the untimely death of that actress. Bernie Taupin, who wrote the lyrics to Elton John's famous hit, has always claimed that the inspiration came from something he read about the death of Janis Joplin, and no doubt that's true, but it is an eerie series of coincidences nevertheless.

HAL FOSTER'S *PRINCE VALIANT*

As a body of work, Foster's *Prince Valiant* remains strangely paradoxical. Essentially modernist in its oeuvre, the comic is set in the Age of Arthur. Ostensibly American in its outlook, the setting is mostly European. Undeniably democratic in its politics, the principal character is, after all, a prince. The success of *Prince Valiant*, therefore, lay in Foster's uncanny ability, if not to resolve those paradoxes, then to facilitate their peaceful coexistence.

Foster's artwork is unmistakably *modernist*. His artistic sensibilities were informed not only by his regard for Pyle and Wyeth, but also by long years of drafting advertising copy and illustrating catalogues. In the decade following the collapse of the Bauhaus in Germany, Foster was bringing the same Art Deco discipline to the new frontier of comic art. Moreover, *Prince Valiant* shares its naissance with the explosion of Social Realism in the United States and parallels can be drawn between Foster's art and that of Grant Wood, John Steuart Curry, and Thomas Hart Benton. Foster must have known of Diego Rivera's murals also, and could not but have been inspired by Santiago Delgado's medievalist contribution to the 1933 Chicago International Fair. How, then, did Foster harmonize his *modernist* artistic vision with the acculturated mysticism of the Arthurian legends?

In fact, Foster's attitude toward mysticism in general is difficult to fathom. The earliest strips clearly elucidate the standard topoi of the genre—witches, sorcerers, demons, and ogres. Against this, however, we have Valiant's own (very modern) skepticism, which is akin to that of Twain's Connecticut Yankee, Hank Morgan. There is also the wisdom of Foster's Merlin, who eventually tells the prince: "magic is but scientific trickery . . . and sorcery the art of implanting in the mind an idea, a belief, which the sorcerer can control."[57] Merlin's revelation comes late in the life of the strip, though, some twelve years into its run, and it is hard at that point to unremember all that has gone before.

The witch Horrit, introduced to the reader in the very earliest strips, seems to have genuinely prophetic powers[58] and, although the powers of the sorceress Morgan le Fey may come from psychotropic drugs, she does seem to be attended by demonic henchmen.[59] It is difficult, also, to imagine the potion concocted by Merlin to combat le Fey in this early storyline as "scientific" given its primary ingredient (le Fey's falcon) and its capacity to induce night horrors without being ingested. There is also Merlin's garden, filled with dragons, gnomes, fairies, and elves.[60]

The ogre of Sinstar Wood seems real enough, although it might be trickery,[61] but is it merely coincidence that Valiant's "cursed" sword Flamberge lives up to its reputation? The sword seems to make Val invincible and bonds inseparably with him. Even after Merlin tells us that there is no such thing as magic, Flamberge continues to act in an uncanny way, returning to Valiant after he throws it into the sea for instance,[62] and conspiring to kill an outlaw who tries to steal it.[63]

The story of the witch-woman and the Cave of Time seems difficult to explain scientifically as well. In a scene reminiscent of Thor's wrestle with Elli ("Old Age") in the *Gylfaginning*, Valiant enters a cave guarded by a witch-woman to battle with an old man, who subsequently steals his youth and overpowers him: "All contend with *Time* and all are vanquished" we are told.[64] The witch-woman returns Val's youth to him before he flees in terror.

During Valiant's protracted quest for Aleta, he also encounters the magus Belsatan and his wife, Acidia.[65] Acidia appears young and beautiful, despite being centuries old, and Belsatan is attended by a retinue of zombies. The old wizard can weave dreams, summon storms, call demons, and transport bodies magically. No attempt is made to explain these phenomena with science.

Prince Valiant lives in the days of Arthur, of course, and the decline of those days began with the quest for the Holy Grail, but Foster kept away from that subject for a very long time. It was only at the very end of the 1950s, more than two decades after beginning the strip, that Foster let Arthur's knight begin that quest.[66] Naturally, there is no "science" to the Grail, but perhaps in Foster's treatment of this topic, as in those other apparently otherworldly occurrences outlined above, we would do well to heed Merlin's earlier advice to Val. Magic may be scientific trickery, but Merlin had also warned the young prince about something else as well. "There are also great powers for both good and evil beyond material things," he told Val, "but of these I dare not speak."[67] Perhaps we are meant to interpret the inexplicable aspects of the *Prince Valiant* storylines in that manner, not as magic and sorcery, but as aspects of a religious ontology that Christian America could not help but believe.

Barbara Tepa Lupack has written that Pyle democratized "not only the Grail but also the concept of nobility itself,"[68] and we see in Foster's *Prince Valiant* the same process continued, perhaps even amplified. Dispossessed of his native lands, Prince Valiant's father, King Aguar, is forced to shelter in the marshes of Britain, but almost as soon as we are introduced to the young Valiant,[69] he is escaping into these swamps to find adventure. Val is joined in the fens by "a half-savage native boy"[70] who teaches the young prince how to hunt. Years later, Valiant meets the boy again and the two, now grown, become companions once more. The Briton is adept at fighting with a heavy staff and Valiant is keen to learn—"you taught me how to use the weighted net and staff," the young prince says, "now teach me this new way of fighting."[71] From the very outset, Foster is at pains to inform his audience that titles mean nothing when it comes to surviving in the real world, and that true nobility, the nobility of spirit, is a product of noble action rather than noble birth. This democratic sensibility continues throughout the entire run of Foster's *Prince Valiant*.

During Val's sojourn in Tambelaine, he becomes aware of the love between Melody, daughter of King Lamorack, and the commoner, Hector. Initially jealous, Val soon conspires to help the couple elope despite the inequality of their birth. When finally we take leave of the young lovers, they are entwined on a small boat, heading out to sea: "neither have they friends nor wealth ... yet all the gods on Mt. Olympus look down and envy them."[72]

The storyline *Back in the Misty Isles*[73] sees Prince Arn (the son of Val and his wife, Aleta) saved from drowning by the timely actions of a street urchin named Diane. Aleta realizes she has been so busy running the kingdom that she has failed to teach Arn how to swim and seeks to encourage his friendship with Diane. Arn is reluctant, though, because Diane is a girl. Aleta, therefore, declares Diane is henceforth to be considered a boy for "a year and a day." Interestingly, it is Diane's gender that serves as a barrier to her friendship with Arn, rather than her class. Later in the story, Diane becomes infatuated with Sir Gawain, Val's close companion. That Diane is a peasant and Gawain a knight of the Round Table appears as no barrier to her desires and when she eventually tires of him, Gawain seems somewhat put out.

In fact, the distinction between noble and peasant is never particularly clear in *Prince Valiant*. Val's companions seem to come from all variety of classes, or their class remains indeterminate. Peasants become knights and lords play at being peasants. In the storyline *The Matchmakers*,[74] for example, Prince Charles, son of King Harloch of Cornwall, is knighted following the Battle of Badon Hill. As the ladies of the court try to match young Charles with various noble companions, he upsets all their plans by marrying a homely peasant girl with whom he has fallen in love.

For his part, Foster had not originally wanted his titular character to be royal. Foster chose an Arthurian setting for his strip and had originally planned for his hero to be the son of a thane. It was King Features's executives who promoted Valiant from thane's son to earl's son to prince during the title development—"I didn't want to make him a prince or a king," said Foster, "because I thought that was a little ostentatious."[75]

Valiant's wife Aleta is, of course, liege of her own kingdom, the Misty Isles, where she rules in her own right as a sort of Amazon queen, but at the height of the Cold War, Foster had Aleta eschew despotism and appoint a "Senate" to take over the running of her country. In a speech to her former ministers, she places power into their hands, like the Senate of "Ancient Rome," putting aside her crown so that she can return to the equally noble role of wife and mother.[76] In doing so, Foster reminds his audience of the overwhelming importance of the family as a basic unit of society and demonstrates a uniquely subversive contribution to American medievalism—the "adventure" of suburban living.

It would be easy to dismiss the "folksiness" of prince Valiant's home life as stereotypical. Surely this is just like the family shenanigans we can see in any comic strip of the time—*Bringing Up Father*, *Blondie*, *Dennis the Menace*—but that is exactly the point. Foster has taken the recognizable family life of everyday Americans and injected it into the hyperreal world of Arthurian romance. Knights-errant slay dragons, or rescue damsels, or storm towers (and Valiant does all these things), but they don't change swaddling, or feed toddlers, or teach their children to swim. Foster's creation, though, was reflecting an American reality.

Following the victories in Europe and the Pacific, with millions of servicemen returning stateside, marriage rates in the United States soared. A 1948 *Parents' Magazine* article reported that 2,250,000 marriages had taken place in America during 1946, a 60 percent increase on prewar marriage numbers, and that by 1947 there were 14 marriages for every 1,000 Americans, giving the United States a higher rate of marriage than "virtually any other (country) in the world."[77] So too, it was in early 1946, after a long and complex courtship, that Foster finally allowed Valiant and Aleta to marry.

Foster was well aware of the genres he was crossing. In a panel appearing at the end of the wedding episode, he addressed his audience directly: "Now here, according to approved writers of romance, the saga of Prince Valiant should end. But the winning of Aleta is one thing, costing Val no more than his heart, but living with her is another story . . . and we think the story is worth telling."[78] America, it seems, agreed.

For the next three decades, Foster continued to interweave the stories of Val's knightly deeds with those of his wife and children. America watched as the Arthurian couple squabbled, separated, made up, had children and raised them. The Arthurian vision subsided gently into the American Dream. And Foster was explicit in his connection of the two.

Foster's strip was always subtitled "In the days of King Arthur," but when a long-anticipated reprint of the first three years of *Prince Valiant* was finally released in 1982, the publication was called *Prince Valiant: An American Epic*. The title page of each edition bears an original Foster drawing of Prince Valiant in his red, white, and blue livery standing before an American flag.

Prince Valiant was well acquainted with America, of course. The storyline *The New World* saw Val and Aleta journey there in 1947.[79] Prince Arn, Val's heir, was an American citizen, being born there in section number 551, and his nurse was a Native American "princess" called Tillicum. Tillicum later married Val's close friend Boltar.[80] Aleta, assumed to be a woodland goddess by the Native Americans, also promised that her American-born son would come back to help them some day, and Arn delivered on that promise in *Arn in the New World*, a storyline that ran for a year and a half in the mid-1960s.[81]

These "New World" stories also allowed Foster to demonstrate another of his unique talents—his capacity to draw the American wilderness. Foster's long exposure to, and deep experience with, the natural landscapes of both his native Canada and his adopted United States, imbued his drawing with an unequaled authenticity. Carl Barks, the famous Disney cartoonist, was a fan of Foster's work: "*Valiant* was beautifully illustrated," Barks said, "Each panel was a work of art."[82] Barks was particularly taken with Foster's coastal imagery and kept a panel handy as an exemplar from which to work.

Foster's capacity to anchor his strip within both the cultural and geographical locus of America was extraordinary. Where Pyle democratized Arthur's knights, and Wyeth popularized them, Foster made them American. It is little wonder, then, that his long-running strip became so central to the medievalist vision of so many Americans and so influential in the art of the comics that followed.

Carl Barks was not the only comic artist to use Foster's work as a model—the comic book legend Jack Kirby thought that Foster's *Prince Valiant* was "astonishing" and "beautiful."[83] Kirby took the mask made by Prince Valiant in the storyline *The Maid Ilene* as the inspiration for his own 1970s character *Etrigan the Demon*.[84] Arn Saba, the artist and comics' journalist who conducted possibly the last recorded interview with Foster in 1979, expressed a deep respect for the man and his art.[85] Marvel stalwart Wally Wood also admired Foster's work (although this didn't stop him from producing his own pornographic version of the strip, *Prince Violate*, in the early 1980s).

Boxes of correspondence held at the E. S. Bird Library at Syracuse University bear witness to a steady string of letters written to Hal Foster by aspiring comic book authors. Many wrote to Foster for stylistic tips or advice on getting into the business. Some—like Art Wood, Jim Logan, Jeff Anderson, Johnny Achziger, John Verpooten, and Tex Lowell—eventually became comic book artists in their own right.[86]

Joe Kubert (*Sgt. Rock, Hawkman, Viking Prince*) and John Severin (*Mad Magazine, Conan the Barbarian, King Kull*) were also fans—Kubert going as far as to say that Foster had "inadvertently fathered an incredible number of cartoonists."[87] Jerry Siegel reportedly based his later (iconic) visualization of Superman on Foster's Valiant, and Alex Raymond (*Flash Gordon*), Shelly Moldoff (*Green Lantern, Hawkman, Black Pirate*), and Bob Kane (*Batman, Robin, Joker*) "swiped" whole sections from the series.[88] Carmine Infantino (*Flash, Green Lantern, Bat Girl*) declared that Foster was an influence on his art. Anyone aware of Mike Mignola's work (*Hellboy, Batman: Gotham by Gaslight*), and especially his use of shadow and powerful blocks of color, would also realize his debt to Foster's earliest work, particularly the swamp scenes in *The Prophecy* storyline.[89]

Following the Second World War, *Prince Valiant* was exported worldwide. As *Prinz Eisenherz*, the strip enjoyed lasting success in occupied Germany. Translations soon began appearing in French, Italian, Spanish, Portuguese, and Dutch. The success of these translations in Spain inspired Victor Mora and Miguel Ambrosio Zaragoza to produce their own version of the hero. In 1956, *El Capitán Trueno* (Captain Thunder) appeared and remained in continuous publication for the next twelve years selling as many as 170,000 copies every week. At the height of its popularity, *El Capitán Trueno* enjoyed translation into Italian, French, Greek, and Portuguese. Meanwhile, *Prince Valiant* became popular in Australia, South Africa, Canada, Scandinavia, and throughout Latin America. Frank Frazetta produced his own derivative version (*Shining Knight*) for DC Comics.

Frazetta eventually moved beyond the world of the comic book to find acceptance as a multimedia visual artist. As such, he is not the only artist to admire Foster's skill, as demonstrated by letters to Foster in the E. S. Bird Collection from Robert Horvath and Philip Steele. This acceptance beyond the borders of comic fandom indicates Foster's impact on the wider world.

During his lifetime, Foster received an astounding number of cartooning and comic book awards, but more significant than those in the context of this chapter, is the praise and acknowledgment he received outside of his artistic fraternity. At a time when America was working hard to shut the comic book industry down, Foster was receiving the *Gold Medal Award* from the American *Parents' Magazine*. He was similarly exempted from the wrath of the *German Teacher's Journal* as they decried the proliferation of the American comic books that "fell into the hands of homeless children" from "the backpacks of alien soldiers" or "the bags of loose women."[90]

This makes particular sense especially when we consider the demographics of Foster's readership. Children read his comics of course, as did families sitting around the Sunday table, but a perusal of the correspondence held at Syracuse University indicates just how many of these readers maintained a lifelong attraction to *Prince Valiant*. A theme that emerges from the correspondence is the imagined authenticity of Foster's work, his historical accuracy. Students asked him questions on matters of history and Arthurian literature. Teachers used his illustrations as tools. University students encountered his work in lectures. The line between artistic license and authenticity that Hearst and Pulitzer had blurred decades before, is very much apparent in these letters.

Foster researched his work intensely, though he never claimed to be presenting accurate representations of a historical subject, indeed, just the opposite, but these claims were made for him by his readers or imagined by generations that consumed his work. Foster became the authority on the Middle Ages for so many Americans and, through the power of the American publishing industry, the world. When Foster met Edward, the duke of Windsor (and formerly King Edward VIII), in October of 1951, the duke, somewhat hyperbolically, called *Prince Valiant* the "greatest contribution to English literature in the past hundred years."[91] In 1955, the city of New Orleans chose *Prince Valiant* as the theme for their annual Mardi Gras, a choice they revisited for an unprecedented second time in 1967. Foster was invited to participate in the planning and execution of the 1964 New York World's Fair. When the John R. Minchew group wanted to develop a housing project called "Camelot" in the suburbs of Washington, scant miles from the house a young Senator Kennedy had lived in with Jackie, they asked for Foster's input.

CONCLUSION

How then do we assess the influence of Hal Foster on the medievalism of the United States? It would be easy to argue that, with so widespread a syndication, Foster's anachronistic vision must have been central to the American understanding of what the Middle Ages should look like. The 1954 *Prince Valiant* movie looked exactly like Foster's strips, and they, in turn, looked exactly like every other sword and shield epic produced during the boom decade. It is more difficult, however, to determine how much of this vision was Foster's invention, and how much of it was informed by the illustrations of Wyeth and Pyle, but certainly, when Hollywood reached for a visual vocabulary with which to define its narrative of medieval life, the lexicon it used was ultimately an amalgam of those three artists—Pyle, Wyeth, and Foster.

It is difficult, also, to separate the particular contributions of these three men to the medievalist sensibilities of postwar America because they shared also those particular preoccupations that made those sensibilities so distinctly American. What can be said, and what lies at the heart of this reception history at hand, is that Foster's work demonstrates a clear engagement with both its audience and with the world that audience experienced.

The birth of the American Century was witnessed by men and women who had grown up on the tales of King Arthur as illustrated by Pyle and Wyeth. When a lost generation of these Americans sought meaning in the aftermath of a brutal and mechanistic war, they framed their narrative in the familiar stories of their childhood and, as they did, Hal Foster's *Prince Valiant* brought to life a vision of a nobler time in a continuous series of meticulously drafted, polychromatic panels.

While the United States fought Germany, Prince Valiant battled the Huns. When the war was over, Val married his sweetheart, Aleta, and settled down to have children. Those children grew up in the temperate forests and verdant fields of North America—the same landscapes Foster journeyed through as a youth, the same landscapes experienced by his audience.

Foster's capacity to adapt his medievalist stories to reflect a contemporary reality was essential in securing his enormous fan base and, with it, his lasting success. Moreover, with such a wide range of important comic artists claiming Foster as their touchstone, it would be easy to argue that if American comic book medievalism did not come in large part straight from the vision of Foster himself, then it came from the vision of those whom Foster inspired.

CHAPTER 2

The Green Arrow (1941)

Robin Hood was, after all, a political activist fighting against a corrupt administration. What am I supposed to do? Steal from myself and give to the poor?
—OLIVER QUEEN (THE GREEN ARROW)

Prince Valiant was not the only cartoon hero to survive the collapse of the so-called Golden Age of Comics. Having debuted in 1941, just four years after the first *Prince Valiant* comic went into publication, the Green Arrow continued to fight injustice in the pages of *Adventure Comics* and *World's Finest Comics* until his rebirth as a Bronze Age[1] icon at the end of the 1960s. It was in this incarnation, drawn by Neal Adams and scripted by Dennis O'Neil, that Green Arrow would begin to dismantle the Comics Code Authority, perhaps the greatest blow for freedom that a comic book character could strike.

Green Arrow's debt to Robin Hood seems obvious, although early versions of the comic book superhero were reluctant to acknowledge this, but the continued success of the former is surely a byproduct of the long reception history of the latter. This chapter, therefore, will explore the complex relationship of the Green Arrow with his Sherwood antecedent. Robin Hood scholarship is dauntingly profuse, of course, and there seems little need to venture into exhaustive detail. Some salient points, however, must be illuminated by a brief survey of the material available—a survey that begins in eighteenth-century Scotland.

THOMAS PERCY AND THE "REBIRTH" OF ROBIN HOOD

James Macpherson was born in Ruthven, near Inverness, in 1736. He was educated in Aberdeen and claimed to speak Scottish Gaelic. In his early twenties he produced a series of "translations" which were printed as *Fragments of Ancient Poetry collected in the Highlands of Scotland*. The poems captured the zeitgeist of post-Jacobite Scotland and Macpherson was funded by public subscription to undertake an expedition to the Highlands and the Western Isles in order to recover more Gaelic texts. Macpherson claimed success in these adventures and proceeded to publish a series of "translations" in the early 1760s, culminating in a collected edition, *The Works of Ossian*, in 1765.

Irish historians, including Charles O'Conor, immediately challenged the authenticity of Macpherson's work and his credibility was seriously undermined. Samuel Johnson's *A Journey to the Western Islands of Scotland* (1775) asserted that Macpherson's "translations" were, in fact, compositions constructed from scattered fragments. Macpherson was never able to produce the manuscripts he claimed as his exemplars, yet his publications both indicated and fueled a hunger for "native" British epics nevertheless. Britons wanted their own ancient literature to augment, or even replace, the dominant paradigms they had inherited from Classical Greece and Rome and whereas Macpherson's contributions remained dubious, another text by Thomas Percy was to satisfy that desire.

Thomas Percy was born in Bridgnorth, Shropshire, in 1729 and was educated at Christ Church, Oxford. In 1753 he was appointed vicar of Easton Maudit, in Northamptonshire and, at about that time, he came into possession of a singular book through quite remarkable circumstances:

> Percy had paid visit to Humphrey Pitt, an old Salopian friend. While there, he noticed that the maids in the parlour were lighting the fire with a bundle of paper that had been lying under a bureau. It was a poetry miscellany, transcribed by hand into a folio book, and Percy, enthralled, asked if he might have the curiosity before it was entirely consumed. He thereby acquired a seventeenth-century commonplace book containing transcripts of ballads, metrical romances, and popular songs, many of which he later learned were extant solely in this "Folio MS."[2]

Upon close reading, Percy realized that the manuscript represented more than just an oddity—it was a unique vestige of the lost world of the English minstrel.

If Percy was fortunate to have found such a treasure, he was equally fortunate in his friends. Humphrey Pitt had the friendship of the poet William Shenstone and thus served as the conduit through which Percy and Shenstone might meet. Shenstone was instrumental in urging Percy to publish the recovered folio, and the two worked closely on the project until Shenstone's death in 1763.[3] Shenstone, in turn, brought Percy into contact with the publisher Robert Dodsley.[4] Shenstone and Percy also shared a common friendship with James Grainger, the Scottish poet and translator, who had introduced Percy to the eighteenth-century luminary Samuel Johnson.[5] It was probably Johnson who inspired Percy to refer to his discovery as *Reliques*, and it was certainly Johnson who worked most closely with Percy on the final draft of the manuscript during a period of Johnson's convalescence at Percy's home.

Johnson's mental health had never been robust, but in the spring of 1764 he found himself "in a deplorable state, sighing, groaning, talking to himself, and restlessly walking from room to room"—he confided to his friend James Boswell that he "would consent to have a limb amputated" if it meant that he might "recover his spirits."[6] Johnson had proposed a critical edition of Shakespeare's plays during the 1740s and his success in publishing *A Dictionary of the English Language* (1755) provided him the opportunity to do so. The task, however, proved herculean. Under contract from 1756, Johnson battled with debtors and his own deteriorating mental state for years until, fearing his own imminent confinement, he accepted Percy's offer to summer at Easton Maudit.

The country idyll suited Johnson, it would seem. He spent eight weeks with Percy, during which he worked on Shakespeare and the *Reliques*, both of which saw publication in 1765. Percy's *Reliques*, therefore, and Johnson's magisterial edition of Shakespeare's plays, came forth from the same summer of convalescence, and were born into print in the same year.

Johnson's *Plays of William Shakespeare* changed the face of English literature, but Percy's *Reliques* were similarly influential in their own way. Whatever the truth of Macpherson's claims, the publication of the Ossian cycles had given the British reading public a taste for native heroes, and it was this appetite that Percy fed.

Of all the characters featured in the *Reliques*, none became so popular as Robin Hood. This is not to say that Percy invented Robin Hood, or even rediscovered him. By the time *Piers Plowman* was composed in the later fourteenth century the tales of Robin Hood were already famous enough to feature in allusion.[7] A few decades after that, Andrew Wyntoun mentioned both Robin Hood and Little John in his *Orygynale Cronykil of Scotland* in an entry for the year 1283.[8] There was a proliferation of Robin Hood tales throughout England and Scotland from about the middle of the fifteenth century, and the stories were integrated into May Day Revels and summer pageants. By the sixteenth century, however, both the tales and the games associated with them were being actively suppressed.

In the earliest ballads Robin Hood was low born, antiauthoritarian, and vociferous in his devotion to the Virgin Mary. The popular veneration of a character such as Robin Hood was something that the centralized and protestant monarchies of the British Isles could ill afford to tolerate. In 1549 Bishop Latimer warned King Edward VI against the "pretence of gathering for Robin Hood, a traitor and a thief"[9] and, in Scotland, the games were banned in 1555. At the same time, efforts were also being made to rehabilitate the outlaw.

John Major's *Historia Maioris Britanniae* (1521) was the first to locate Robin's outlawry within the "tyrannical" rule of King John. Major presented the woodsman as a loyal subject of the rightful king (Richard) who stole only from the wealthy (especially greedy and corrupt Abbots) that he might give to the poor.[10] The *Chronicle* of Richard Grafton, first published in 1569, expanded on Major's innovations by inventing a noble lineage for Robin. Rather than a common yeoman, Grafton maintained that the outlaw was an earl who had fallen into debt. Robin's adventures, therefore, were no longer the illegitimate actions of a social upstart, but the expression of his "manly courage," "chiualry," and "noble dignitie."[11] By the time the *Reliques* were published, Robin Hood had not disappeared, but he had been radically changed. Percy's publication, therefore, was to resurrect not only the ancient poetry of England, but also the ancient Robin Hood.

Three decades after the first publication of Percy's *Reliques*, the English antiquary Joseph Ritson published his edition of the Robin Hood cycle in 1795.[12] A fervent supporter of the political activist Tom Paine and a passionate Jacobin himself, Ritson kept the calendar of the French revolutionaries (the decimalized, antimonarchial, antireligious calendar adopted in France by 1792). Little wonder, then, that his *Robin Hood: A Collection of all the Ancient Poems, Songs and Ballads, now extant, relative to that celebrated Outlaw* emphasized Major's "revolutionary" outlaw and promoted the woodsman as a social activist and quasi-terrorist. Ritson's twelve-page preface to his publication, "The Life of Robin Hood," was the first academic discussion of the Robin Hood tradition and 117 pages of scholarly apparatus entitled "Notes and Illustrations" supported the work. Thomas Bewick's illustrations, which accompanied Ritson's text, were intended to broaden the publication's audience, and that they did—the book remained in print long after Ritson's death in 1803. Moreover, Ritson's scholarship built on that of Percy to imbue the Robin Hood legend with an academic capital. By the early nineteenth century, even antiquarians could no longer ignore this folk hero.

William John Thoms featured Robin Hood in his three-volume *Early English Prose Romances*, the last volume of which was in print by 1828. Thoms was still a young man when he published the *Romances*, and somewhat ahead of his time. He had been encouraged in his endeavors by Francis Douce, former keeper of manuscripts in the British Museum, and had anticipated strong demand for his scholarly work, but sales were disappointing. Nevertheless, the *Romances* did help to establish his reputation as an antiquary.

He was soon made a fellow of the Society of Antiquaries and, by 1838, he was secretary to the influential Camden Society. In 1845 he was appointed clerk, and subsequently deputy librarian, to the House of Lords, and in 1849 became the founding editor of *Notes and Queries*. Thoms was an avid admirer of the German mythologists Jacob and Wilhelm Grimm, and in the later 1840s he began a column entitled "Folk-Lore" in the *Athenaeum*. The *Athenaeum* was largely the product of Charles Wentworth Dilke, close friend to both John Keats and Leigh Hunt, and Thoms's use of the term "folklore" in so prestigious a publication soon saw its use eclipse previously used terms such as "antiquities" or "popular literature." By 1858, the general interest in Thoms's folklore warranted a second, extended, edition of his *Early Prose Romances*—a situation that "mitigated" the disappointment of the first edition's lack of sales.[13]

In the meantime, John Keats had himself produced *Robin Hood: To a Friend* in 1818, the same year that John Hamilton Reynolds published *On Robin Hood*. Thomas Love Peacock, the English novelist and close friend to Percy Bysshe Shelley, had begun writing his *Maid Marian* that same year, but publication was delayed until 1822, by which time Robin Hood had appeared as a patriotic rebel with a cheerful disposition in Walter Scott's *Ivanhoe* (1819).

Scott secured Locksley as a dominant toponym in the developing mythos and introduced the incident in which Robin splits his opponent's arrow at an archery contest. The entry of such details into the Robin Hood canon attests to the significance of Scott's contribution not only to the legends of Sherwood Forest, but also to medievalism in general. This significance, of course, has been acknowledged for some time.

In 1965, before medievalism had acquired the academic currency it enjoys today, Alice Chandler wrote that it was "impossible to trace all the ramifications of Scott's portrait of feudalism, especially in relation to popular belief," but that "such books as Southey's *Sir Thomas More*, Carlyle's *Past and Present*, Pugin's *Contrasts*, Disraeli's Young England novels, and many of Ruskin's works come immediately to mind."[14] The effects of Scott's medievalist vision, though, shaped more than just popular literature—Chandler also argued that "the influence of Scott" ripened "a generation or two later into the Parliamentary activities of Disraeli's Young England Party."[15]

Influential as Walter Scott was in his own country, his impact across the Atlantic was even more profound, and generations of scholars have illuminated the complex interrelationship of American medievalism with the works of this British novelist.[16] Mark Twain famously blamed Scott's writing for stifling progress and promoting retrograde practices, particularly in the southern United States:

> Then comes Sir Walter Scott with his enchantments, and by his single might checks this wave of progress, and even turns it back; sets the world in love with dreams and phantoms; with decayed and swinish forms of religion; with decayed and degraded systems of government; with the sillinesses and emptinesses, sham grandeurs, sham gauds, and sham chivalries of a brainless and worthless long-vanished society. He did measureless harm; more real and lasting harm, perhaps, than any other individual that ever wrote.[17]

Even so, Scott's Robin Hood, though not as republican as some of his literary predecessors, is still a yeoman, and a steadfastly independent one at that. It could be argued that, whatever *Ivanhoe*'s contribution to the ideology of slavery and class division in the *antebellum* South might (or might not) have been, the inclusion of the Sherwood outlaws did, at worst, little to add to this and, at best, possibly served to undermine it.

Scott's conflict-based narrative of Anglo-Norman relations, and Robin Hood's position within that narrative, were both further augmented in the popular imagination by the publication of Jacques Nicolas Augustin Thierry's *Histoire de la Conquête de l'Angleterre par les Normands* in 1825. John Matthew Gutch produced a new scholarly collection of the Robin Hood tales in his *Lyell Geste of Robin Hode with other Ancient and Modern Ballads* in 1847. Leigh Hunt published *How Robin and His Outlaws Lived in the Woods* in 1855. Nor was the Sherwood outlaw confined to the pages of literary works and academic journals, for he soon began appearing on stage as well.

James Robinson Planché staged his three-act opera *Maid Marian, or The Huntress of Arlingford* in 1822, and in 1846 a pantomime was performed (*Robin Hood and Richard Coeur de Lion*) in which a woman played Robin. Sometime in 1849, Joachim Hayward Stocqueler produced *Maid Marian, the Forest Queen*, a play he followed up with a comic opera soon after.

Stocqueler was one of those raconteurs produced by a burgeoning British empire. By the time he arrived in London in 1841, the forty-year-old had already traveled widely in India, Afghanistan, Persia, and Egypt. Pierce Egan (the Younger) had produced a wildly successful serial entitled *Robin Hood and Little John: or, The Merry Men of Sherwood Forest* in 1838 and turned it into a book in 1840.[18] Stocqueler's *Maid Marian* was intended as a theatrical companion to Egan's book, and it is easy to imagine the two men working closely on the project. Egan's own politics were famously liberal and his *Robin Hood* was just one of several popular works he had produced with antiauthoritarian themes.[19] Stocqueler, who eventually immigrated to the United States and assumed the surname Siddons, also published the script to *Maid Marian* sometime in 1849.[20]

By the middle of the nineteenth century, then, Robin Hood had become immortal. Liberated from the dusty anonymity of an antiquarian's bookshelf, he lived outside of time, but he was still a prisoner of place. While the Scots fought the Irish for possession of Fionn mac Cumhaill, and King Arthur's ghost slipped borders between western England, Wales, and Cornwall, Robin was very much English, and northern English at that. It was an American who was to change all that.

FRANCIS JAMES CHILD

If the liberal democracy of the young United States had promised its citizens the chance of success according to talent, then Francis James Child was fruit born of that promise. The third of eight children born to the sailmaker Joseph Child and his wife, Mary, Francis grew up in the rugged North End of Boston, Massachusetts. His receipt of a Medal of Merit from the Boston School's Committee in 1837 must have assuaged any fears his tradesman father might have had about his continuing education, and Francis went on to the free English High School, where he graduated second in a class of fourteen in 1840. Epes Sargent Dixwell, a Harvard graduate and former teacher at the English High School, then convinced Joseph to allow his son to attend the Boston Latin School, where Francis met Charles Eliot Norton. Both the Eliots and the Nortons were established families within Boston's elite, the so-called Brahmins, and the young Charles, inheritor to the prestige of both families, began a friendship with Francis that would last the rest of their lives.

Francis excelled at the Latin School and was offered a place at Harvard. His father gave him $826 toward the cost of his college education and Francis contributed $431.11 that he had earned himself. Dixwell procured the rest of the necessary funds, some $680, from his brother-in-law Jonathan Ingersoll Bowditch, a local merchant involved in trade with the Far East.[21] Bowditch was himself a talented student in his day and much enamored of the mathematical sciences, but he had chosen a mercantile career over an academic one.[22] Nevertheless, he retained a philanthropic interest in the Boston school system throughout his life, an interest that extended to the support of talented scholars like Child.

Harvard expanded Child's frontiers even further, both intellectually and socially. Henry Wadsworth Longfellow, the first American to translate Dante's *Divina Commedia*, taught at Harvard until 1854. Nathaniel Hawthorne, Longfellow's friend, delivered frequent lectures there. Child attended Harvard at the same time as the poet James Russell Lowell, and would have been well aware of the controversy sparked by the infamous "Divinity School Address" of 1838 in which Ralph Waldo Emerson discounted both the veracity of biblical miracles and the divinity of Christ. Child, the son of a Boston sailmaker, found himself at the oldest and most prestigious university in the United States during a decade in which American literature was individuating itself from its European forebears and asserting its own independence. Nor was Child at that time the only Harvard scholar of humble origins—Mary Ellen Brown's research into the biographical accounts of the graduating class of 1846 indicates that a number of them came from even "less privileged backgrounds."[23]

Child accrued the nickname "Stubby" at Harvard because of his stocky build, but the jibe was well intentioned. Charles Eliot Norton believed that Child's working-class origins contributed to his "shy and diffident" manner, but, for Norton at least, the story of Child's rise was the epitome of republican democracy—Joseph Child, wrote Norton, belonged to "that class of intelligent and independent mechanics which has had a large share of developing the character of our democratic community, as of old the same class had in Athens or in Florence."[24] By the time of his graduation, Child was extremely popular with his peers and recognized as "the best writer, best speaker, best mathematician, the most accomplished person in knowledge of general literature" among them.[25] Child initially tutored mathematics at Harvard, before transferring to history, political economy, and English literature in 1848. That same year, Child published a critically annotated edition of Elizabethan plays.[26]

Working from a rare 1820 printing of these plays probably obtained for him by Norton,[27] Child became increasingly aware of the dearth of such cultural materials available to him at Harvard and determined to undertake an extended tour of Europe.[28] Child had dedicated his first book to Jonathan Bowditch and Bowditch, who had loaned Child the money to enroll in Harvard, agreed to fund the expedition.

Already fluent in Greek and Latin, Child used his time in Europe to develop proficiency in Italian, French and, most importantly, in German. The importance of the "Grand Tour" was not a new concept in the middle of the nineteenth century, and the educated elites of the United States still saw the European sojourn as an essential qualification among people of quality, but continental Europe held a particular attraction for the young republicans of Francis Child's day. In France, the February Revolution had swept aside the *Orleanais* monarchy and ushered in the Second French Republic. Garibaldi, following heroic defeats in Italy, was on the run. Germany had been convulsed by uprisings and revolts. Everywhere in Europe the talk was of republics and democracy and for the young graduates of Harvard the heady mix of politics and scholarship particular to Germany made these northern states a "Camelot of erudition"—as early as 1819, Boston intellectual George Ticknor had declared that a knowledge of the German language was essential for real scholarship.[29]

Child sent a copy of his *Four Old Plays* to Jacob Grimm and was accepted as a student, initially at Göttingen and then in Berlin. He collected political material, especially pamphlets, for Norton[30] and returned to Harvard in 1851, at the age of twenty-six, to take up the Boylston Professorship of Rhetoric and Oratory, a position he held until 1876.

Child's contact with Grimm must have excited him to the possibilities of further research into the fields of "primitive" literature and popular balladry. Poets and scholars within the German states were pressing their native folk traditions into use as distinct ethnic and political signifiers, and the centrality of this research to the politics of a new Germany had been verified by Grimm's appointment to the abortive Frankfurt Assembly following the March Revolution of 1848. Child studied under the German scholar while the latter was writing the new edition of his *Deutsche Mythologie* (German

Mythology) that would appear in two volumes in 1854, the same year that his monumental *Deutsches Wörterbuch*, upon which he worked with his brother Wilhelm, would appear. Outside of Germany, however, the brothers Grimm were probably best known for their *Kinder- und Hausmärchen* (Children's and Household Tales), which had been in publication since 1815 and which would serve as the immediate inspiration for Child's most ambitious work.

Upon his return to Cambridge, Child found Longfellow at work on what was to become *Hiawatha*, an epic poem that sought to render the dubious research of Henry Rowe Schoolcraft into an epic poem in trochaic tetrameter. Schoolcraft, a self-trained ethnographer and Indian agent, had published a collection of stories he purported to be of Ojibwa origin as *Algic Researches* in 1839. The relationship of Longfellow's poem to Schoolcraft's research, and the ethnographical shortcomings of both, have been detailed elsewhere.[31] What is significant about Longfellow's poem in the context of my argument here, however, is its attempt to recreate a distinctly, albeit imagined, American past in the language of the European folk epic.

Longfellow used the stories in Schoolcraft's publication as the basis for a poem composed in the style of the Finnish *Kalevala*. Longfellow had obtained an early edition of Finnish poetry that had been translated into German by Hans Rudolf von Schröter.[32] The Finnish philologist Elias Lönnrot greatly expanded on this early edition to produce the national epic *Kalevala* by 1835 (a second, further expanded version was in print by 1849). Longfellow chose to present the stories published by Schoolcraft in the distinctive meter of the *Kalevala*, the trochaic tetrameter. We know also that Child conversed with Longfellow about the *Finnische Runen*.[33]

By 1853, Child had been awarded an honorary doctorate from the University of Göttingen, and had begun editing editions of both Spenser and Chaucer for publication. Child's plan was to produce American editions of English poetry, but somewhere about this time he determined to incorporate early ballads into those editions. Child's decision to include these "primitive" poems was an unprecedented one in as much as ballads had hitherto been seen as rustic—important steppingstones in the evolution of English poetry, but not worthy of study in their own right. Child, emboldened by the examples of Percy, Ritson, Grimm, and Lönnrot, proposed to include the ballads as legitimate exemplars of the poetic canon, thus equating poems such as *Robin Hood and the Monk* with Spenser's *Fairie Queene* and Chaucer's *Troilus and Criseyde*. This was Child's great innovation, to offer his "valorization of the ballad as coeval with received canonical poetry."[34]

The first fruits of this project, Child's *English and Scottish Ballads*, were published in eight volumes between 1857 and 1858. The entirety of volume five, more than 400 pages in itself, was devoted to the tales of Robin Hood. For Child, Robin Hood was an exemplary hero:

> There is no one of the royal heroes of England that enjoys a more enviable reputation than the bold outlaw of Barnsdale and Sherwood. His chance for a substantial immortality is at least as good as that of stout Lion Heart, wild Prince Hal, or merry Charles. His fame began with the yeomanry full five hundred years ago, was constantly increasing for two or three centuries, has extended to all classes of society, and, with some changes of aspect, is as great as ever.[35]

These introductory remarks, published as a preface to the fifth volume of his series, are significant.

By the mid-nineteenth century, American intellectuals in general, and Boston intellectuals in particular, were beginning to claim a place on the greater stage. Harriet Beecher Stowe, Ralph Waldo Emerson, Henry Wadsworth Longfellow, Oliver Wendell Holmes (Sr.), and James Russell Lowell worked together to establish a new literary and cultural journal, the *Atlantic Monthly*, in 1857 and Lowell, editor of the *Atlantic*, thought that Child's comments on the English outlaw were important enough to publish independently from the *English and Scottish Ballads*.[36] A close reading of the article quickly illustrates why.

For the democratically minded Yankees, Robin Hood was a hero for the "New World," one whose nobility arose from action rather than an accident of birth. From rude, yeoman stock, Hood's fame had "extended to all classes of society." Child sought also to distance the hero from the (Catholic) Marianism of the original ballads and to emphasize, instead, the democratic nature of Robin's endeavors and his struggle against injustice. In doing so, Child fell into line with Ritson's earlier analysis of a socially radical Robin Hood. "Those who desire a full acquaintance with the fabulous history of Robin Hood," wrote Child, "will seek it in the well-known volumes of Ritson."[37]

With the publication of the *English and Scottish Ballads*, Child's world widened even further. In 1860 he secured his place within the foremost families of Boston by marrying Elizabeth Sedgwick. The investment by the Boston Brahmins in institutions such as Harvard University provided funds for Child to purchase manuscripts and collections of correspondences and to mount expeditions to record oral traditions firsthand. Through his close friendship with Charlie Norton, he was brought into the orbit of John Ruskin, Thomas Carlyle, and Frederick James Furnivall. Nor was all this trans-Atlantic intellectual commerce unidirectional.

Child's innovation in his Chaucerian scholarship popularized the fourteenth-century poet on both sides of the Atlantic and facilitated new readings of this foundational English author. He worked closely with Furnivall in the establishment of the *Early English Text Society*, an enterprise that turned rare manuscripts into easily accessible library books. Moreover, Child's continued work on manuscripts such as Percy's *Reliques* ensured their survival, as William Chappell once explained to Child: "We English ... feel that we all owe you a debt of obligation for having rescued Percy's manuscript, by a generous offer, which no Englishman has made."[38]

Child's political agenda in all this was clear enough. The fragile democracy of the United States had been sorely tested in the middle decades of the nineteenth century as factions divided over state's rights. In the 1860s, this division erupted into the crucible of a brutal war. Kim Moreland has argued that the American Civil War ushered in profound and widespread cultural disruptions that drove a "medievalist impulse" in the postwar United States, an impulse that functioned "not in the ordinary way as an individual memory of a past experience but as a cultural memory, a trace of an earlier time that the American consciousness linked itself to in the past as a source, measured itself against in the present as contrast, and aspired to in the future as an ideal."[39] Child's own initial desire to foster a cultural unity in his country gave way to an even more driving need to heal the rift caused by the Civil War: "to rescue from oblivion ... evidence of the cultural childhood of the American community, in order to suggest a path towards achieving an ideal cultural unity in the newly United States."[40]

Robin Hood seemed a likely conduit for such endeavors. Where earlier commentators, such as Shenstone,[41] had seen a moral dubiousness in the outlaw, Child was unperturbed, and championed Robin Hood in both his *English and Scottish Ballads* and his monumental *English and Scottish Popular Ballads*, the final volume of which was not to be published until 1898, two years after Child's death. By that time, though, Robin Hood had become a truly "popular" character.

ROBIN HOOD IN AMERICA

The second half of the nineteenth century witnessed a dramatic widening of public interest in medievalist literature. Robin Hood, with his yeoman origins, rustic lifestyle, and antiauthoritarian achievements, was perfectly positioned to exploit this change in taste.

A new, less expensive, edition of Ritson's *Robin Hood* appeared in the 1850s. Pierce Egan's serial was still in print and featured copious illustrations by W. H. Thwaite. Indeed, so popular had Egan's serial become, that it passed across the Channel and was translated into French. This translation served as the basis for the Robin Hood novels of Alexandre Dumas, *Robin Hood, prince des voleurs* (*Robin Hood, Prince of Thieves*) and *Robin Hood le proscrit* (*Robin Hood the outlaw*), both published in the mid-1860s. Dumas's recensions of the English legends were translated, in turn, into Spanish by the editor of the Columbian journal *Oveja Negra* (*The Black Sheep*), although the Colombians mistakenly believed the Dumas novel to be a French translation of a novel by Walter Scott. In 1904, Dumas's novel, based on Egan's, was translated back into English.

Ritson and Egan were selling well, then, and editors were convinced that a market existed for less academic, more prosaic, retellings of the ballads. In 1859, *The Life and Exploits of Robin Hood* was published, not "for the critic or the antiquary, but for the large proportion of the reading public who have no leisure, and but little inclination, for recondite discussions."[42] A decade later George Emmett published his similarly populist and handsomely illustrated *Robin Hood and the Outlaws of Sherwood Forest*.

This popularization of the cycle, however, did nothing to lessen upper-class enthusiasm for the hero. In the early 1880s, Alfred Lord Tennyson turned his attention away from his Arthurian labors, momentarily, and toward Sherwood Forest. The product of this effort, *The Foresters, or Robin Hood and Maid Marian*, was published in 1881. A year later, Child began publication of his magnum opus, *The English and Scottish Popular Ballads*.

As important as Child was to the study of the European past and to the resurrection of studies into pre-Shakespearean literature, it was not *The English and Scottish Popular Ballads* that gave birth to the modern Robin Hood. As crucial as Scott's medievalism might have been in the burgeoning consciousness of an emergent America, and as profusely illustrated as Egan and Emmett's publications were, it was not from them that a lasting vision of Robin Hood was to come. That honor belongs, for the most part, to Howard Pyle.

More than twenty years before Pyle published a single volume of his Arthurian series, before *Otto of the Silver Hand* or *Men of Iron*, before even his first pirate story "The Rose of Paradise," Pyle published *The Merry Adventures of Robin Hood*. It was an audacious project. Stephanie Barczewski has written "the popular ballads and chapbooks featuring the legend of Robin Hood . . . emphasized populist values which appealed to working people. At the legend's core were basic aspirations virtually identical to their own—justice, equality, and above all, independence."[43] Pyle took those aspirations and wrote them for an American audience.

Pyle was probably working on his *Robin Hood* scripts as early as 1876 when he wrote to his mother from New York and asked her to send him her copy of "Percy's Robin Hood"[44]—undoubtedly one of the new editions made possible by Child's conservation efforts. The first of these stories appeared in *St. Nicholas* some three years later, but, in 1883, Pyle published *The Merry Adventures*. This was the first time anyone had written *and* illustrated a book about the Sherwood outlaw specifically for an American audience. Pyle adapted the stories to suit his purpose, emphasizing the hero's innate nobility, rather than his birthright, and concentrating on his fight for social justice. Robin's devotion to the Virgin was prominent once again as well, Pyle's own adherence to the philosophy of Emanuel Swedenborg probably made him less antagonistic to Catholic Marianism—Swedenborg had conversed with the Madonna in his visions, after all.[45]

Pyle's artistic style seemed to combine modernity with nostalgia in a fresh, new way. His crisp line-work was reminiscent of both medieval engravings and Walter Crane's illustrations of the Grimms' *Hausmärchen*.[46] Pyle's hero, too, was visually different from his predecessors in Egan or Emmett. The *poulaine* slippers, the distinctive hunter's cap, the pointed beard, these were all Pyle's innovations, innovations that were to become standard for at least the next century. *The Merry Adventures of Robin Hood* was an outstanding financial success for Pyle as well, and provided him with not only an immediate income, but also considerable leverage in his next contract negotiations.

The American public warmed to Pyle's version of Robin Hood immediately, and it became a touchstone of American literary culture. It is indicative of the position of *The Merry Adventures* in the cultural life of America that the Classified Catalogue of the Public Library of Fitchburg, Massachusetts, that was published in 1886, the year after the library's foundation, lists a copy of Pyle's book among its inventory. Significantly, the library's collection also included copies of both Ritson's *Robin Hood* and *The Life and*

Exploits of Robin Hood from 1859.[47] Small regional libraries like Fitchburg were making decisions about the literary future of Middle America, and that future featured Robin Hood very strongly.

The outlaws' adventures continued to be staged in theaters throughout the second half of the nineteenth century. George Alexander Macfarren produced *Robin Hood* in 1860 and William Henry Birch produced his operetta *The Merrie Men of Sherwood Forest* in 1871. In 1879 Robin Hood made it onto the German stage with Albert Dietrich's production entitled, simply, *Robin Hood*. Reginald de Koven and Harry Smith presented *Robin Hood: A Comic Opera* in 1890 and, a year later, Sir Arthur Sullivan presented Tennyson's poem, set to music, on stage. The stage version of *The Foresters* met with little critical acclaim.

In 1902, more than a decade after the success of their first staging of the Robin Hood legends, de Koven and Smith returned to familiar territory with *Maid Marian*. This sequel to their earlier comic opera was nowhere near so successful, but this may have had more to do with the waning of the stage as a medium of entertainment than with the material itself, for theater was giving way to a new form of mass entertainment—motion pictures.

The Robin Hood legends were passing irrevocably into the visual lexicon of America. Barely had the new medium of motion picture began than it was pressed into this service. In 1908 Percy Stow directed *Robin Hood and His Merry Men*. Etienne Arnaud and Herbert Blanche followed up with *Robin Hood* in 1912 and Herbert Brenon directed *Ivanhoe* the following year. In 1922, Allan Dwan directed the muscularly athletic Douglas Fairbanks in his own version of *Robin Hood*, a version unsurpassed until Michael Curtiz and William Keighley's 1938 blockbuster *The Adventures of Robin Hood* immortalized Errol Flynn in the lead role. Nineteen thirty-eight was also the year in which White's *The Sword in the Stone*, discussed in the previous chapter, first saw publication.

Louis Rhead's illustrated book *Bold Robin Hood and His Outlaw Band* appeared in 1912, but his plates drew heavily from Pyle. In 1917, Paul Creswick published his version of *Robin Hood*, illustrated throughout by Pyle's protégé, Newell Convers Wyeth. Wyeth's drawings did more than compliment those of Pyle, they served to cement further in the minds of American audiences the centrality of Pyle's vision.

ROBIN HOOD IN COMIC BOOKS

With such a well-established and long-term popularity in the United States, it must come as no surprise to learn that Robin Hood was one of the first heroes to appear in comic book form. In fact, the debut of the outlaw in *New Adventure Comics* predated that of Superman by six months.

Issue number 23 of the first volume of *New Adventure Comics* appeared in January 1938 and followed Pyle's script closely. Robin, a yeoman, is tricked into killing one of the king's deer by a group of royal foresters who then arrest him. He is eventually freed by another commoner and, over the course of the next eight issues of *New Adventure Comics*, we follow the young outlaw as he gathers his band of merry men, fights injustice, and redistributes unfairly gathered taxes. The serial stopped abruptly in September of 1938, and the company who published *New Adventure*, Detective Comics (forerunner to DC Comics), was not to revive the series for more than a decade.

This is not to say that Robin Hood was not popular with comic book audiences, quite the contrary, but he was a problematic property. With the sudden proliferation of Golden Age heroes, the comic book business quickly realized the importance of maintaining exclusive control over their products. Epic legal battles such as the one between Fawcett and National Comics (successor to Detective Comics) as to the originality of Captain Marvel were to become commonplace in the industry as sales rose and revenues soared. Robin Hood, on the other hand, was a character in the public domain. Who could legally justify their ownership of such a famous legend?

In February 1956, Quality Comics put this question to the test when it began a new series, *Robin Hood Tales*. Impetus for this series had come from the recent success of the British ITV series *The Adventures of Robin Hood*, which had begun airing in early 1955. Although the production was based in Great Britain and used English actors, the producer was former New York journalist Hannah Weinstein.

During the 1930s and 1940s, Weinstein had been an activist in various Communist projects in the United States, but had left America for Britain in 1952 to escape the scrutiny of the House Un-American Activities Committee. As the producer of *The Adventures of Robin Hood*, she hired a number of blacklisted American writers to script and edit the series. Ring Lardner Jr., Waldo Salt, Robert Lees, Adrian Scott, and Howard Koch were all credited under pseudonyms and their storylines revolved, unsurprisingly, around the central themes of the redistribution of wealth and the importance of communal strength in the face of despotism and tyranny.[48]

Given the success the British TV series was enjoying on American television, DC Comics, as it was by then, could not afford to let ownership of their character slip. DC's *The Brave and the Bold* already boasted a number of characters from the Middle Ages (Silent Knight, Viking Prince) and so Robin Hood appeared alongside them in issue 5, May 1956.

Quality Comics was still crowding the Robin Hood market, of course, but legal action against them was impossible because copyright on the traditional hero would have been unenforceable. DC chose, instead, to simply "buy out" their opposition. Quality Comics ceased to trade in December 1956, having been subsumed into National Periodical Publications, and when *Robin Hood Tales* issue 7 appeared in February 1957, it did so with a DC logo in the top left-hand corner of the cover. This victory, however, was to be short lived. In January 1958, Robin Hood ceased to appear in *The Brave and the Bold* and by April of the same year *Robin Hood Tales* had ceased publication as well.

ITV's *Adventures of Robin Hood* fared far better, and continued in production until 1960. The iconic series inspired a spate of movies: *Robin Hood's Greatest Adventures* (1956), *Robin Hood, the Movie* (1958), *Robin Hood: The Quest for the Crown* (1958), *The Son of Robin Hood* (1959), and *Sword of Sherwood Forest* (1960). ITV also capitalized on the success of their *Robin Hood* by producing a parallel serialization of Scott's *Ivanhoe* that ran from 1958 until 1959.

In France, Jean-Claude Deret scripted 52 episodes of *Thierry la Fronde* (*Terry the Sling*), which aired on French television from November 1963 until March 1966. *Thierry* later screened in Canada as *Thierry la Fronde* and *The King's Outlaw*, in Poland as *Thierry Śmiałek* (*Thierry the Daredevil*), in Australia as *The King's Outlaw*; and in the Netherlands as *Thierry de Slingeraar* (*Thierry the Sling*). In 1966, German TV aired *Robin Hood der edle Räuber* (*Robin Hood the Noble Bandit*).

With such widespread success for the character on both the small screen and in theaters, DC's decision to axe the series would appear as little more than a cynical exercise in character retention—comic book characters that remained unused for a considerable period of time became fair game for other companies to pick up. DC seemed to publish just enough Robin Hood comic books to justify their claim to the character. It was an atypical strategy, though, to produce whole series in order to retain characters. Far more common was the practicing of guesting, and Robin Hood guested frequently in DC comic books.

DC's own vigilante archer, Green Arrow, had visited Sherwood Forest as early as the August 1942 issue of *More Fun Comics*. Having confiscated "time pills" from the evil Professor Wurm, Green Arrow and his sidekick Speedy ventured back to twelfth-century England and proved themselves the equal of the famous bowman. Green Arrow switched places with Robin Hood again in issue 40 of *World's Finest Comics* (May 1949), and in issue 264 of *Adventure Comics* (September 1959) Green Arrow and Speedy travel back to Sherwood yet again. As late as September 1972, Green Arrow was still getting Robin Hood out of trouble (in issue 101 of *The Justice League of America*).

Wonder Woman twice used the "Amazon time-and-space transformer" to travel back in time and meet Robin Hood, once in May 1956 (issue 82 of *Wonder Woman*) and again in November 1957 (issue 94). Interestingly, in the second instance, the legendary archer seems to have sent some form of, possibly psychic, message to Wonder Woman while she was watching *The Adventures of Robin Hood* on her television.

In issue 22 of *Superman's Girl Friend, Lois Lane* (January 1961), Lois visits a new Robin Hood museum only to scratch herself on one of the ancient arrows. In the dream sequence that follows, she is transported back to Sherwood Forest to become "The Sweetheart of Robin Hood!" This story was obviously so good that it deserved a revisit in May 1967 (*Superman's Girl Friend, Lois Lane,* issue 74). In October 1964, time traveler Rip Hunter also ventured back to twelfth-century England to meet Richard I, Robin Hood, Maid Marian, and the Merry Men in issue 22 of *Rip Hunter, Time Master*.

Nor was the influence of Robin Hood felt only in direct representations of the original character. Jerry Robinson's inspiration for Batman's sidekick Robin came from Wyeth's version of Robin Hood, and so the young superhero took on both the name and the costume of the legendary outlaw.[49] In issue 116 of *Detective Comics* (October 1946), the Dynamic Duo met and rescued Robin Hood.

Robin Hood appeared quite frequently then, but rarely in his own comic, and DC still claims him as part of their "multiverse." The character, however, was obviously a popular one on television and at the movie theaters. Why, then, has DC failed to exploit this success? The answer lies in copyright.

THE GREEN ARROW

While Robin Hood, as a copyrightable property, was always problematic, the Green Arrow was not. Written by Mort Weisinger and drawn by George Papp, Green Arrow appeared for the first time in issue 73 of *More Fun Comics* (November 1941). The Green Arrow might have looked like Robin Hood and behaved like Robin Hood, but he was entirely paid for and owned by what was to become DC Comics.

The creators of the Green Arrow owed as much to the pulp fiction of the 1920s and 1930s, as they did to Pyle's *Merry Adventures*. Edith Heal had published her *Robin Hood* in 1928 and Geoffrey Trease's *Bows Against the Barons* appeared in 1934, but Green Arrow's genesis lay in the particular pulp of Edgar Wallace.

The prodigious Richard Horatio Edgar Wallace was, by turns, a crime writer, a journalist, a novelist, a screenwriter, and a playwright, and is perhaps best known today as the cocreator of *King Kong*. In 1923 he published *The Green Archer*, a widely popular novel about a bow-armed vigilante. The book itself went into multiple republications throughout the 1920s and 1930s, and was still being published in the 1970s. French (*L'Archer Vert*) and German (*Der grüne Bogenschütze*) translations appeared early. Spencer Gordon Bennet turned the book into a ten-episode cinema serial in 1925, and the legendary James Horne produced another fifteen-episode version in 1940. *Der grüne Bogenschütze*, directed by Jürgen Roland in 1961, also became a foundational film in Cold War Germany.

Wallace, of course, took much of his inspiration from Pyle. The Green Archer was a modern-day crime fighter dressed as Pyle's Robin Hood, so Weisinger took Wallace's creation and melded him with Batman to create the Green Arrow. Like Batman, the Green Arrow had a boy sidekick (Speedy), some custom-made vehicles (an Arrow-Car and an Arrow-Plane), a secret lair (the Arrow-Cave), and a special way for law enforcement officers to contact him (the Arrow-Signal). There was no way to know how popular the Green Arrow might become, but in the fast-paced world of the disposable Golden Age superhero, no one really cared. As it turned out, the Green Arrow was remarkably long lived.

The Green Arrow ran continuously in *More Fun Comics* from his debut late in 1941 until January of 1946, when he switched over to another DC publication, *Adventure Comics*.[50] His run in that publication lasted until February 1960, which meant that the Green Arrow survived both the postwar slump in comic book sales and the United States Senate Subcommittee on Juvenile Delinquency. The end of their run in *Adventure Comics* did not mean the end of Green Arrow or Speedy, however, as they continued on in *World's Finest Comics*, a magazine they had featured in since 1942.[51]

Green Arrow suffered his share of indignities, though. His storylines were made more family friendly and a female counterpart (Miss Arrowette) was introduced, albeit spasmodically.[52] His origin story was also retconned[53] so that his alter ego, Oliver Queen, could become a millionaire playboy like Bruce Wayne.[54] Reading these early adventures, however, one is keenly aware of the elephant in the room—with his trademark costume, replete with Pyle's plumed hunter's cap, and distinctive weaponry, surely the Green Arrow *is* Robin Hood.

The comics themselves are markedly taciturn on this matter. Green Arrow visits Sherwood of course, as noted above, and there is some limited interaction with Robin Hood, but, on the whole, the writers seemed keen to keep a distance between the two heroes. When we meet Green Arrow for the first time (*More Fun Comics* #73), we hear of Joan D'Arc and William Tell, but not of Robin Hood. This lack of acknowledgment, however, is compensated for by a distinct playfulness in the ensuing storylines.

In *More Fun Comics* issue 76 (February 1942), Green Arrow and Speedy come to the aid of Andrew Bowling, an eccentric millionaire. Guards working for the tycoon have imprisoned him in his own "medieval" castle and have equipped themselves with armor and weapons stolen from Bowling's extensive collection. DC, of course, did not rely on William Randolph Hearst for syndicated comics.

Green Arrow storylines went on to reference William the Conqueror, King Arthur, and Merlin as well as King John and Robin Hood. One storyline invoked Twain's *Connecticut Yankee*,[55] another saw Robin Hood's statue used to good effect (Speedy overturns the statue to trap some fleeing villains).[56] The very last Green Arrow story featured in *Adventure Comics* has the superhero in the offices of a major comic book producer arguing for up-and-coming artist Bill Nixon. Bill wants to pen a comic book about the "Golden Archer," but the editor in charge dismisses his superhero pitch as unrealistic.[57] In the next issue of *Adventure Comics*, Green Arrow was gone.

For the most part, though, by the early 1960s the only part of the Green Arrow that seemed at all like Robin Hood was the costume. The essential and timeless elements of the Robin Hood legend, those which had made the outlaw so accessible to American audiences, "justice, equality, and ... independence," were absent from the Green Arrow mythos—but that changed in 1969.

When Green Arrow reemerged in issue 85 of *The Brave and the Bold* (August–September 1969), he was new man. He looked new, thanks to artist Neal Adams's redesign, more muscular and taut, although still wearing a recognizably Pyle-inspired uniform. The storyline, however, more than anything else about the comic, promised change.

On June 6, 1968, Senator Robert Kennedy, an active opponent of organized crime, was shot dead in Los Angeles. Issue 85 of *The Brave and the Bold* was on the newsstands less than a year later with a storyline that saw Batman and Green Arrow react to the shooting of Gotham's anticrime crusader, Senator Paul Cathcart. Unlike Kennedy, Cathcart survived. The positive response to this publication within the DC readership was instrumental in the company's shift toward current-affairs-driven plotlines aimed at an older and more informed audience.

Dennis O'Neil was a journalist with an English literature major from Saint Louis University who began freelancing for Charlton Comics in the mid-1960s. When Charlton editor Dick Giordano moved across to DC Comics in 1968, he passed some work on to O'Neil. O'Neil's contributions to DC were extensive. He located his storylines within topical events, reflected significant real-world issues within the animated fantasy of the DC universe, and rewarded an expanding adult readership with a challenging, multifaceted exposition.

It was O'Neil who invented Arkham Asylum to house Gotham's insane. In the wake of Bobby Kennedy's assassination by Sirhan Sirhan, a Palestinian Arab, and the rise of the Palestinian Liberation Organization, it was O'Neil who created the terrorist Ra's Al Ghul, leader of the "Demon's Head" and former commander of the League of Assassins (Ra's Al Ghul is Arabic for *Demon's Head*). In the words of Michael McAvennie, "O'Neil rescued Batman from the cozy, campy cul-de-sac he had been consigned to in the 1960s and returned the Dark Knight to his roots as a haunted crime fighter."[58] Most importantly for this chapter, though, it was O'Neil who reinvented Green Arrow as a modern-day Robin Hood.

In issue 75 of *Justice League of America* (November 1969) Dennis O'Neil stripped Oliver Queen of his wealth. Defrauded by greedy capitalists, Green Arrow is forced to fend for himself on the "mean-streets" of Star City. He begins to question his role in society. This questioning began an odyssey for which Dennis O'Neil teamed up with Neal Adams in issue 76 of *Green Lantern* (April 1970).

Charged with reinvigorating sales for the "moribund" *Green Lantern* series, DC editor Julius Schwartz gave O'Neil free reign to "combine comics writing with . . . journalism" and to "dramatize the real-life issues that tormented the country in the context of superheroics."[59] Green Lantern was one of DC's least multidimensional characters—fearless, law abiding, sworn to uphold an ancient and intergalactic code of justice. He was not a hero for a troubled and rebellious America. In *Green Lantern 76*, the hero apprehends a gang of juvenile offenders, only to find out that the target of their attacks is a greedy landlord whose corrupt abuse of power is compelling mass evictions. "I been readin' about you," says an African American bystander to the Green Lantern, "how you work for the blue skins . . . the orange skins . . . the purple skins! Only there's skins you never bothered with . . . the black skins! I want to know . . . how come?!" A dejected Green Lantern hangs his head in shame, unable to answer the question.

O'Neil introduced Green Arrow into the series as the counterpoint to Green Lantern. His wealth gone, Green Arrow has become radicalized by living in the slums. "On the streets of Memphis a good black man died," he says to Green Lantern, "and in Los Angeles, a good white man fell"—behind the proselytizing superhero are portraits of Martin Luther King Jr. and Robert Kennedy. "You call yourself a hero! Chum, you don't even qualify as a man. You're no more than a puppet . . . Listen . . . forget about chasing around the galaxy! And remember America. It's a good country . . . beautiful . . . fertile . . . and terribly sick! There are children dying, honest people cowering in fear, disillusioned kids ripping up campuses."[60]

Thus began a journey across the country to find themselves, and America. Over the next fourteen issues, the two heroes confronted crises of corporate greed, environmental vandalism, overpopulation, small-town conformity, racism, religious cults and, most famously, heroin addiction.

The Comics Code Authority had always been explicit in forbidding any depiction of illegal drug use, but in 1970, the United States Department of Health, Education and Welfare had asked Marvel Comics to feature a strong antidrug message in one of its main series. A story arc in issues 96 to 98 of *The Amazing Spider-Man* (May to July 1971) chronicled the plight of Peter Parker's friend, Harry Osborn, in his struggle against pill addiction. The CCA refused to sanction the storyline, but strong sales of these issues undermined the Authority's control and the code was subsequently revised.[61] O'Neil took advantage of this revision to explore the problem further.

Issues 85 and 86 of *Green Lantern* (August and October 1971) revealed Speedy's heroin addiction. Battling feelings of abandonment by Green Arrow, and forced into association with the criminal elements of Star City, the young sidekick becomes addicted. Although Speedy kicks his habit by issue

86, a very rapid recovery indeed, O'Neil was unequivocal in his treatment of drug abuse and Adam's artwork featured explicit depictions of heroin paraphernalia, including a syringe that took up almost the entire cover of issue 86.

Most important, though, throughout this short-lived series Green Arrow *is* Robin Hood. O'Neil self-consciously places the superhero within that referential with the very first issue of the revised series, and we watch as Green Arrow works ceaselessly for the next fourteen episodes to uphold his independence in the face of a growing tyranny, to seek "true" justice, and to champion the underdog. At the series' end, unable to cope with the limitations of his capacity to change an unjust world, Green Arrow fakes his own death and "little Robin Hood me," as he describes himself, retreats to an ashram.[62]

O'Neil's experiment was a fascinating one from the perspective of the reception history of Robin Hood in America, but it proved financially unviable. The Green Lantern/Green Arrow series finished in 1972 and was not to be revisited until 1976. When it did resume,[63] it was without the artistic talents of Neal Adams and, although Dennis O'Neil was still writing the scripts, the social consciousness of the previous incarnation was gone. Green Arrow remained as Green Lantern's foil until the end of 1979, at which point he passed back into an unspoken retirement.

Green Arrow returned in his own title in May 1983, which lasted only four issues.[64] In 1985, DC killed him off in their *Crisis on Infinite Earths*. Death, of course, is never permanent in the world of comic books, and so the archer was revived, again as a political activist, in 1986.[65]

By this time, O'Neil's depiction of Green Arrow had become canonical and so, in issue 38 of *Secret Origins*, we see Oliver Queen (once again a multimillionaire) wrestling with his role in society: "Robin Hood was, after all, a political activist," he muses, "fighting against a corrupt administration." Still, the incongruity of Queen's privilege is obvious. Robin Hood, in his recension as an outlawed nobleman, had this problem taken out of his hands. Queen, on the other hand, finds himself asking: "What am I supposed to do? Steal from myself and give to the poor?"

The new Green Arrow, at least, seemed much more comfortable with his Robin Hood origins, and the central themes of the Robin Hood legend have not been absent from the hero's storylines since the mid-1980s. Nor have his writers ceased to be playful—in Mike Grells's *Green Arrow: The Longbow Hunters*, Oliver Queen lives above his girlfriend's flower shop, the appropriately named *Sherwood Florist*.[66]

The final decades of the twentieth century and the first decade of the twenty-first saw a return to Robin Hood movies and television serials. At the same time Green Arrow, now firmly established as a comic book superhero who carried the spirit of Robin Hood into the modern world, continued to grow in popularity. By 2013, Green Arrow had transitioned into a hit television series, *Arrow*, produced by the CW Network, and by 2015, *Arrow* was airing its fourth season.

CONCLUSION

Just as *Prince Valiant* functions as a polyvalent locus in the reception history of Arthuriana, so too Green Arrow serves to demonstrate the continuities of the Robin Hood mythos in the medievalist comic books of the American Century. Indeed, significant as the Arthurian legends have become in the cultural imaginings of the United States, the connection between state and story seem even more significant in the case of Sherwood Forest's most famous son.

Whereas America received from Britain a fully formed Arthur, a king that could be modified perhaps, certainly adapted, but never wholly assimilated, Robin Hood emerged from a contentious past seemingly ready-made for the iconoclastic ideals of a boisterous democracy. In this reception history, America was not merely a recipient. It was American money that ensured the physical survival of those few artifacts central to the yeoman's story. It was American scholarly interest that elevated the bandit from a position of relative obscurity to one of legitimate academic pursuit. Most important, though, it was American popular culture that made Robin Hood into a contemporary legend—American movies, American television shows, American comic books. And through all of these myriad incarnations the legacy of Francis James Child and the vision of Howard Pyle can still be seen.

CHAPTER 3

The Mighty Thor (1962)

Force rules the world still, has ruled it, shall rule it; meekness is weakness, strength is triumphant, over the whole earth still it is Thor's-Day!
—HENRY WADSWORTH LONGFELLOW (1807–1882)

The comic book superhero that eventually came to feature in his own Marvel title, *The Mighty Thor*, has always stood astride two mythological universes. As the latest avatar of the Norse God of Thunder, Thor rests one foot on the long transmission history of Teutonic literature, while, with the other, he rests on the alternate folklore of comic book publishing. As a series, *The Mighty Thor* has maintained a steady popularity for more than five decades and has gone on to spawn numerous animated serials, several major motion pictures, and a plethora of tie-in merchandise and memorabilia. Some of this success, to be sure, must be a result of the creative talents behind the comic book, but much of it has to do with timing—marketing the right product at the right time.

Just as the achievements of *Prince Valiant* and Green Arrow were predicated upon decades of reception history that preceded their entry into mainstream popular culture, Marvel's was not the first comic book version of the Norse hero to find publication. It was, however, the first to enjoy success and, for *The Mighty Thor*, as with so many other comic book ventures, the cultural environment that facilitated this success was the product of a great many other people working over a very long period of time.

THE "VIKING" REVIVAL IN EUROPE

The success of *The Mighty Thor* owes much to the promulgation of Scandinavian studies in the universities of America and the subsequent dissemination of that study into the wider community by way of popular literature. Just as academic interest in Arthurian myths or the legends of Robin Hood bled into the popular consciousness of America through the works of Howard Pyle and Newell Wyeth, so too the Norse *Eddas* transitioned from general obscurity, to academic curiosity, and finally to popular artifact through the agencies of nationalism, Romanticism and, in this particular case, widespread immigration.

The great bulk of what we know about Teutonic mythology comes from three sources alone: the *Poetic Edda*; the *Prose Edda*; and the *Song of the Nibelungs*. Only the first two of these sources are technically Norse (that is, they describe the mythological world of ancient Scandinavia), whereas the third pertains more to the legends of the ancient Germans. That being said, all three contain significant amounts of shared material, or story variants dealing with characters held in common, and the linguistic or cultural divisions drawn between the different traditions have at least as much to do with nineteenth-century nationalism and modern politics as they do with any inherent textual differences.

The *Poetic Edda*, also known as the Sæmundar Edda or the *Elder Edda*, is a collection of Old Norse poems contained in an Icelandic medieval manuscript now referred to as the *Codex Regius*. The material in the codex would appear to deal with pre-Christian Scandinavian mythology, although the codex itself does not predate the thirteenth century. In 1643, the *Codex Regius* came into the possession of Brynjólfur Sveinsson, bishop of Skálholt, who attributed the manuscript to Sæmundr the Learned, a twelfth-century Icelandic priest. Modern scholars reject this attribution, but the codex is still sometimes referred to as the *Sæmundar Edda*.[1]

The *Prose Edda*, also referred to as the *Younger Edda* or *Snorri's Edda*, was already well known when Brynjólfur "rediscovered" the *Poetic Edda*. The Icelandic scholar Snorri Sturluson composed the *Prose Edda* around 1220, and it survives in seven main manuscripts inscribed between 1300 and 1600. Snorri's *Prose Edda* consists of a prologue, the *Gylfaginning* (concerning the creation, destruction, and rebirth of the Norse mythical world), the *Skáldskaparmál* (a dialogue between the sea-god Ægir and Bragi, the god of poetry), and the *Háttatal* (an exposition of verse forms used in Norse mythology).[2]

The *Song of the Nibelungs*, often referred to by its German title *Das Nibelungenlied*, is an epic poem composed in Middle High German probably toward the end of the thirteenth century. It tells the story of the dragon slayer Siegfried, his murder at the court of the Burgundian king Gunther, and of the revenge exacted by Siegfried's wife, Kriemhild. Both the *Poetic Edda* and the *Prose Edda* contain Old Norse parallels of the Siegfried legend, which also survive in the Norse *Völsunga Saga* and Þiðrekssaga, indicating the close interrelationship of Norse and Germanic mythology. As the reception history of these Teutonic sources has been covered in detail by a number of experts in this field,[3] it will be necessary here to offer but a summary of their scholarship.

There are more than thirty extant manuscripts of the *Nibelungenlied* that date from before the sixteenth century, and eleven of these manuscripts are essentially complete. Despite this, the poem itself was virtually unknown before its "rediscovery" in the eighteenth century, at which point it became a major focus of German cultural nationalism. It was at that point that an academic interest in these Northern mythologies began in Denmark with a book written by a Swiss intellectual that was subsequently taken up by the English.

Paul Henri Mallet was born in Geneva in 1730 and, by the age of twenty-two, he was professor of *Belles Lettres* to the Academy at Copenhagen. His research there focused on the ancient history and literature of Denmark and, by 1756, he had published his *Monumens de la Mythologie et de la Poesie des Celtes et Particulièrement des Aciens Scandinaves*. Mallet's *Monumens* included a general introduction on pre-Christian civilization in Scandinavia along with a translation of the *Gylfaginning*, and synopses of the *Skáldskaparmál* and the *Háttatal*.

Thomas Percy, whose *Reliques* had already begun the important work of reestablishing the position of the English ballad, published a translation of Mallet's work in 1770 under the title of *Northern Antiquities*. Percy claimed to have known at least some of the manuscripts that Mallet had worked from and his translation prompted immediate interest among British scholars. Walter Scott later augmented Percy's translation and republished it at Edinburgh in 1809. Later still, Joseph Andrew Blackwell produced a third, expanded edition in London in 1847. It is significant, of course, to find both Percy and Scott once again involved so actively in the reclamation of medieval literature.

Interest in such poetry might well have remained scholarly and marginalized had it not been for a corresponding rise of continental nationalism, coupled, as it was at the time, with a widespread engagement with the new Romanticism. Amos Cottle and Robert Southey produced their translations of Norse poetry in 1797 as *Icelandic Poetry or the Edda of Saemund*.[4] Southey's contribution to the project was probably far less than that of Cottle, but Southey's connections ensured publication. Moreover, the combination of Southey's Republican politics and his Romantic sensibilities brought the work to the notice of a politically minded elite at a time when British interest in the North was just beginning.

By the end of the eighteenth century, Iceland lay within the orbit of British territorial ambitions. In the 1780s, Denmark had offered to cede their dependency, Iceland, to Great Britain in return for a naval base in the Caribbean. The short-lived "protectorate" established in Iceland during the Napoleonic Wars by the adventurer Jørgen Jørgensen was achieved with British ships (and possibly their collusion) and, as late as the 1860s, Britain was still requesting Iceland as compensation for their support of Denmark in the Schleswig-Holstein Wars. British interest in, and enthusiasm for, Iceland and Nordic culture grew dramatically at exactly the same time their political focus began to alight on this northern island, an island that supported a sizable fishing and whaling fleet.

At the same time, the impact of the Napoleonic Wars on the kingdoms of Scandinavia had led to a corresponding rise in nationalist movements. Norwegians had always held a strong sense of their national history and traditions, but their aspirations for nationhood had been frustrated for centuries. The former kingdom of Norway had passed into personal union with the Danish crown in 1524 and Norway had been dissolved as a separate state some twelve years later. Denmark was allied to France during the long wars that followed the French Revolution and, in the wake of Napoleon's initial defeat in 1814, Denmark was forced to cede Norway to the kingdom of Sweden. A subsequent Norwegian uprising was quickly crushed by the Swedes, but Norwegian nationalism was in no way diminished—rather, it was buoyed by the promulgation of Old Norse literature and by the impact of archaeological discoveries within Norway.

In 1867, the first Viking ship to be unearthed, the Tune ship, was excavated in Østfold and, in 1880, a ship burial was excavated at Gokstad by Nicolay Nicolaysen. Nicolaysen was Norway's first state-employed antiquarian and a founding member of the Society for the Preservation of Ancient Norwegian Monuments, which he served as president from 1851 to 1899. He was active in the founding of the *Nasjonalmuseet for kunst, arkitektur og design* (National Museum of Art, Architecture and Design) and was a strong proponent of the Norwegian National Academy of Craft and Art Industry.

Scandinavian Romanticism was a powerful force within the intellectual circles of Sweden as well. A cadre of Swedish poets and authors formed the *Götiska Förbundet* (Gothic League or Geatish Society) in 1811 as a social club for literary studies among academics. Their long-term view was to raise the moral tone of society through the contemplation of Scandinavian antiquity and to offer these "native" traditions as a counterpoint to the biblical and Classical orientation of the academies. For some involved in the *Götiska Förbundet*, it had been moral degeneracy that had led to Sweden's territorial loss of Finland to Russia in 1809.

The *Götiska Förbundet* published a periodical, *Iduna*, and it was in this publication that the poem *Vikingen* (The Viking) by Erik Gustaf Geijer first appeared. Geijer thus popularized the term "Viking." Geijer also collaborated with Arvid August Afzelius in producing the three-volume collection of Swedish folk songs, *Svenska folk-visor från forntiden*, which appeared between 1814 and 1816. Another member of the *Götiska Förbundet*, Esaias Tegnér, wrote a modern version of *Frithiofs Saga*, which became popular and influential not only in Scandinavia and Germany, but also in Great Britain and the United States.

In Denmark itself, Mallet's work was continued by a number of important scholars. Rasmus (Christian) Rask studied at the University of Copenhagen where he evidenced a remarkable talent for the acquisition of languages. In 1808 he was appointed assistant keeper of the university library and, in 1811, the same year that the *Götiska Förbundet* was founded, he published the introduction to his *Anvisning till Isländskan eller Nordiska Fornspråket* (Grammar of the Icelandic or Old Norse Language).

Rask's colleague, the antiquarian Carl Christian Rafn was also influential at that time and his scholarship focused largely on the translation of Old Norse literature and related Northern European history. In 1837, Rafn published his *Antiquitates Americanæ*, which advocated the theory that the Vikings had explored North America centuries before Christopher Columbus, an idea that was later to become important to Scandinavian studies in the United States. Henry Wadsworth Longfellow, the Harvard poet, was an avid reader of Rafn and wrote a series of Norse-inspired poems, some lines from which began this chapter.

These developments in Scandinavia were linked to similar phenomena in Germany, of course, where nationalism and Romanticism had combined to produce similar scholarly effects. Jacob and Wilhelm Grimm's publications including *Kinder- und Hausmärchen* (1812–1815), *Die Lieder der alten Edda* (1815), and *Deutsche Sagen* (1816–1818), as well as *Deutsche Mythologie* (1835) written by Jacob Grimm alone, combined with the compositions of Richard Wagner to amplify the resonance of Nordic mythology within the cultural life of the emergent German nation. Wagner's Norse influences further enhanced the allure of the Viking era during the later nineteenth century with his Ring cycle (*Der Ring des Nibelungen*), a set of four operas based loosely on figures and elements of Germanic mythology, making use of the *Poetic Edda*, the *Völsunga Saga*, and the *Nibelungenlied*.[5]

Scandinavian studies in England were further augmented in the meantime by the studies of Benjamin Thorpe. Thorpe is principally known as a scholar of Anglo-Saxon, but he began his academic apprenticeship with Rask under whom he studied for four years at Copenhagen University. In 1866 Thorpe produced his two-volume edition of the *Edda Sæmundar Hinns Froða: The Edda Of Sæmund The Learned*.

Oxford graduate George Webbe Dasent had become acquainted with Jacob Grimm while on a diplomatic post in Stockholm, and it was Jacob Grimm who suggested that Dasent study old Scandinavian literature. In 1842, Dasent produced his own translation of *The Prose or Younger Edda*. The following year Dasent translated Rask's Icelandic grammar for an English audience.

The same year that Thorpe published his *Edda*, Guðbrandur Vigfússon came to Oxford. Vigfússon, who was to become one of the foremost Scandinavian scholars of the nineteenth century, eventually became the Reader in Scandinavian at Oxford University, a post created for him in 1884. At Oxford, Vigfússon worked closely with the historian Frederick York Powell, and together they produced both the *Corpus Poeticum Boreale* in 1887 and the *Grimm Centenary* papers in 1886. Powell was made Regius Professor of Modern History after the retirement of James Froude in 1894, after which he assisted Vigfússon with his *Icelandic Prose Reader* (1897) and the *Origines Islandicae* (1905).

The point being made here, and one that is sometimes overlooked, is that the advent of serious scholarly interest in northern mythologies was not some airy academic pursuit removed from the drives of contemporary society. Rather, it was a direct result of the political needs of the day—national legitimacy on the part of those emergent countries that imagined these sources as part of their linguistic inheritance, and political expediency on the part of Great Britain that was seeking to exploit continental disunity for its own imperial gain. America was not unaffected by British scholarship, or imperialism, for that matter, but when millions of Germanic-speaking migrants poured into the United States during the second half of the nineteenth century, they brought this new and widespread folk chauvinism with them.

VIKINGS IN AMERICA

Interest in ancient Scandinavian history and literature, of course, were by no means limited to European universities. The American institutions so integral to the recovery of British medieval literature were equally interested in Teutonic parallels. In America, however, the imperative for study in these fields was driven not only by academic curiosity, but also by the politics of immigration.

German immigration into the Americas was at its zenith during the middle decades of the nineteenth century. The catastrophic crop failures that blighted Ireland also ravaged central Europe in the 1840s and prompted many Germans to leave their farms. Economic downturn generated conditions of underemployment and poverty. The nationalist aspirations that blossomed in the wake of Napoleon's armies went unrealized as monarchs scrambled to reestablish their *antebellum* kingdoms. The revolutions of 1848 miscarried, and the German states became the domain of secret police forces and systematic repression. Small wonder then, that many Germans chose to find a new life in America.

Between 1840 and 1880, Germans constituted the largest single group of immigrants into the United States. In cities such as Cleveland, Milwaukee, Hoboken, and Cincinnati they made up more than 40 percent of the civic population. By 1900, there were more than two and a half million Americans who had been born in Germany and there were more than 800 German language publishers in the United States.[6]

By the turn of the twentieth century, German immigrants had established themselves within all echelons of American society. Americans knew intimately such (Anglicized) German names as Rockefeller, Astor, Westinghouse, and Guggenheim. Americans drank beer from breweries established by German immigrants: Budweiser; Miller; Pabst; and Yuengling. Within decades they would drive in cars made by Chrysler and fly in planes made by Boeing. American musicians played on Steinway pianos and flocked to hear concerts conducted by German Americans. Indeed, when America looked for someone to compose new music for the Centennial in 1876, German-born Theodore Thomas, musical director for the celebrations, commissioned Richard Wagner to do the honors.[7]

In his *The German Element in the United States*, German American Albert Faust was keen to elucidate what this immigration had meant for his America. Faust's research had indicated that for every American born in Germany, there were 2.9 Americans of German parentage, which meant that, by the turn of the twentieth century, more than 10 percent of the population of the United States were either German or the children of Germans.[8] To this could be added German-speaking immigrants from other countries such as Austria, Russia, and Poland, amounting to more than one million additional immigrants. Faust was also at pains to point out the contribution of the democratically minded German Americans to the Civil War—they constituted the single largest population of immigrant volunteers—and the fact that German immigration to America had surpassed Irish immigration every year since 1851.[9]

Simultaneously with this German immigration, Scandinavians also left their northern homelands for a new life in America. Many made landfall in Quebec and from there traveled overland into the northern United States. Wisconsin, Iowa, and Minnesota saw the largest congregations of people from Norway, Sweden, and Denmark and, by 1900, there were almost one million Americans of Scandinavian birth. With so many Scandinavians settling in Wisconsin, in particular, it could only be a matter of time before local academic institutions began to engage with the same Scandinavian studies that had been exciting their European colleagues.

Rasmus Bjørn Anderson's parents had emigrated from Stavanger in Norway to settle in Albion, Wisconsin, where he was born in 1846. Upon graduating from the University of Wisconsin, Madison, Anderson began teaching courses there in a number of subjects including Latin, Greek, German, and Anglo-Saxon.[10] Cognizant of movements within British universities, though, Anderson was also keen to promote Scandinavian studies at Madison and, to this end, he was ultimately aided by the violinist Ole Bull.

Bull was a world-famous virtuoso and ardent Norwegian nationalist. Having toured the United States on numerous occasions, and having met with considerable success there, Bull had established a colony, which he called New Norway, in Pennsylvania early in 1852. By the 1870s, he was living in Madison where he met Anderson and began supporting the young scholar's attempts to establish Scandinavian studies in the university curriculum.

Bull was, by this time, also promoting Edvard Grieg. Bull's brother had married Grieg's aunt, and their combined celebrity was a benefit for Anderson. Against this support, though, Anderson battled the innate conservatism of the Norwegian immigrants who saw the American education system as "godless and destructive of the Christian faith."[11] Still, he encouraged students of Scandinavian descent to enroll in his courses, and he urged other students of medieval literature to do so as well. By 1875 he was able to establish the first Department of Scandinavian Studies in an American university. It was probably the first such department outside of Scandinavia.

For Anderson, it was clear that his department was a unique product of the demographic environment of his own university. He knew that no such chair existed in any British university at that time and that his own position had more to do with exploiting a local market than it did with any notions of academic diversity:

> While Prof. Sterling, as acting president, and his successor, President Twombly, were without any interest in or appreciation of the Scandinavian languages as a branch of university instruction, still they knew that there was a large and growing Scandinavian population in the Northwest; they noticed that a considerable number of Scandinavian students were attending the university, and so they came to look upon it as a matter of good business policy to give this group of our population some sort of recognition in the department of instruction in the university.[12]

Anderson was also active in propagating the theory that Vikings had settled North America centuries before Columbus's expedition.

In 1874 Anderson had published his research as *America Not Discovered By Columbus*. As Martin Arnold has argued, the prospect of a Norse discovery and settlement of America was attractive not only to Scandinavian Americans, but also to many German and British Americans as well.[13] Such settlements were attested to by early Norse writings (*Eiríks saga rauða*, *Grœnlendinga saga*, *Hauksbók*, and the *Flateyjarbók*), but details were inconsistent and unclear. It was not until the excavations at L'Anse aux Meadows, Newfoundland, during the 1960s, that definitive proof of this settlement would be found.

During his time as head of the Department of Scandinavian Studies, Anderson also published a number of books on Norse subjects, including his *Norse Mythology* (1875), *Viking Tales of the North* (1877), and his own translation of *The Younger Edda* (1880). He left the university for diplomatic postings in 1883, but continued to be active in supporting the department he had established.

In 1905, Anderson founded the Norrœna Society, a publication company dedicated to republishing translations of texts that promoted "the History and Romance of Northern Europe." Among the society's projects was a reprinting of Thorpe's *Edda Sæmundar Hinns Froða*, as well as Dasent's *Story of Burnt Njal* and his *Collection of Popular Tales from the Norse and North*

German. In all, between 1905 and 1911, the Norrœna Society published some fifteen volumes of Norse sagas, poetry, and history that provided an accessible source of material for college libraries, thus paving the way for more universities to follow in Wisconsin's wake. By the turn of the twentieth century, Scandinavian studies had established itself in a number of American universities, universities that were to produce scholars who would dominate this field in the decades to come.

In 1880, Lee Milton Hollander was born in Baltimore to the children of German immigrants. Upon the death of his father, Hollander's mother returned to Germany, and so he spent his school years in Frankfurt, eventually returning to the United States to complete a doctoral thesis at Johns Hopkins University. Upon graduation, he spent the next two years traveling and studying in Scandinavia and, upon his return to the United States, taught German and Norwegian first at the University of Michigan and then at Anderson's old department at the University of Wisconsin. In 1920, Hollander moved to the University of Texas and, by 1929 he held the chair at the Department of Germanic Studies, a position he retained until his retirement in 1967.

Hollander's scholarly output was considerable, and among his most significant contributions to Norse studies was his translation of *The Poetic Edda* that appeared in 1928. He also published *Old Norse Poems: The most important non-skaldic verse not included in the Poetic Edda* (1936), *The Skalds: A selection of their poems* (1945), *The sagas of Kormák and the Sworn brothers* (1949), *Njál's saga* (1955), *The saga of the Jómsvíkings* (1955), *Eyrbyggja saga* (1959), *Heimskringla: History of the Kings of Norway* (1964), and *Víga-Glúm's saga and The story of Ögmund Dytt* (1972).

Arthur Gilchrist Brodeur was born in Franklin, Massachusetts, in 1888 and obtained his doctoral degree from Harvard in 1916. Following graduation, he took up a position teaching English and German philology at the University of California, Berkeley, eventually becoming a full professor in 1930. Brodeur was integral in establishing a Department of Scandinavian Studies at the university and served as its first chairman from 1946 until 1951. He retired from Berkeley four years later and moved to the University of Oregon.

Brodeur had begun translating Old Norse for the American-Scandinavian Foundation even before completing his doctorate at Harvard. His edition of *The Prose Edda* appeared in 1916. Unlike many of his contemporaries, however, Brodeur did not limit his output to scholarly editions alone. By the 1920s, Brodeur, often working with his close friend Farnham Bishop, was publishing fiction for popular magazines such as *Argosy* and *Adventure*. A good many of these stories made use of Norse themes and storylines. The novella *Vengeance* (1925) was a retelling of *Völsunga saga*, while the serialized novel *He Rules Who Can* (1928) focused on Harald Hardrada's career in the Varangian Guard. Nor was Brodeur the only scholar seeking publication through the American-Scandinavian Foundation.

In 1923, Henry Adams Bellows's translation of *The Poetic Edda* appeared under the same imprint. The Danish American industrialist Niels Poulson had established the American-Scandinavian Foundation in 1910 and, by 1914, their output had expanded to include publications through the *Scandinavian Classics* and *Scandinavian Monographs* titles. The foundation also financed the publication of an accompanying *Scandinavian Review*. It was not only academics who benefited from all these labors, for a popular interest in Norse mythology had also begun to permeate mainstream American society thanks to the work of educators like James Baldwin.

Baldwin was a contemporary of Rasmus Anderson but, unlike Anderson, was largely self-taught. Born in Indiana in 1841, Baldwin's literacy owed much to the school-readers collected by his father and, in later life, he recalled with some fondness Emerson's *Primer*, McGuffey's *First Reader*, and *The Child's Instructor*.[14] By 1865 Baldwin was teaching in Indiana neighborhood schools and in 1870 he founded a high school in Noblesville. Three years later he organized a public school system in Huntington where he also established the first school library. In 1883, Baldwin became superintendent for the Rushville Public Schools.[15]

Baldwin's publishing career began in 1882 when he produced *The Story of Siegfried*. The work consisted of a loose retelling of the Norse legends and was illustrated with six engravings, the original artwork for which was done by none other than Howard Pyle. The book was an immediate success and remained in print for several decades. A second edition appeared in 1888 and a third in 1901. Six years after Baldwin's death, yet another edition was to appear, this one with new artwork commissioned from Peter Hurd, the student and son-in-law of Pyle's disciple Newell Wyeth.

In 1887, after twenty-two years as an educator, Baldwin left Indiana to join the Education Department of the publishing firm Harper's. There he added his input to the publication of Harper's Readers, editing five of the six-volume series. From 1890, Baldwin was the assistant editor of Harper's periodicals.

The American Book Company bought Harper's in 1894, and Baldwin joined the new editorial department, working there until 1924, by which time he was editor-in-chief. In 1897 he published *The Baldwin Readers* and in 1911 he coauthored *The Expressive Readers* with Ida Bender. In all, Baldwin published more than fifty books in his lifetime that sold more than 28 million copies.[16] His impact on American education was substantial, and his collaboration with Pyle significantly popularized Norse legends in America. It was Baldwin who took this ancient literature out of the universities and presented it to American schoolchildren, and it was Pyle who gave those schoolchildren a vision to accompany that literature.

Martin Arnold has already detailed the extent to which this "Norsemania" also manifested in the literature of late-nineteenth-century America.[17] If children were being bought up on Baldwin's *Siegfried* at this time, their parents were being no less influenced by the plethora of popular novels that featured the same themes, or the more respectable poetry of Lanier, Longfellow, Whittier, and Lowell.

Just as with Pyle's Robin Hood, a popular appreciation of all things Viking was soon translated into the cinematic experience. Stuart Blackton directed a very early motion picture entitled *The Viking's Daughter*, which was released in 1908. *The Oath of a Viking*, directed by Searle Dawley, was released in 1914, and *The Viking Queen*, directed by Walter Edwin, was released a year later. *The Viking*, directed by Roy William Neill and released in 1928, told the story of Leif Ericson, credited by Rasmus Anderson as the first European to set foot in the Americas. *The Viking* was also the first feature-length Technicolor film that boasted a soundtrack. Vikings, of course, were also the principal villains in the 1954 production of Prince Valiant. Roger Corman's classic B-Grade *Viking Women and the Sea Serpent* was released in 1957 and originally carried the even more impressive title *The Saga of the Viking Women and Their Voyage to the Waters of the Great Sea Serpent*.

In 1958 Richard Fleischer, the son of an Austrian emigrant, directed the big-budget film *The Vikings*. Fleischer had started out in animation (*Betty Boop*, *Popeye the Sailor*, *Superman*), but had made a name for himself with his adaptation of Jules Verne's *20,000 Leagues under the Sea*, which saw release in 1954. Adapted from Edison Marshall's 1951 novel of the same name, *The Vikings* was based loosely on the stories of the ninth-century raider Ragnarr Loðbrók. Fleischer cast Ernest Borgnine as Ragnar, Tony Curtis as an enslaved Prince Erik, and Kirk Douglas, his hero from *20,000 Leagues*, as Ragnar's villainous son Einar.

The Vikings was a sensation in its day, returning excellent results both in America and in the United Kingdom. It inspired the Italian director Mario Bava to produce his own version, *Gli Invasori* (The Invaders) in 1961, a film he followed with *L'ultimo dei Vikinghi* (The Last of the Vikings) later that same year and *I Coltelli del Vendicatore* (The Knives of the Avenger) in 1966. Other Italian directors also exploited the success of Fleischer's original with *I Normanni* (The Normans) appearing in 1962 and *Erik, il Vichingo* (Erik the Viking) released three years later. In America, the sets from *The Vikings* were used to produce a short-lived television series, *Tales of the Vikings*, from 1959 until 1960.

In 1964, Jack Cardiff made his contribution to the genre with *The Long Ships* starring Richard Widmark and Sidney Poitier and, the following year, Charlton Heston appeared in the Franklin Schaffner film *The War Lord*. In 1969, Clive Donner directed David Hemmings and Michael York in *Alfred the Great*.

By the time that verifiable Viking remains were discovered at L'Anse aux Meadows, therefore, an interest in ancient Scandinavian history and mythology was a long-established component of both academic and popular culture in the United States. The Newfoundland discoveries added impetus to claims that North America had been discovered by the Norse, a theory popularized by Rasmus Anderson almost a century before. In 1930, Wisconsin had instituted October 9 as Leif Ericson Day, a state holiday recognizing the Norse settlement of America. A year later, Minnesota did the same. By 1956 only seven states of America and one Canadian province were celebrating the holiday, but the finds at L'Anse aux Meadows swung opinion in favor of Anderson's proposal. In 1964, the United States Congress authorized the observance of a national holiday to commemorate the arrival of the first Europeans to the Americas—the Vikings. It was in the midst of all this Viking frenzy that *The Mighty Thor* emerged.

A COMIC BOOK THOR

The Mighty Thor, together with *The Amazing Spiderman* and *The Incredible Hulk*, lies at the heart of one of comic book's greatest sagas—the blood feud between Stan Lee and Jack Kirby. Kirby went to his grave in 1994 still bitterly resentful of the treatment he received at the hands of Lee, his former employer. Lee, to this day, remains adamant that his is the correct version of the story.

That story began in 1962 when Stan Lee "created" a "new" superhero called Thor: "I had already given birth to the Fantastic Four, the Hulk, and Spider-Man. Next, I wanted to come up with something totally different."[18]

Different meant more powerful, but nothing was more powerful than the Hulk (the strongest man in the world). Then:

> It finally came to me; don't make him human—make him a god . . . Mulling it over, I decided readers were already pretty familiar with the Greek and Roman gods. It might be more fun to delve into the old Norse legends . . . so I picked Thor, the Norse God of Thunder.[19]

Lee's younger brother Larry Lieber wrote the script and Jack Kirby did the artwork. Lee determined to place the Thunder god in the ailing *Journey into Mystery* title and Thor appeared for the "first" time in issue 83 (August 1962).

It might seem pedantic to place inverted commas around terms such as "create," "new," and "first," but it is precisely these terms that fueled the controversy that was to drive Jack Kirby away from Marvel Comics and cast such a pall over the entire industry for decades to come. Who, after all, "creates" a comic book character, the scriptwriter or the artist? How "new" is a mythological character that has existed in literature for more than a millennium? And how can either Lee or Kirby have claimed that Thor debuted in August 1962 when both of them had used the character years, even decades, before?

Thor's early appearances in *Journey into Mystery* carried no credits. Later, Kirby was acknowledged as penciler, but Lee's name still headlined, and this soon became a major bone of contention between the two.

By 1965 Marvel Comics were selling 35,000,000 copies a year and 40,000 readers had paid to join the Merry Marvel Marching Society, Marvel's in-house fan club.[20] For the first time in a decade, Marvel was approaching sales parity with their longtime rival DC. The *New York Herald Tribune* ran an article on Stan Lee's up-and-coming company, and Nat Freedland, the reporter sent to cover the story, cast Lee as the face of Marvel and the reason for its success. Kirby was furious.

Lee, who had no control over Freedland's take on the industry, acknowledged that Kirby had a right to feel aggrieved and changed the credits on subsequent issues of *The Mighty Thor* (and the *Fantastic Four*) to read "A Stan Lee and Jack Kirby Production," but the damage was done. Later, Kirby was to claim full credit for creating not only Thor, but also the Fantastic Four, the Hulk, and even Spider-Man: "(a)ll of them came from my basement," Kirby said.[21]

The Lee/Kirby dispute fed, in turn, into a larger ugliness that lay at the heart of comic book creation in general. On the surface the argument was about who got the credit for creating a cultural icon, but these icons were also salable products, so at the heart of this debate was a question of money. As comic book heroes transitioned from ten-cent pulp-fiction rags into a multimillion-dollar industry, the debate as to their origins, and, therefore, their copyright ownership, became more heated.

Jerry Siegel and Joe Shuster had famously sold their rights to *Superman* for $130 in 1938. By 1940, *Superman* was selling more than a million copies per month and although Siegel and Shuster were being paid annual salaries of $75,000 each to write those comics, this was nothing compared to the millions of dollars that National Comics was making from the publication and merchandising of the superhero. Siegel and Shuster determined to sue their employer, but a New York court ruling in 1948 upheld their original contract with National. For industry insiders, the brewing storm between Lee and Kirby seemed to be history repeating itself. By 1970, Kirby had left Marvel to join DC.

Kirby's decision to leave Marvel was based on more than a falling out over credits, of course, but it is this aspect of the dispute that draws our attention here particularly because, in terms of *The Mighty Thor* at least, the claims of both men are so obviously wrong. Lee claims to have come up with the idea by himself, but his own admission that he "pictured Norse gods looking like Vikings of old, with the flowing beards, horned helmets, and battle clubs"[22] shows how little input he must have had in the final product, for *The Mighty Thor* has none of these things. Kirby's counter that *The Mighty Thor* came from his basement needs more than a little qualification as well.

The first Thor to make it into comic books was the creation of Dan Gormley. *Thor: God of Thunder* first appeared in the first issue of Fox's *Weird Comics* (April 1940) where the awkward and "unworldly" Grant Farrel is transformed into an avatar of the Norse god in order to carry out Thor's "work" on earth. Gormley's terrestrial Thor is blond and clean shaven, just as Kirby's Thor would be some twenty years later. Gormley's Thor also started out with the magical hammer and cloak associated with the Eddic legends of the Thunder god, but also a curiously atypical winged helmet.

By 1940, Vikings were usually depicted wearing horned, not winged, helmets, as Lee's comment quoted above indicates. This trend had begun in 1875 when Richard Wagner's costume designer, Carl Doepler, had pioneered the look for the first Bayreuth production of the full *Ring des Nibelungen*.[23] Vikings wearing winged helmets, as had been common in earlier nineteenth-century artwork, would become exceedingly rare after the sensational, and international, success of Wagner's ring cycle.

Over the course of the first five issues of *Weird Comics*, Gormley's hero lost most of his costume as the artist streamlined his visual style. By issue five (August 1940), Thor appeared in a pair of short trunks only. By issue 6 he had transformed into "Dynamite Thor," a superhero whose invulnerability facilitates a unique form of propulsion—by exploding sticks of dynamite attached to his belt, Dynamite Thor is able to fly. Not surprisingly, Dynamite Thor disappeared after only two issues, although he reappeared briefly in issues 6 to 8 of Fox Feature Syndicate's *Blue Beetle* (February to June 1941).

As an interesting aside, Gormley initially scripted his *Thor: God of Thunder* under the pseudonym Wright Lincoln, probably a pun involving a popular children's toy of the time. Frank Lloyd Wright, the famous architect, had patented his interlocking construction kits, "Lincoln Logs," in 1920. By 1940, Wright's Lincoln Logs were a household name, hence Wright Lincoln.

Soon after Gormley launched his short-lived *Thor: God of Thunder*, a young Jack Kirby began penciling his own mythological superhero, Mercury, in issue one of Timely Comics' *Red Raven* (August 1940). Kirby's Mercury was blond and bore a winged crown and, curiously, was transformed into Hurricane, "son of Thor, god of Thunder, and the last descendant of the ancient Greek immortals" in the first issue of *Captain America Comics* (March 1941). The first *Mercury* story was reprinted in issue 14 of *Marvel Super-Heroes* (December 1967) where it was claimed that the writer, Martin A. Bursten, was actually a pen name for Jack Kirby (implying, therefore, that Kirby had scripted the story as well as drawing it).

At about the same time *Wham Comics* also featured their hero *Detective Craig Carter*, whose magical ring allowed him to summon celestial help. In the first issue of *Wham* (November 1940), Carter summoned Thor. A circus strongman called Thor also appeared in issue 10 of the *Captain Marvel Adventures* (May 1942) written by Charles Beck and Otto Binder.

Kirby revisited the Norse legends in 1942, when he presented Thor once again, but this time as a villain. In issue 75 of *Adventure Comics* (June 1942), the Joe Simon/Jack Kirby hero Sandman was confronted by a hammer-wielding (and mortal) supervillain who had taken on the name of Thor. This Thor, however, looked nothing like the Thor that Marvel fans were to see in the early 1960s. Instead, Lee's vision of a Viking with flowing beard and a horned helmet appeared. Thor was quickly defeated and did not return to bother the Sandman again until Neil Gaiman resurrected Simon and Kirby's character almost four decades later. In the "Season of Mists" issue of Gaiman's *Sandman* (1992), Thor is portrayed once more as a red-bearded giant. As a side note, there has also been some fan speculation that Shadow, the hero of Gaiman's 2001 novel *American Gods*, might also have been intended by the author as a representation of the Norse Thunder god.[24]

Fawcett's *Whiz Comics* was also using Thor as a character during the Second World War. That company's popular magician, *Ibis the Invincible*, found himself battling the evil god Loki in issue 50 (January 1944) and was obliged to call on Thor to vanquish him. Some years later, another Fawcett staple, *Marvel Family*, featured a story by Otto Binder called "The Hammer of Thor" in issue 23 (May 1948). In Binder's story, a down-on-his-luck mechanic unleashes supernatural powers when he discovers the hammer of the Thunder god hidden in his garage.

Finally, Marvel's long-running postwar comic book, *Venus*, also featured a cameo by the Thunder god in issue 12 (February 1951). The story was drawn by Werner Roth, but the script, significantly, was executed by Stan Lee himself. Both Lee and Kirby, therefore, had dabbled with Thor long before either of them ever "dreamed" up their "new" comic in 1962. With the exception of Gormley's Thor, however, none of these early versions looked anything like *The Mighty Thor*. They were, just like Lee's description, archetypal Vikings with flowing beards and horned helmets. They were not the only Vikings in comic books, though.

The notion of the Norse "discovery" of the Americas was satirized in Carl Barks's *Donald Duck and the Golden Helmet*, which first appeared in 1952 and drew at least some of its narrative impetus from American disillusionment with German nationalism in the wake of the Second World War. Nine years later, however, Barks's *Mythic Mystery* appeared in print with Thor, replete in winged helmet, cape, and hammer, teaming up with the much wiser Scrooge McDuck (with Donald, Huey, Dewey, and Louie along for the ride). *Mythic Mystery* appeared in the year after the first finds were made at L'Anse aux Meadows.

When DC Comic's *The Brave and the Bold* started publication in 1955, it featured three "historical" superheroes: the Golden Gladiator; the Silent Knight; and the Viking Prince. The last of these three, Jon the Viking Prince, enjoyed a four-year run, appearing in the first twenty-four issues.

In issue 3 of *The Brave and the Bold* (December/January 1955–1956), fishermen discover an ancient hammer inside their nets, and Jon determines that it must be one of two hammers forged by Thor. Thor appears only in flashback in the story, but it may be significant that Jon's enemy here, the Baron Thorvold, does sport a winged helmet. Jon himself is always represented as clean shaven with long blond hair.

After his run in *The Brave and the Bold*, Jon disappeared from comic books until he was revived in 1966. In a two-issue story arc in *Our Army at War*,[25] DC's Sergeant Rock finds the Viking Prince frozen inside a glacier. The arctic ice has both preserved the Viking Prince and retconned his backstory, for now it seems that he has been banished from Valhalla by Odin for having fallen in love with a Valkyrie. Odin has cursed the prince to be separated from his sweetheart until he dies a heroic death, a task made more difficult by Odin's rendering him invulnerable to all known weapons. Jon joins Rock in his battle against the Nazis and eventually achieves his goal when he is blown up by "plastique" explosive (a weapon unknown to the ancient All-Father, Odin). Jon's death, of course, was no permanent barrier to his reappearance in subsequent comic books, but that part of his story is more directly relevant to our analysis of *Northlanders*, and so it will be covered later, in chapter 7.

Kirby's Thor reappeared more than a decade after his appearance in *The Sandman*, in issue 16 of *Tales of the Unexpected* (August 1957). In the story "The Magic Hammer," Kirby's Thor boasts a full red beard, horned helmet, and fur loincloth, but we can see the advent of several round bosses on his tunic and the hammer itself is now identical to that which we will see in issue 72 of *Journey into Mystery*. "The Magic Hammer" also introduces the audience to Kirby's first version of Loki, a recurrent character in the later stories.

In 1959, Steve Ditko drew "The Hammer of Thor" for issue 11 of Charlton Comics' *Out of This World* (January 1959). In Ditko's story, a young Viking chances upon Mjölnir in a cave and subsequently uses the weapon to thwart a Hunnic invasion of Scandinavia, thus elevating himself to godlike status among his people. Ditko's hero is blond and, initially, beardless.

In issue 127 of *Batman* (October 1959) the Dynamic Duo must battle against the Thunder god as well. In this case, Thor turns out to be Henry Meke, the proprietor of a small museum. Meke possesses an ancient hammer, the haft of which was forged from a meteorite. Having passed through space, the meteorite took on cosmic powers that it then transferred to Meke during thunderstorms, thus convincing the antiquarian that he had become Thor. DC's Thor stays true to the original with red hair and a full beard, although the artist, Sheldon Moldoff, opted for a winged helmet instead of a horned one.

A DC Comics' Thor appears again in issue 135 of *World's Finest* (August 1963). In the story "Menace of the Future Men," writer Bill Finger returns to the meteorite-powered hammer of *Batman* #127 although this time it is in the hands of the "real" Thor, a "Norseland" warrior from the year 522. Batman, having traveled back in time, notes that this Thor is not the mythological god but, in fact, a "minor tribal chief." The story is interesting in that it shows DC's continued engagement with their Thor, even in the face of booming sales of the new Marvel superhero.

Neither Lee nor Kirby's claim as to the origins of Marvel's Thor seem particularly credible then. The Norse god appeared before, during and after his Marvel "genesis" in a number of forms. So why did the Thor that appeared in issue 83 of *Journey into Mystery* achieve a success that none of his previous incarnations could manage, even those versions created by Lee and Kirby?

The hero of *The Mighty Thor* differed significantly from his earlier avatars. His distinct image consisted of his hammer, of course, but also long, blond hair without a beard, an embossed tunic, a heavy red cape, a winged helmet, and thigh-high boots secured by *vindingr* (strips of cloth or leather wound about the legs). During the 1950s Kirby had given us the tunic and the hammer in *Tales of the Unexpected*, and Jon the Viking Prince had boasted long, blond hair in *The Brave and the Bold*, but none of the comic book versions of the Norse god had combined all these elements. That does not mean, however, that it had not been done before.

By the time that the Mighty Thor appeared in 1962, James Baldwin's *Story of Siegfried* had been in publication for almost eighty years. It is hard to imagine a public library or school in the United States that could not, by the middle of the twentieth century, boast multiple editions of this American classic authored by a man who did so much to influence pedagogy in his homeland. For forty years, Baldwin's prose had been illuminated by Pyle's vision, and when young Americans leafed through their copies of *Siegfried* they were presented with a youthful, clean-shaven hero with long, blond hair, a heavy cape, an ornately winged helmet, thigh-high boots, and *vindingr*—and, just for good measure, the illustration in the frontispiece of Baldwin's best-seller even shows the hero wielding a hammer.[26]

Thor had appeared in a plethora of comics before his "debut" in *Journey into Mystery*, but it was not until the artist's vision was brought into line with that of the audience that the comic book hero could enjoy real success. Kirby and Lee finally gave America what they had wanted, what they had been programmed to expect, and Marvel was rewarded for it. This is not to say that Marvel's contribution to the mythos was not considerable, however, as they brought the ancient god into the world of the twentieth-century superhero.

THE MIGHTY THOR

Marvel's recension of the Norse god was plagued from its outset by a series of story holes and by plot lines that could lead nowhere. While on vacation in Norway, an American doctor, Donald Blake, witnesses the arrival of the Stone-men from Saturn. These aliens are an advance scouting party, sent to ascertain the Earth's vulnerability to invasion. Blake, partially handicapped, flees into a cave where he finds a stick. This stick, when struck against the ground, performs two magical transformations: it changes itself into the legendary hammer Mjölnir (simplified to Mjolnir for the comic book); and it transforms the American doctor into the Norse god of Thunder.[27]

Thor defeats the aliens, of course, and the invasion is averted—who would dare to attack a planet with so powerful an ally—but where can a story like this one go? Thor is, after all, a god. Foiling petty crimes (like Spider-Man), or running from the authorities (like the Hulk), or even outwitting supervillains (like the Fantastic Four) could hardly be taxing to a god. Immortal and all-powerful, there could be little suspense in any regular comic book storyline involving this newest Marvel creation. And what did Marvel mean by a "god" anyway?

Audiences were immediately perplexed by the inconsistencies of the deity/hero. Only the Thunder god, the comic book stipulates, can handle Mjolnir, so Don Blake must actually be Thor, not just a mortal transformed into Thor, otherwise he could not have picked up the magical artifact in the first place. Why, then, did Don forget that he was a god and why did he forget about the hammer he had apparently lost in a cave in Norway, a country to which he had apparently never been before? Furthermore, Mjolnir, once thrown, will always return to Thor's hand so, having been misplaced in the cave in Norway, why did it not return to him immediately? Most important of all, if Thor is a god, what can that mean for Christianity?

All these questions might seem fatuous, it is just a comic book after all, but they are the questions that were posed by a considerable number of readers at the time. The initial *Journey into Mystery* comic books carried only stories, but, by issue 109 (October 1964), one or two pages of every copy were set aside for "The Hammer Strikes." This section consisted of letters from the fans, and the fans were perplexed.

Using these fan letters as a source of information is admittedly problematic. We have no way of knowing how representative such correspondences were. Editorial comments that appeared in the letters pages regularly stated that the few letters published were selected from hundreds or even thousands of examples. The editors stated that they had tried to select letters that represented their audience and the sort of questions they were asking. Even so, we know that at least some of these letters were written by the editors themselves, or by the writers involved with the comic book.[28] The letters often contain encrypted taunts at other employees or jibes from rival comic companies. Many, however, were genuine, and through them we can glean at least some insight into the audience of comic books like *Journey into Mystery* and the issues that motivated these fans to write in.

Reading "The Hammer Strikes" in *Journey into Mystery* one is immediately struck by the number of letters from service personal and university students. There are very few (in fact virtually no) letters from younger readers expressing childish delight in Thor's superheroic antics, the sort of letters we might read in Batman comics, for example. Rather, we find long and detailed musings on the nature of the deity, proposed resolutions of plot holes, and debates over variations in mythologies. Vietnam is discussed, the *Eddas* are mentioned, Tolkien's *Lord of the Rings* is compared to Marvel's *Tales of Asgard*. Readers cite their senior English texts, their university professors, and *Bulfinch's Mythology*. Addresses given for these letters include the University of Massachusetts, the California Institute of Technology, Bridgeport, Pennsylvania State College, the University of Pennsylvania, Cornell, the University of Washington, Ohio State University, and the Royal Shakespeare Theatre in Stratford-upon-Avon.

We know from editorial responses printed in these letters pages that Thor, like the Hulk, was popular with college students, and that by the mid-1960s *Journey into Mystery* was one of Marvel Comic's biggest sellers.[29] We know, also, that the editors listened to these fans and adopted plot resolutions proposed first in "The Hammer Strikes." It was eventually revealed, for example, that it was Thor's father Odin who, having decided that his son needed to be taught humility, had transplanted Thor, without memories of his godhood, into the frail body of Donald Blake. Blake was too human for Mjolnir to return to him it seems, and so the hammer lay waiting for the predestined day when its owner would stumble upon it. This resolution, first revealed in issue 159 of *The Mighty Thor* (December 1968), was actually proposed by Dwight Decker in the readers' pages of the previous issue.

Thor's other dilemma, who to fight, was quickly solved by dipping back into mythology. Marvel transformed the fire god Loki into Thor's adoptive brother (Balder's filial relationship with Thor was dissolved and he became, instead, Thor's best friend) and pitted him against the Thunder god in a series of contests based on Loki's feelings of paternal rejection and the resultant sibling rivalry.

After various unsuccessful attempts to destroy Thor,[30] three of his principal enemies (the Absorbing Man, the Destroyer, and the Wrecker) were unleashed through Loki's connivance.[31] The destruction thus unleashed by Loki prompted the formation of a new superhero team, the Avengers, which Lee had hoped would capture some of the market then being exploited by DC's Justice League of America. The first issue of *The Avengers* appeared in September 1963.

Loki's malice ensnared Thor in increasingly epic adventures. He teamed up with Balder and his own Asgardian father to battle the fire-demon Surtur and the storm-giant Skagg in issue 104 of *Journey into Mystery* (May 1964). Thor also encountered the Olympian god Hercules,[32] who became another close ally, especially after Thor saved Hercules from the malevolence of Pluto.[33] Thor went on to halt the rapacious advance of Ego the Living Planet, rescue his human love-interest Jane Foster from the High Evolutionary, and defeat the Evolutionary's flawed creation, the Man-Beast.[34]

Having fallen in love with Jane, much to his father's disapproval, Thor and Odin clashed repeatedly over the relationship[35] until Odin finally relented and allowed his son to love the human woman, on the condition that she pass an Asgardian test. Jane failed that test, unfortunately, and was returned to Earth as the heartbroken Thor was introduced to the warrior-woman Sif.[36]

Journey into Mystery covers had featured the larger subtitle "The Mighty Thor" since issue 104 (May 1964), but with issue 126 (April 1966), Marvel decided to change the publication's title. Henceforth, *Journey into Mystery* was no more. Now there was to be only *The Mighty Thor*. Issue 126 also marked a change in plotline trajectory.

Thor's divine nature had dictated Asgardian storylines from early on in his career, but the writers had also augmented the "god on Earth" scripts with additional material taken straight from the *Eddas*. Beginning in issue 97 of *Journey into Mystery* (October 1963), these traditional stories appeared in pages at the back of the comic book under the heading "Tales from Asgard." With the advent of *The Mighty Thor*, the writers decided to tie the two halves of the comic more closely together. From issue 126, Thor's adventures became increasingly divorced from the real world of Jane Foster and more closely aligned with the mythological world of the *Eddas* and the *Nibelungenlied*.

Once returned to his Asgardian realm, following his separation from Jane, Thor went on to battle other foes taken from Norse mythology. He fought the troll Ulik for the first time when the creature attempted to steal Mjolnir.[37] Soon after, he joined with his fellow Asgardians to take on the Enchanters Three.[38] Thor avoided being claimed by the death goddess Hela in issue 150 (March 1968) and returned to Asgard to prevent Mangog from drawing the Odinsword and ending the universe.[39] As the 1960s came to a close, Thor learned the origin of the cosmic entity Galactus, encountered Ego once more,[40] stopped the childlike deity Him (who would eventually become Adam Warlock) from kidnapping Sif,[41] and battled Surtur a second time when the fire-demon teamed up with Loki and attempted to storm Asgard yet again.[42]

At the same time Marvel attempted to expand upon Thor's success by producing spin-offs. *Tales of Asgard*, removed from *The Mighty Thor* in early 1968, was launched as its own title in October of the same year. It was discontinued after only one issue. The Warriors Three were Marvel creations rather than borrowings from Norse mythology. These three Asgardian warriors (Fandral, Hogun, and Volstagg) had appeared in issue 119 of *Journey into Mystery* (August 1965), but, after frequent appearances in *The Mighty Thor*, they had brief outings in their own comic book in 1976 and again in 1984.[43] *Balder the Brave* began production in 1985, but was discontinued after only four issues.[44]

In 1980, Roy Thomas, whose contribution to medievalist comic books will be explored more fully in the following chapter, began introducing material from the *Eddas* and the *Nibelungenlied* directly into the storylines of *The Mighty Thor*. Starting with issue 293 (March 1980), Thomas interwove the ancient tales with an ongoing storyline that ran for the next eight issues until he left Marvel for DC. It seems no coincidence that, following Thomas's transfer, DC then produced its own four-part series *The Ring of the Nibelung*, which was written by Thomas.[45]

With Thomas leaving Marvel, the plotlines of *The Mighty Thor* moved further away from Norse mythology and closer toward the convoluted, but self-contained, mythos of the Marvel universe. Thor's popularity continued unabated, sales remained strong, and he appeared often in parallel titles. By the early twenty-first century, the Marvel hero had transitioned into a box-office hit and merchandising goldmine, and so it seems appropriate to finish this chapter as it started, with *The Challenge of Thor*.

When Longfellow first published his poem in 1863, in the midst of the Viking Revival, he was looking to breathe tension into the story of Iceland's tenth-century conversion to Christianity, to pit Thor against Christ, as it were: "Thou art a God too, O Galilean! And thus singled-handed unto the combat, gauntlet or gospel, here I defy thee!" With one of the longest running comic book series still in publication, and with more fans than ever thrilling to the adventures of the Norse god on the big screen, perhaps Thor defies Christ still.

CONCLUSION

The correlations between the reception histories of the Arthurian legends, the stories of Robin Hood, and the tales of Valhalla as they appear in the medievalist comics of the American Century must seem obvious at this point. Over these last three chapters we have seen remarkable similarities in the reemergence of medieval literature, its use in the creation of complex nationalist ontologies, and in the transmission of those concepts into a new and popular cultural form.

What must be equally obvious, also, is the centrality of the names Pyle and Wyeth within that reception history. We have seen, so far, European textual scholarship both adopted and fostered by American academics and used in a number of ways, but the translation of that literary tradition into a popularly recognizable form would seem to have been pioneered and, to a large extent, orchestrated by these two men. Comics, no less than movies, took a great many cues from both Pyle and his protégé.

This is not to say that talented individuals like Hal Foster, or Dennis O'Neil, or Jack Kirby merely transferred the visions of Pyle and Wyeth into their work. All the medievalist comics so far assayed labored to transmit the tales of the European Middle Ages across the Atlantic, to interpret those narratives for a new audience, and, at times, to create an entirely new art form. In the next chapter, however, we will turn our attention toward another vein of comic book medievalism, a medievalism less indebted to its European antecedents and more uniquely American.

CHAPTER 4

Conan the Barbarian (1970)

Let me live deep while I live; let me know the rich juices of red meat and stinging wine on my palate, the hot embrace of white arms, the mad exultation of battle when the blue blades flame and crimson, and I am content. Let teachers and priests and philosophers brood over questions of reality and illusion. I know this: if life is illusion, then I am no less an illusion, and being thus, the illusion is real to me. I live, I burn with life, I love, I slay, and am content.
—CONAN, FROM ROBERT E. HOWARD, *QUEEN OF THE BLACK COAST* (1934)

The overnight success of *The Mighty Thor*, much like that of *Prince Valiant* or Green Arrow, was a long time in the making. Decades of scholarship had washed down from the New England universities, flowing into the curricula of American schools that, by the early twentieth century, were bursting with enrollments. Wave upon wave of immigrants pushed their children forward with the promise of education and the hope of a better future. These children found textbooks that brought the heroes of their parents' homelands into the bright modernity of their adopted country, proffering some stability against the threat of change, and continuity in the face of innovation. Arthur and his knights, Robin and his Merry Men, Thor and the gods of Valhalla, all of them found a place at the Thanksgiving table.

From the 1930s on, comic book authors wisely borrowed from the literary traditions that had preceded them, and borrowed heavily, especially from the wealth of children's literature that had filled the shelves of the more affluent families, the school repositories, and the district libraries. There had always been unresolved questions at the heart of American medievalism, though, and these questions were inherited by this new medium. Was magic (or *is* magic) real? Was magic (or *is* magic) evil?

The magic of the late-nineteenth-century Arthurian legends was problematic and ambiguous, the magic of the Norse revival, no less so. As we have seen, comic book authors skirted around issues of divinity and diabolism with an opaque prevarication, seemingly unwilling to make definitive statements about the Christian God, or pagan gods, or the Devil, or sorcery. Following the early lead of Mark Twain, comic book medievalists like Hal Foster tended to come down on the side of rational explanation and "science as magic," although, as we have also seen, they did not always do so, and they did not do so unequivocally. Comic book heroes, for all the absurdity of their narrative, tended to be scientific as well. Superman was an alien, Batman was an inventor, and the uncanny ability of Green Arrow to perform ludicrous feats of archery apparently required no explanation whatsoever. Still, there was an uncertainty there.

White's Arthurian retellings were popular as soon as they appeared in print, but they had, at their heart, a disconcerting weirdness—a quality that remained unresolved in the early storylines of *Prince Valiant*. As we have seen, fans of *The Mighty Thor* seemed challenged by the superhero's divinity and his interaction with a world of magic. The medievalism of these comics was nostalgic and, for the most part, utopian, but there was a darker strain of medievalism taking root in America as well, an alternate medievalism that would play upon American fears of dark magic and the unquiet dead. Far from the gothic-revivalist towers of the Ivy League colleges, far from the urban sophistication of the East coast metropolises, a grim, cynical, violent medievalism was stirring to life in the most unexpected of places—the Wild West.

ROBERT E. HOWARD

It is difficult to say what Robert Ervin Howard would have made of Conan's popularity had he lived long enough to see it. With the single exception of Tolkien, no other fantasy writer has ever outsold Howard,[1] and yet Howard himself undervalued his work in this genre: "if I ever do anything of lasting merit," he wrote, only weeks before his death in 1936, "it will be fiction laid in the early west."[2]

Howard was both a product and a prisoner of the West. Born in 1906, the son of a traveling country doctor, Howard spent his earliest years traipsing through the boomtowns of Texas, eventually settling in Cross Plains, a small town whose population would swell from some 1,500 to more than 10,000 with the discovery of oil in 1920. The young Howard was proud of his settler heritage and fascinated by the "yarns" he heard from old-timers in the district, but he hated the oil boom and resented both the crime and the human flotsam that washed in with it.[3] Cosseted by his mother and bullied at school, Howard read voraciously.

The authors favored by the young Texan wrote about rugged individualists and tough, determined men. Among his preferred writers, Howard listed Arthur Conan Doyle, Jack London, Mark Twain, Zane Grey, Sir Henry (H.) Rider Haggard, and the war hero and Hearst journalist Ambrose Bierce. We know also that Howard engaged with medievalism through the works of James Macpherson, Walter Scott, and Alfred Lord Tennyson, names we have encountered repeatedly in the course of this study. Perhaps most important, though, Howard was exposed to fantasy writing through the works of Edward Plunkett, Baron Dunsany, and with what he called "weird" writing through the works of his close correspondent Howard Phillips (H. P.) Lovecraft.[4]

Although they never met in person, Lovecraft and Howard wrote to each other often, each deeply supportive of the other's talent. They shared a high regard for the work of Baron Dunsany, whose innovative *The Gods of Pegāna* (1905) marks the watershed between the literate fantasy of Shakespeare and Spencer, and the popular fantasy of writers like Howard and Tolkien. Dunsany's popularity in the years around the Great War had also seen him embark upon lecture tours of the United States and Lovecraft, an inveterate fan, had thrilled to hear him speak in Boston.[5]

Like Lovecraft, Howard was also obsessive in his reading of history, developing lifelong passions for pre-Christian mythologies, the sunken continents of Atlantis and Lemuria, and the barbarian tribes of northern Europe, particularly the Picts. Howard identified strongly with the Celtic people and took exception to the work of scholars like Rasmus Anderson in attempting to establish the Norse as the first Europeans to discover America. In a brief autobiographical piece, Howard claimed that the Celts visited America before the Spanish or the Vikings: "St. Brandon came to America," he wrote, "and others before him, and in frailer craft than the *Santa Maria* or any long serpent."[6]

Howard's passion for history had been ignited when, at the age of thirteen, he had come across a schoolbook written in an "interesting and romantic style" in a library on Canal Street, New Orleans.[7] Leon Nielsen has identified this book as George Scott-Elliot's *Romance of Early British Life*, first published in 1909.[8] Scott-Elliot—adventurer, explorer, military hero—was exactly the sort of writer the young Howard would have gravitated toward and his amateur histories are full of drama, action, and high adventure. More important, for a book of its day, *Romances of Early British Life* is also copiously illustrated with some twenty-eight plates, executed by artists steeped in the medievalist traditions of Victorian England. Thus we find paintings by Frederick Leighton, John Campbell, and Lancelot Speed (the last of whom, coincidentally, was also a celebrated cartoonist).[9]

By the age of twenty-one, Howard had determined to pursue a career of writing full-time. Income, rather than literary authenticity, was the primary objective of Howard's writing and, as such, he submitted numerous articles to pulp-fiction magazines. He wrote about boxers, pirates, detectives, and cowboys. He wrote funny stories, he wrote adventure stories, he wrote historical stories, he wrote weird stories, he wrote poetry. He wrote anything he thought might get published. In 1929 Howard's first fantasy story was published.

Weird Tales published "The Shadow Kingdom" in August of that year. The story introduced audiences to the hero Kull, a former gladiator turned mercenary who had become the King of Valusia, in an age before Atlantis was swallowed by the sea. The readership responded well to Howard's story, and he followed it up with several more. "The Mirrors of Tuzun Thune" was published that September and "Kings of the Night" was published in November of the following year. Howard wrote a further nine Kull stories, and a poem, but none of these found publication.

In 1932, a frustrated Howard took the rejected Kull story "By This Axe I Rule!" and rewrote it. He swapped Kull the Conqueror for Conan the Barbarian, transplanted the action into a postdiluvian (but still ancient) kingdom called Aquilonia, and renamed the novelette "The Phoenix on the Sword." *Weird Tales* accepted the revised script for publication in its December 1932 issue, and Conan was introduced to the world.

CONAN THE BARBARIAN

In all, Howard wrote some twenty-one Conan stories of which seventeen were published in his lifetime. The other four found publication in the years following his suicide in 1936, as have a number of other unfinished fragments and synopses. Delineating the reception history of Conan the Barbarian is a relatively straightforward task, but explaining the eventual popularity of Howard's creation is somewhat more complicated. What becomes immediately obvious to anyone reading the original stories, however, is the essentially American flavor of them. Conan is a cowboy—albeit a cowboy in a strange, medievalist world.[10]

Howard's preference for "fiction laid in the early west" informed his fantasy writing. The essential elements of the modern western—"larger-than-life hero, love story, western landscape ... and occasional violence"[11]—are all standard features of the Conan stories. Howard imagined the Cimmerians, the barbarian nation from which Conan hails, as a proto-Celtic people inhabiting the lands that would eventually become Britain, and yet the landscape through which Conan rides is in no way European. He traverses deserts adorned with mesas and buttes, rides through open prairies where the grass is so high it can hide a horse, looks out over cactus-studded plains, and cuts his way through verdant jungles. On his journeys he fights off wolves and bears—European fauna to be sure—but also panthers, lions, monkeys, and giant snakes.

It is easy to see Conan as that quintessential western figure, the semi-nomadic gunfighter (albeit without a gun), wandering from town to town, righting wrongs, and looking for a place to belong. Nor should we see this stereotype as antithetical to the same medievalist elements that also informed Howard's work—indeed, as Jennifer Moskowitz has noted, "the mythological construction of the cowboy, built on the foundation of the medieval English knight, was a crucial element in the creation of nationalist sentiment in post–Civil War America."[12]

This ontological association of the knight with the cowboy adds further context to Twain's criticism of Scott's "enchantments," as it is an analogy that carried some weight even during the heyday of the Wild West. As early as 1884, a newspaper in the town of Deadwood, South Dakota, referred to cowboys as "knight(s) of the lariat."[13] To ascribe to the transient cattlemen of a tough town like Deadwood the epithet of knights is exactly the sort of "sham chivalry" that Twain was lamenting and, despite the article's protestation that the "genuine" cowboy is "hardly ever known to do a mean and cowardly act," it should be remembered that it was in Deadwood that James Butler ("Wild Bill") Hickok was famously gunned down in 1876—shot in the back while playing cards. The association between cowboys and knights kept its currency, however, and in 1899, the North Adams Evening Transcript advertised a "cowboy tournament" in St Louis under the same banner: "Knights of the Lariat."[14]

Whatever the limitations of this comparison, it must be said that the violence of the modern western does come, at least in part, from the realities of the lives lived in frontier towns like Deadwood. Moreover, for one famous commentator, the violence that defines the western genre is both a product and a defining characteristic of the society in which that literature is produced. "The essential American soul is hard, isolate, stoic, and a killer," wrote D. H. Lawrence, "A man who turns his back on white society. A man who keeps his moral integrity hard and intact. An isolate, almost selfless, stoic, enduring man, who lives by death."[15] Conan, like the gunfighter or the cowboy, is a hard, isolate, stoic killer—but he is also more than that.

When Luce wrote his editorial on the American Century some five years after Howard's death, he extolled to his readership a series of core values, "a love of freedom, a feeling for the equality of opportunity, a tradition of self-reliance and independence," values he believed to be "infinitely precious and especially American."[16] These values might just as readily define Conan's character.

Conan is also a traveler, and Luce maintained that Americans were "the least provincial people in the world," that they had "traveled the most," and that they knew "more about the world than the people of any other country."[17] Like Conan, though, Americans were not altogether impressed with what they found on their travels. There was value in other nations to be sure, but theirs was not the same caliber of dynamic spirit that invigorated the New World: "Other nations can survive simply because they have endured so long," wrote Luce, "But this nation, conceived in adventure and dedicated to the progress of man—this nation cannot truly endure unless there courses strongly through its veins . . . the blood of purposes and enterprise and high resolve."[18]

Conan the Barbarian, uneducated but powerful beyond measure, is driven by his lust for life. Drawn into lands far more civilized than his own, he is simultaneously disparaging of their learning, awed by their achievements, and desirous of their wealth. He walks a world made claustrophobic with the ruined towers of fallen empires, and scorns the vicious intellect of bookish wizards and greedy priests.

It is important to note that, at the time of his death, Howard's increasing success meant that he was able to express a preference for his writing, and that preference was not for fantasy. Edgar Hoffmann Price, one of Howard's literary heroes, did not care for the Conan stories (Howard "at his un-best!" he would later write[19]), and Howard seems to have taken Price's criticisms to heart. Had Howard continued, it seems likely that he would have begun to specialize in the westerns that he loved so much. Indeed, at the time of his death, Howard had just secured a deal with the English publisher Herbert

Jenkins to print his first book, the western collection *A Gent From Bear Creek*.

Such speculation, of course, remains just that. In June 1936, Howard's mother slipped into a coma. Informed by a nurse that his mother was unlikely to recover consciousness, Howard took his own life. *A Gent from Bear Creek* was published posthumously, and Howard was mourned by his friends and fans. Lovecraft was deeply affected by Howard's suicide and, diagnosed with cancer of the small intestine at about the same time, died within the year.

Two years later, Donald Wandrei and August Derleth founded the small independent publishing firm Arkham House, ostensibly to preserve the heritage of Lovecraft, their literary hero. Their focus extended eventually to Lovecraft's circle as well and, in 1946, Arkham published Howard's second book *Skull-Face and Others*, which included five Conan stories previously published in *Weird Tales*.[20]

In 1951, Glenn Lord had come across a copy of Arkham's *Skull-Face* and become curious about the book's author. Lord was instrumental in getting Arkham to publish a collection of Howard's poetry, *Always Comes the Evening*, in 1957, and in 1961 he began the seminal fanzine *The Howard Collector*. By 1965, Lord had become the executor of the Howard estate, such as it was—in an interview for another fanzine, *REH: Lone Star Fictioneer*, Lord commented that he was "just the agent for the Howard heirs. [There] actually isn't such an entity as a 'Howard estate' ... though it is a convenient term."[21] Lord's control over what was left of Howard's material, however, did not ensure his control of Howard's literary creations, particularly Conan.

Arkham was one of several publishing ventures that sought to exploit both the easing on paper restrictions that followed the end of the Second World War and the increased market for cheap fiction brought about by postwar literacy programs. Gnome Press, founded in 1948 by David Kyle and Martin Greenberg, was another. In 1950, Gnome released Howard's only Conan novel, *The Hour of the Dragon*, as *Conan the Conqueror*.

The Hour of the Dragon had originally appeared in serial form in *Weird Tales* between December 1935 and April 1936. John Clark, a longtime Howard fan, edited the serial for Gnome, turning it into the first Conan hardback. In 1952, Gnome followed up with *The Sword of Conan*, an anthology of Conan stories edited by Clark and another Gnome author, Lyon Sprague de Camp.

In 1953, while yet another company (Ace Books) produced a soft-cover version of *Conan the Conqueror*, Gnome produced a third Conan hardback,

King Conan. De Camp, by this time the only editor involved, saw fit to substantially alter some of Howard's original material for this publication, a pattern he continued for the next few years—*The Coming of Conan* (1953) and *Conan the Barbarian* (1954) both contained rewritings by de Camp. Even more worrying for Howard purists, *Tales of Conan* (1955) and *The Return of Conan* (1957) contained stories so transformed by de Camp as to be almost unrecognizable from the original material.

None of these early Conan books seem to have sold well. It took Arkham almost a decade and a half to sell the three thousand copies of *Skull-Face* they printed in 1946. Gnome Press produced similarly small runs of their Conan hardbacks and found them equally difficult to shift, even at half price.[22] *Space Science Fiction* had printed one of Howard's previously unpublished Conan stories, "The God in the Bowl," in September of 1952, and *Fantasy Magazine* printed "The Black Stranger" in February of the following year, but Conan was still not a marketable commodity outside a small fan-based genre. It was to be another fantasy writer who would launch Conan into stardom, albeit unwittingly.

JOHN RONALD REUEL TOLKIEN

De Camp and Lord had saved Conan from oblivion, but they had not made him a household name. The Cimmerian lingered in the Gnome Press editions as a shibboleth, rewritten by Howard's greatest fans for the enjoyment of a dedicated cadre of "sword and sorcery" adepts. It was Tolkien who was to change all this.

John Ronald Reuel Tolkien was nearing retirement when his best-known work, *The Lord of the Rings*, finally achieved publication. Formerly the Rawlinson and Bosworth Professor of Anglo-Saxon from 1925 to 1945, and then Merton Professor of English Language and Literature from 1945 to 1959, the Oxford Don had enjoyed reasonable success with his 1937 children's book *The Hobbit*. Tolkien had commenced work on a sequel that same year and, after more than a decade of writing, found himself trying to convince his publishers to accept the result, an epic fantasy novel for adults that ran for several thousand pages.

By this time Tolkien had already parted company with George Allen and Unwin, the firm that had produced *The Hobbit*, and so the new novel was offered to the publishing house of Collins. Milton Waldman, Tolkien's contact at Collins, advised the professor to drastically reduce his manuscript, but

Tolkien remained adamant that the book should be printed in its entirety.[23] Tolkien evidently believed that fantasy novels would find a ready audience and that the length of his offering would prove no barrier—as early as 1947 he had written that it "may be a large book, but evidently it will be none too long in the reading for those who have the appetite."[24]

Tolkien's views were not unfounded. By 1952, the year that Tolkien asked Collins to publish his novel in its unabridged form, demand for *The Hobbit* had seen reprintings in both the United Kingdom and America. Moreover, Tolkien's close friend and fellow fantasy author, Clive Staples (C. S.) Lewis, was enjoying considerable success with his new Narnia series. Geoffrey Bles had published Lewis's *The Lion, the Witch and the Wardrobe* in 1950, and his *Prince Caspian* the year after. In 1952, Lewis was preparing to launch his third Narnia novel, *The Voyage of the Dawn Treader*. Lewis's novels, though, were still aimed at children, and Tolkien was asking Collins to publish an adult fairy tale. They refused. Tolkien returned to George Allen and Unwin somewhat chastened and willing to do what was necessary to see his novel in print.

Tolkien agreed to remove the supporting material from his manuscript (portions of which would eventually see publication as *The Silmarillion*) thus reducing it by half. George Allen and Unwin split the remaining prose into three books and published the first, *The Fellowship of the Ring*, in July of 1954. *The Two Towers* appeared a few months later, in November, and the final in the trilogy, *The Return of the King*, was in print by October of the following year. The Houghton Mifflin Company of Boston acquired the rights for an American edition of the novel and had released the final installment by January 1956.

By 1956, Wystan Hugh (W. H.) Auden was well established within the cultural hierarchies of his adopted America. A lifelong fascination with medieval literature, which was to result in the publication of his own translations from the Norse during the 1960s,[25] led Auden to eulogize Tolkien's trilogy as "a masterpiece of its genre," albeit a genre which he acknowledged some critics found "trifling by definition."[26] Tolkien's friend Lewis was even more laudatory. For him *The Lord of the Rings* was "like lightning from a clear sky; as sharply different, as unpredictable in our age as *Songs of Innocence* were in theirs."[27]

It is important to note at this point, despite the opinions of Lewis and Auden, just how few copies of Tolkien's novel were initially produced. George Allen and Unwin had reason to believe that the *Hobbit* sequel would attract a good readership, and they were confirmed in this belief when the first printing of *The Fellowship of the Ring*, some 3,000 copies, sold out almost immediately. Even so, only 3,250 copies of *The Two Towers* were printed in Great Britain, and 7,000 copies of *The Return of the King*. In America, 1,500 copies of *The Fellowship of the Ring* were produced, a mere 1,000 copies of *The Two Towers,* and some 5,000 copies of *The Return of the King*.[28] Sales were good, but hardly phenomenal, and this is where the cultural influence of *The Lord of the Rings* might well have finished, had it not been for loopholes in the American copyright law and the advent of the paperback in mass culture.

Paperback books were no new invention in the 1950s, but they were achieving a new level of status. Originally developed during the second half of the nineteenth century to provide passengers of the new rail systems with inexpensive traveling copies of well-known works of literature, by the middle of the twentieth century, paperbacks had become an integral component in the promulgation of learning to a burgeoning and less class-bound readership.

In 1935 the British publisher Allen Lane had begun its Penguin Books imprint and, in the United States, Simon and Schuster followed suit four years later with their Pocket Books label. American paperback companies were also closely associated with both pulp-fiction publishers and comic book houses—Ace, Dell, and Fawcett all produced both pocketbooks and comic books.

This association with more innovative forms of publishing further allowed these groups greater freedom in their ambitions. Paperback publishers attached to companies that produced hardbacks editions needed to ensure the viability of both products. Original editions of new work were to be produced in hardback and only once sufficient hardback copies had been sold could cheaper paperback editions be commissioned. With no hardback sales to protect, companies like Ace, Dell, and Fawcett soon began to experiment with the paperback publication of original material. The first of these to appear was the Gold Medal Books published by Fawcett in 1950.

These new paperbacks had to work hard to overcome a public perception of illegitimacy. New books that appeared only in paperback were seen as second rate and even paperback editions of successful hardback books could seem a little tainted. As late as 1960, Tolkien himself had expressed the idea that paperback editions of his work would "cheapen" it.[29] It is unlikely, therefore, that *The Lord of the Rings* would have ever passed into a paperback edition had it not been for the spectacular audacity of the pulp-fiction industry.

Donald Wollheim, editor of the paperback specialists Ace Books, claimed that Houghton Mifflin had neglected to copyright *The Lord of the Rings* in the United States. Utilizing an ambiguity in the American copyright law, Ace produced a staggering 150,000 copies of an unauthorized edition of Tolkien's novel in 1965. These Ace paperbacks sold for 75 cents apiece, compared to six dollars for the Houghton Mifflin hardbacks.[30]

Although Houghton Mifflin did not produce paperbacks, they worked closely with another publisher who did, Ballantine Books. Tolkien worked quickly to produce a new edition of the novel that was copyrighted in the United States and printed by Ballantine. The author also wrote letters to his American supporters asking them to boycott the Ace edition. Newspapers across the country ran with the story. In October 1965, Ballantine produced some 125,000 copies of an authorized United States edition of *The Lord of the Rings*, which sold for 95 cents a copy. Another 10,000 copies were printed for sale in Canada. Within ten months Tolkien, who had been dubious, at best, about ever allowing his work to appear in paperback form, had sold a quarter of a million copies of *The Lord of the Rings*.[31]

The rising status of the paperback novel was signaled in the 1960s by the addition of a Paperback Bestsellers list in the *New York Times*. On September 4, 1966, *The Lord of the Rings* debuted on that list at number three. By December 4 it had climbed to the top position, where it spent the next eight weeks. In total, *The Lord of the Rings* appeared for forty-nine weeks on the bestseller list, and this at a time when the list ranked only five titles. Eight years later, when the list had been expanded to ten titles, *The Lord of the Rings* appeared on it once again, suggesting, perhaps, that Tolkien's epic was a strong seller for a good many years.[32]

Tolkien's largest readership, much to his eventual chagrin, was on American campuses, and these campuses were booming as never before. Whereas in 1940 only 5.5 percent of men in America and 3.8 percent of women had spent a full four years at college, by 1960 this number had swelled to 9.7 percent and 5.8 percent respectively. By the end of that decade, the first year that Conan the Barbarian appeared in his own comic book, these numbers had grown to 14.1 percent and 8.2, and with the population of the United States growing from just over 123 million in 1940, to more than 203 million in 1970, these percentage increases represented an unprecedented growth in college enrollments.[33] Not only were scholars like those of the previous chapter—men such as Hollander and Brodeur—now teaching their medievalist courses, they were teaching them to larger and larger classes.

Across America, both on campus and off, the very appearance of Tolkien's novel in paperback format was soon seen as an indicator of its counterculture status. Hardback novels were the prescribed texts of crusty professors, while paperbacks were new and rebellious. Moreover, Tolkien's nostalgic medievalism and his focus on rustic simplicity also paralleled the hippie ethos of a rejection of technology and a return to nature. Unlike Howard's grim individualism in the face of an ultimate, possibly inescapable, defeat,

> [the] moral and religious allegories, parables and fables informing the stories of . . . Tolkien move away from the unsettling implications which are found at the centre of the purely fantastic. Their original impulse may be similar, but they move from it, expelling their desire and frequently displacing it into religious longing and nostalgia.[34]

For some, visions of Middle Earth became part of a greater whole that involved communes and flower power. Some even took the message far more literally.

On May Day 1966, less than a year after the paperback editions of *The Lord of the Rings* had flooded American colleges, medieval studies graduate and author Diana Paxson led a medieval parade through the campus of the University of California, Berkeley, as a "protest against the 20th century."[35] Another participant in that May Day parade, Marion Zimmer Bradley, who would soon become famous for her feminist contributions to the Arthurian legends, eventually coined a name for their movement, the "Society for Creative Anachronism," and new chapters were soon seeded across the country. Michael Cramer has rightly pointed out that the "genesis" for this new movement lay in the "confluence of the counterculture and fantasy literature,"[36] the same confluence that accounts for the commercial success of Tolkien in the 1960s. By 1968 there were three SCA kingdoms in America, and the society itself had been incorporated as a nonprofit organization in California.

For those who preferred literary escapism, rather than dressing up, Tolkien's success convinced publishers that paperback fantasy novels would return a healthy profit and these companies increasingly began to open their doors to young writers. Michael Moorcock found a publisher for the first of his Elric books, *Stormbringer*, in 1965.[37] Elric, a cultured and sickly albino aristocrat, heir to an ancient and corrupt empire, represents a self-conscious antithesis to Howard's dark barbarian, Conan. Moorcock's postcolonial narrative, however, found less favor with American audiences, and has yet to ignite the same kind of enthusiasm generated by the muscle-bound Cimmerian.

Three years later, Fritz Leiber, the author generally credited with coining the term "sword and sorcery," published his *Swords in the Mist*.[38] Like Howard, Leiber's work had originally found publication in pulp-fiction magazines and, like Howard, it was to be paperback publication that rescued Leiber's vision from obscurity. That same year, 1968, Ursula Le Guin also published the first book of her Earthsea quadrilogy, *A Wizard of Earthsea*.[39]

While all this was unfolding, Lyon Sprague de Camp also chose to attempt a relaunch of Conan. He approached Ace Books about releasing a paperback series but Ace refused, partly because of the financial failure of their 1953 *Conan the Conqueror* and partly because of their ongoing problems with Tolkien. De Camp then approached another paperback publisher, Lancer Books, who was interested, but Gnome instigated a lawsuit against their former employee claiming sole ownership of Howard's material.[40] Conan reprints, therefore, at least at that moment, seemed to be impossible.

Undaunted, de Camp teamed up with another writer, Lin Carter, to produce a series of original Conan stories and adaptations to augment the Howard material. In 1966, Lancer produced the first in an eleven-volume series, *Conan the Adventurer*. Gnome's *Return of Conan* had featured cover art by renowned comic book artist Wally Wood and feedback had been positive. For *Conan the Adventurer*, Lancer turned to another comic book artist, Frank Frazetta, to produce the cover art. As mentioned in chapter 2, Frazetta, a lifelong fan of Hal Foster, had previously produced his own medieval series, *Shining Knight*, for DC Comics.

Lancer's Conan series produced eleven paperbacks in less than four years and sold more than ten million copies.[41] A twelfth installment was printed by Ace Books in 1977, four years after Lancer went bankrupt. It seems unlikely that de Camp could have interested Lancer in the Conan franchise without the phenomenal success of *The Lord of the Rings*, which, in itself, seems somewhat appropriate—Tolkien enjoyed Howard's Conan stories, although we do not know what he thought of de Camp and Carter's later adaptations.[42]

At the same time, original Conan material was also appearing thanks to the work of Glenn Lord and other loyal Howard fans who were discovering new material in the papers left by Howard. The fragmentary "Hall of the Dead" appeared in *The Magazine of Fantasy and Science Fiction* in February of 1967 and "The Vale of Lost Women" appeared in *The Magazine of Horror* that same spring.

In 1968, a Texan fanzine called *Star-Studded Comics* featured possibly the first adaptation of a Conan story into a comic book format. Although *Star-Studded Comics* ran to only eighteen issues in all, from September 1963 until mid-1972, it still managed to launch the careers of comic book artists like Alan Weiss and Dave Cockrum, and comic book writers like Roy Thomas. Thomas was to become an ardent fan of Howard's work. Indeed, it was Thomas's appreciation of Cross Plains's own weird writer that was to usher in the next chapter in the Conan saga.

By the dawn of the 1970s, publishing houses could no longer work fast enough to supply the market with fantasy literature, and it *was* being seen as literature by this time thanks to the publication of studies by European academics like Tzvetan Todorov.[43] Moreover, some of those companies that were producing sword and sorcery titles, Dell and Fawcett for example, were also actively producing comics. Little wonder then that Conan's next foray would be into the world of the comic book.

A COMIC BOOK CONAN

There had been sword and sorcery heroes of Conan's ilk in a few early comic books. Crom the Barbarian appeared very briefly in a 1950 issue of *Out of This World*, which was reprinted later in Avon's *Strange Worlds*. In 1966 Harvey Comics published a story about Clawfang the Barbarian in the first issue of their *Unearthly Spectaculars* and, three years after that, DC Comics featured their Nightmaster in issues 82 through 84 of *Showcase*. Such limited runs, however, clearly indicated that none of these heroes succeeded in gaining audience approval. That all changed in 1970 with the first issue of Marvel's *Conan the Barbarian*.

Roy Thomas, having written for *Star-Studded Comics* and edited the fanzine *Alter Ego*, moved to New York in 1965 and, after a brief stint at DC, began working for Marvel. As assistant editor he was privy to the fan letters that poured in to Marvel's New York office and the fans were asking for fantasy, specifically Tolkien, Burroughs and, most of all, Howard. Thomas began to read Howard's work and he was impressed, but with the phenomenal success of the Lancer paperbacks, he thought it unlikely that he could acquire the rights to Conan. He began negotiations, instead, to publish a comic featuring Lin Carter's Conanesque Thongor. These negotiations, however, soon stalled.[44]

Marvel was nervous about branching out beyond their superhero mainstays and worried about the potential audience. As sword and sorcery heroes were violent and nihilistic, it would be difficult to script stories that would satisfy both the intended audience and the Comics Code Authority.

After a period of fruitless haggling with Lin Carter's agent, Thomas decided to contact Glenn Lord and pitch him the idea of licensing Conan to Marvel for a comic book title. To Thomas's surprise, Lord agreed.[45] The first *Conan the Barbarian* comic appeared in mid 1970. It was an immediate and unequivocal success.[46]

By this stage Thomas had become an advocate for Robert E. Howard and was working closely with both Lord, the executor of Howard's estate (such as it was), and the comic book artist Gil Kane, who had apparently acquired Conan as a copyright property sometime late in the 1960s.[47] With the success of *Conan the Barbarian*, Thomas was able to convince Marvel to publish *Savage Tales*, which appeared just months later, in early 1971.

Savage Tales was Marvel's attempt to encroach on the comics-magazine field then dominated by Warren Publishing, whose noncode publications (*Creepy, Eerie, Vampirella*) were aimed at an older readership. The Comics Code Authority prohibited adult content in comic books, but these pulp-style magazines featured a different format—they were larger and they included articles and stories with minimal, or even no, graphics. Publishers of these magazines claimed that they were not comic books and that they were, therefore, outside the self-imposed restrictions of the CCA. Even so, there was no guarantee that what publishers said about their product would prove defensible in court or, more importantly, in the minds of parents who remembered only too well the anticomics crusades of the 1950s.

Issue 1 of *Savage Tales* was not followed by issue 2 for more than two years, so nervous had Marvel become about upsetting their main target audience, but the continued success of *Conan the Barbarian*, and Thomas's growing appreciation for Howard's work, dovetailed to provide the impetus for a continued series.

Meanwhile, by June 1971, Marvel had double-dipped into the Howard legacy to produce another comic title, *Kull the Conqueror*. Kull was not Conan, however, and the series ran for only ten issues, culminating in September 1973. The following month, the long-awaited second issue of *Savage Tales* appeared with more adult-oriented Conan material.

English artist Barry Windsor-Smith worked with Roy Thomas to turn their *Conan the Barbarian* stories into black-and-white masterpieces. The self-stated aim of the invigorated series was to showcase the work of Robert E. Howard[48] and, to that end, the magazine was to include not just comics, but also stories, essays, and photographs pertaining to Conan and his creator. Thomas worked closely on the project with Lord and was in contact with de Camp. A letter from Fritz Leiber appeared in issue 5 conferring both recognition and respect.[49] By this stage Thomas was himself amassing a considerable Howard collection that included all the available hardback and paperback releases, copies of *Skullface* and *Always Comes the Evening*, and a good number of the original pulps that featured Howard's work.[50]

Conan's run in *Savage Tales* was to prove short lived, five issues in all, but not because it was unpopular. The success of the magazine comic, and a change in Marvel's administration, convinced the company that it was time to commit to its older readers. Issue 5 of *Savage Tales* (July 1974) was the last to feature the Cimmerian, but it was augmented immediately by a new title, *The Savage Sword of Conan*. Nor was the publication of Conan comics the limit of Marvel's ambitions in the sword and sorcery genre, for they were busy acquiring the rights to other Howard creations as well.

"The Shadow of the Vulture" had been published in *Magic Carpet Magazine* in January 1934. A work of historical fiction set against the backdrop of the Battle of Mohács in 1526 and the Siege of Vienna in 1529, the story introduced the character of the sword mistress Red Sonya of Rogatino. Buoyed by the success of the various Conan titles, Thomas adapted the character to become the Hyrkanian Red Sonja, the "she-devil with a sword" whose comic book career will be discussed at length in the next chapter.

At about the same time Marvel also put other sword and sorcery heroes into print, if only to gain copyright over them. Thus, Michael Moorcock's Elric appeared in early issues of *Conan the Barbarian*[51] and Lin Carter's Thongor eventually appeared in a short-lived run in *Creatures on the Loose*,[52] the same title that had originally launched Kull.

Marvel's competitors were no less hesitant to cash in on the sword and sorcery boom. Western Publishing, the home of Gold Key Comics, produced nineteen issues of *Dagar the Invincible* starting in 1972.[53] DC Comics launched their version of Fritz Leiber's Fafhrd and the Gray Mouser with *Sword of Sorcery* in 1975, and followed it up with *Claw the Unconquered*, *Stalker*, and *The Warlord*.[54] The short-lived Atlas/Seaboard Comics commissioned *Ironjaw* and *Wulf the Barbarian* at about the same time, and Wendy Pini, famous by this stage for her risqué appearances as Red Sonja at various comic conferences, began *Elfquest* with her partner Richard Pini in 1978.[55]

For the most part, though, these other series enjoyed only temporary success. Conan was still king.

Thomas's *Savage Sword of Conan* appeared by August 1974 and would remain in continuous publication for more than twenty years, eventually running to some 235 issues. The magazine boasted Glenn Lord as technical advisor and featured cover art by Frank Frazetta and Boris Vallejo, the same artists whose work had adorned the Lancer series of paperbacks. Like the earlier *Savage Tales*, each issue of *Savage Sword* began with the same excerpt from Howard's Nemedian Chronicles with which he began the very first Conan story, the "Phoenix on the Sword":

> Know, O prince, that between the years when the oceans drank Atlantis and the gleaming cities, and the years of the rise of the Sons of Aryas, there was an Age undreamed of, when shining kingdoms lay spread across the world like blue mantles beneath the stars . . .

Barry Windsor-Smith, increasingly frustrated with the limitations of working for a CCA publication, was at last allowed to publish his unedited, adult, artwork. Now, for example, Atali, the frost-giant's daughter, could appear naked, as Windsor-Smith had originally drawn her, rather than coyly draped in loose cloth or hidden by her long tresses.[56]

In between new or reinvigorated Conan stories, articles appeared by Howard fans like Fred Blosser and Robert Yaple fleshing out the Hyborian mythos. Lin Carter and Lyon Sprague de Camp wrote pieces, underground comic book artists like Richard Corben contributed material, articles on the Society for Creative Anachronism and comic book conventions were featured.

The short stories, the books, the comic books, the fanzines and, by 1978, the syndicated comic strips that appeared in some twenty-five newspapers across America, all continued to simultaneously feed and create a demand for Conan. In 1976, Glenn Lord published his "bio-bibliography" of Howard, *The Last Celt*, along with a series of Conan audio books on long-play record. Robert Weinberg's biographical *Annotated Guide to Robert E. Howard's Sword and Sorcery* was published by Starmont House the same year.

The mid-1970s, therefore, saw an unprecedented surge in sword and sorcery comic books. The counterculture embracing of Howard and Tolkien at the end of the 1960s had led to a boom in paperback sales that had then translated into a comic book explosion in the decade that followed. In

1980, Marvel released yet another Conan series, *King Conan*, which was to last until almost the end of the decade, but Howard's sullen hero had not reached the height of his appeal just yet, for the paperback boom and the comic book explosion were both leading toward a new nexus of fantastic interaction, a point at which fans could completely immerse themselves in their longed-for fantasy worlds and interact in an ingenious way with their favorite heroes.

PLAYING OUT OUR FANTASIES

Fantasy literature and, in particular, fantasy literature from the sword and sorcery genre, seems to attract devotees who crave active participation with their literary heroes to an extent seldom seem in other art forms. A recent psychological study on participants in a fantasy-based card game offers some insights into the mechanisms at work here.

Researcher, and gamer, Brett Martin posited that the appeal of interactive fantasy games lies in their ability to offer tangible "participation in a fantastic realm," a realm that has "occupied a special meaning" in the life of the gamer "since childhood." He argues that, unlike fiction "where the story is predetermined and the reader is a passive observer," such games allow participants to become "a central character of influence to the events that unfold in the realm of the imaginary."[57] Kurt Lancaster has similarly noted that people "are drawn to role-playing games because these games combine the innate need for people to interact socially, to observe, create, and perform stories"—in short, fantasy role-playing games allow the participant "to play with fantasy."[58]

Fritz Leiber was an early proponent of such games and his most famous sword and sorcery creations, Fafhrd and the Gray Mouser, were based on a game he had developed with his friend and fellow fantasy writer Harry Fischer. The two characters—a tall, powerful barbarian and a short, mercurial thief—together with their fictional world of Nehwon had been sketched out in conversations between Fischer and Leiber as early as 1936. In 1937 the two writers spent some time designing a board game set in Nehwon and, possibly to promote the game, each began composing a story utilizing their new mythos. The results, Fischer's "The Lords of Quarmall" and Leiber's "The Adventure of the Grain Ships," were not to see publication for many years, but the project stayed with Leiber and he continued to produce fiction using the characters and the settings. In 1939, the pulp-fiction magazine *Unknown* published Leiber's "Two Sought Adventure" and Fafhrd and the Gray Mouser were in print. Leiber was to go on to publish thirty-six Fafhrd and Gray Mouser stories, novellas, and novels, and the repackaging of his earliest pulp fiction into paperback collections during the early 1970s ensured Leiber's place within the hierarchy of the sword and sorcery A-list.

Leiber was a pioneer in many ways, but, by the mid-1970s, role-playing games were shedding their marginal status and emerging as a major medium through which readers of fantasy stories could engage more deeply with the sword and sorcery genre. The history of fantasy role-play games has been explored in some depth elsewhere,[59] and so a brief history will suffice here.

It is significant that the birth of the modern wargame (a game using military miniatures to simulate combat) can trace its origins to the idiosyncrasies of pioneering science-fiction writer Herbert George (H. G.) Wells. Wells's publications *Floor Games* (1911) and *Little Wars* (1913) began the hobby in earnest, although Fred Jane, author of the reference series *Jane's Fighting Ships*, had developed a set of rules for recreating naval battles using model ships as early as 1898. Such games enjoyed a steady growth in popularity during the first half of the twentieth century and, by the early 1960s, there existed several companies dedicated to the production of miniature figurines and models to use in the large-scale restaging of historical battles. By about this time also, some wargame enthusiasts were beginning to see the attraction of smaller-scale combats using fewer figures and concentrating on squad-level tactics.

Henry Bodenstedt's small-scale skirmish wargame, *Siege of Bodenburg* was published in issues 6 through 10 of the magazine *Strategy and Tactics* in 1967. Gary Gygax and Jeff Perren of the Lake Geneva Tactical Studies Association, a Wisconsin wargaming club, modified Bodenstedt's original rules to produce their *Chainmail* rules in 1971.[60] *Chainmail* included a supplement that facilitated individual fantasy-based combat, which Gygax and Dave Arneson developed into *Dungeons and Dragons* by 1974.[61] One thousand copies of *Dungeons and Dragons* (D&D) were sold that year, 4,000 the year after—sales were multiplying exponentially. Gross profits for TSR, the company that produced the game, rose from some $2 million in 1979, to $8.5 million in 1980, to $20 million in 1981.[62]

Interest in interactive fantasy games and the success of D&D instigated a number of imitations that began appearing soon after—*Tunnels and Trolls* in 1975, *Chivalry and Sorcery* in 1977, and *Runequest* in 1978.[63] Marc Miller's *Traveller*, a game designed to facilitate role-playing set in space, was also published by the Games Designers' Workshop in 1977. By the late 1970s, role-playing was emerging as a mass culture phenomenon.

At the same time, the Society for Creative Anachronism had continued to grow since its foundation in 1966. By the mid-1970s membership was soaring, and there was a well-established nexus between wargamers, role-players, and reenactors. Robert E. Howard, of course, was no stranger to such pastimes himself, and his biographies are peppered with photographs taken by his friends as they play with swords, or spears, or pistols, passing themselves off as pirates, or barbarians, or waterfront toughs.

It was only a matter of time, therefore, before sword and sorcery fans combined this love of dressing up and role-playing to create Live-Action Role-Playing (or LARPing) where participants dress as fantasy characters and play out their role-playing games in public areas. Other fans, more interested in the costumes of their sword and sorcery heroes than in recreating their battles, reproduced these outfits and began to wear them to comic book conventions and fanzine meetings—a practice now referred to as Cosplay.

Wargaming, role-playing games, historical reenactment, LARPing, and Cosplay, it would seem, were all broadly attractive to the same fan base, as even the most casual observers would have noted. *Savage Sword of Conan* featured numerous articles on the SCA and on Cosplay from its earliest editions, and companies like TSR and Strategy and Tactics regularly advertised their products in its pages and in the pages of its CCA-approved companion-title *Conan the Barbarian*.

Readers of the comic book, as opposed to the magazine, might also have noticed advertisements for Joe Weider's bodybuilding courses inserted between the panels of Conan's adventures. Had they noticed, they would have seen a bikini-clad beauty held aloft on the shoulder of an outrageously proportioned strongman with an equally outrageous name. By the middle of the next decade, however, there would be few Americans who did not know the name Arnold Schwarzenegger and few who did not know him as Conan the Barbarian.

CONAN THE MOVIE

Filmmaker and comic book historian Edward Summer was instrumental in bringing Conan to the big screen. It was he who suggested the project to Hollywood producer Edward Pressman in 1975, and it was his use of

Roy Thomas's and Barry Windsor-Smith's Conan comic books that secured funding.[64] The success of the Lancer paperbacks, recent sales of Frank Frazetta's original artwork, and the sales figures for Marvel Comics' various Conan titles worked together to convince the producers of the viability of the endeavor.[65] Procuring the film rights would prove more difficult, however, as Glenn Lord and Lyon Sprague de Camp had begun legal action against each other to determine ownership. Undaunted, Roy Thomas and Edward Summer began writing a script for the film.

The rights were eventually procured and John Milius, a longtime fan of Richard Fleischer's previously mentioned 1958 film *The Vikings*, was brought in as director. Oliver Stone then replaced Roy Thomas as scriptwriter. Stone, suffering the ill effects of his addiction to cocaine and depressants, produced a script described by Milius as a "total drug fever dream."[66] Stone's postapocalyptic Conan, possibly inspired by Gil Kane's *Blackmark*, which had also appeared in early issues of *Savage Sword of Conan*, was soon abandoned for Milius's more operatic rewrite.

Milius's *Conan* opens with a Siegfried-like sword-forging sequence, but there is much in the film that the Howard fans would recognize. Paraphrases from Howard's stories bracket the film, the first borrowed from the *Nemedian Chronicle* that introduced "The Phoenix on the Sword," the same chronicle that introduced each issue of *Savage Tales* and *Savage Sword*. Readers of Howard could recognize any number of inspirations taken from his stories, but fans of the comic books, perhaps unacquainted with the longer-form literature, would also recognize the crucifixion scene from issue 5 of *The Savage Sword*, or the monstrous snake from issues 2 and 10, or the ascent of the tower from issue 24. Milius also paid his respects to later inheritors of Howard's legacy—Conan's discovery of the sword in an ancient barrow being taken from de Camp and Carter's "The Thing in the Crypt"—as well as homage to Japanese cinema—the final battle scene in *Conan* references Akira Kurosawa's 1954 *The Seven Samurai*, and the "wizard of the mounds" owes much to the 1965 *Kwaidan* directed by Masaki Kobayashi.

Tony Shaw has argued that the film was the product of its time, the cinematic expression of Reaganite individualism in the final bleak days of the Cold War.[67] Certainly, it seemed to strike a chord with its audience. Milius's vision of Conan did not find release until 1982, but, when it did, it was a brilliant success, returning some $130 million for the $16 million investment.

Interest in Conan had also sired an interest in his creator. Darrell Schweitzer's controversial *Conan's World and Robert E. Howard* had been released as part of the Milford Series in 1978. After Milius's *Conan the*

Barbarian finished in the cinemas, Lyon Sprague de Camp released his similarly problematic *Dark Valley Destiny: The Life of Robert E. Howard* through Bluejay Books in 1983. In 1984 Don Herron released his biographical *The Dark Barbarian* through Wildside Press.

Conan the Barbarian also spawned a series of inferior imitations. Don Coscarelli's *Beastmaster* and Albert Pyun's *The Sword and the Sorcerer* were both rushed through postproduction to find release in 1982. Peter Yates's *Krull* was released the following year, and Giacomo Battiato's *Hearts and Armour* the year after that. That same year, 1984, a company called Datasoft exploited the potential of personal computers to provide fans with an interactive fantasy experience when they marketed *Conan: Hall of Volta* for use with the Apple II, the Atari 800, and the Commodore 64.

With the sword and sorcery genre becoming increasingly popular, Universal Pictures was keen to follow up on their initial success, but John Milius was unable to reprise his role as director. Universal, therefore, turned to Robert Fleischer (director of *The Vikings*) to produce a less-violent, more family-oriented sequel. This time the script was written by Roy Thomas and another comic book writer Gerry Conway. Although the movie was successful, returning some $30 million for an estimated $18 million investment, it was clear that audience ardor was beginning to cool. Fleischer later directed *Red Sonja*, which saw cinematic release in 1985 (the same year as Richard Donner's *Ladyhawke* and Paul Verhoeven's *Flesh and Blood*). The release of the Ron Howard–directed fantasy *Willow* in 1988 seemed to mark a hiatus in fantasy movie production. Plans to release a third Conan film stalled.

In 1992 Conan began appearing on television—sixty-four episodes of an animated series called *Conan the Adventurer* began screening that year. These were soon followed by another thirteen episodes of *Conan and the Young Warriors* in 1994. In 1997, twenty-two episodes of a live-action *Conan the Adventurer* were screened. That same year the final installment of the Conan trilogy appeared in cinemas, although without Arnold Schwarzenegger in the lead role. Unsure as to how audiences might react to actor Kevin Sorbo replacing Schwarzenegger, Universal did the opposite of what Robert E. Howard had done when he changed a Kull story into "The Phoenix on the Sword"—they released the final Conan film as *Kull the Conqueror*. The $30 million film recovered less than $7 million at the box office and in postrelease sales.

If Conan fortunes at the box office were turning, the same could not be said of his career in print. Although the comic book *Conan the Barbarian* wound up in 1993, after 275 issues, and *The Savage Sword of Conan* did likewise in 1995, they were seamlessly succeeded by shorter run serializations such as *Conan the Adventurer* (14 issues from 1994 until 1995), *Conan the Savage* (10 issues from 1995 until 1996), and *Conan* (11 issues from 1995 until 1996). Marvel then released their *Conan the Barbarian* miniseries after that: *Stalker of the Woods* (1997); *The Usurper* (1997–1998); *Lord of the Spiders* (1998); *River of Blood* (1998); *Return of Styrm* (1998); *Scarlet Sword* (1998–1999); *Death Covered in Gold* (1999); and *Flame and the Fiend* (2000).

Soon after, Marvel sold their copyright of Conan to Dark Horse Comics, who immediately began production of a new range of tales featuring the Cimmerian hero. Dark Horse's own *Conan* ran for fifty issues from 2003 until 2008 and was immediately succeeded by *Conan the Cimmerian*, which ran for twenty-five issues from 2008 until 2010. At the time of writing, their latest offering, *Conan the Barbarian*, is still ongoing and, with Schwarzenegger about to reprise his role in a new Conan film, there seems little chance of our seeing an end to Conan comic books in the near future.

CONCLUSION

Conan is no less a product of the Lost Generation than was Jay Gatsby or Jake Barnes, and if Howard had trouble selling his creation at the outset of the American Century, then he is in good company with Fitzgerald and Hemingway. If America had already embraced the enormity of the task put to them by Luce, after all, there would have been no need for his editorial. By the 1970s, though, with campus populations soaring and a new generation of Americans navigating their way through Middle Earth—a landscape similarly redolent with ruins—a comic book Conan could come into his own. Once again we see the interplay of literature and contemporary history in determining the reception of a medievalist comic, once again the reflection of society in the mirror of popular culture.

Conan's rise in the imagination of America marks a significant watershed, then, both in US popular culture and in the narrative of the study at hand. The previous three chapters have concentrated on medievalist traditions that were transplanted from Europe—the Arthurian romances that underlie *Prince Valiant*, the tales of Sherwood forest that inform Green Arrow, and the Norse myths upon which *The Mighty Thor* are based, are all products of parent cultures. As such they represent significant engagements with an imagined and translocated past, but they are also essentially immigrant traditions—unashamedly utopian and self-consciously nostalgic.

Robert E. Howard's medievalism, by comparison, while not entirely dystopian, was dark and nihilistic, and it took the best part of half a century before a new generation of Americans could embrace it as their own. Even then, it was the reassuring familiarity of Tolkien's "Old World" medievalism that eased the passage of Howard's bleak vision into the popular mainstream. And yet, once that vision took hold, it changed popular American medievalist culture forever.

Howard facilitated the reception of an American Middle-Age in which errant knights rode through cactus-studded deserts. While *Prince Valiant* and *Green Arrow* reflected America's engagement with a lost Albion, and *The Mighty Thor* tapped into the legacy of a Germanic diaspora, it was with Conan that America began to live out its own, native-born fantasies—and in the next chapter we will examine what happened when those fantasies became gendered.

CHAPTER 5

Red Sonja (1973)

My simple point has always been: if you demolish most of the characters girls like, then girls won't read comics. That's it!
—GAIL SIMONE, *WOMEN IN REFRIGERATORS* (1999)

In many ways the engagement with medievalism demonstrated by heroes such as Prince Valiant, Green Arrow, and the Mighty Thor are not as complex as those considered in the previous chapter. The narrative underlying the first three comic books is one of migration, translation, and transformation, whereas the development of fantasy medievalism, especially in regards to the work of the early pulp-fiction authors, is something that comes directly from the American experience. The ambiguity of this medievalism and the centrality of modern American history to the interpretation and analysis of the genre make it both intensely complex and infinitely rewarding. The saga that underlies this chapter is made even more intricate by the inclusion of gender as a further point of reference, and by the reading of the underlying history of both the comic book and its creators as constituting an almost irreducible interrelationship of historicized subjectivities.

There are, today, two great female players left on the field of action heroes in comic books, and the history of both is significant and contested. *Wonder Woman* has been in continuous circulation for more than seventy years now, but her backstory is classical rather than medieval and, thus, outside the scope of this present volume.[1] Red Sonja, on the other hand, has been in print since 1934, although in comic books only since 1973, but her backstory, like that of Conan, is medievalist.

RED SONYA OF ROGATINO

Like Conan, the genesis of Red Sonja lay in the pulp fiction of Robert E. Howard. "The Shadow of the Vulture," which appeared in the *Magic Carpet Magazine* in January 1934, introduced Howard fans to Red Sonya of Rogatino, a soldier of fortune defending Vienna against the forces of Sultan Suleiman the Magnificent. In that story, Sonya claims to be the sister of Suleiman's favorite concubine Roxelana, and Howard describes Sonya, a Ruthenian mercenary, as

> tall, splendidly shaped, but lithe. From under a steel cap escaped rebellious tresses that rippled red gold in the sun over her compact shoulders. High boots of Cordovan leather came to her mid-thighs, which were cased in baggy breeches. She wore a shirt of fine Turkish mesh-mail tucked into her breeches. Her supple waist was confined by a flowing sash of green silk, into which were thrust a brace of pistols and a dagger, and from which depended a long Hungarian saber. Over all was carelessly thrown a scarlet cloak.[2]

As the tale progresses, Sonya is quickly revealed to be an expert warrior, a heavy drinker, and a steadfastly stoic companion.

Red Sonya was one of several female heroes that Howard was experimenting with, but it would seem that none was particularly successful for him. Red Sonya did not appear again after "The Shadow of the Vulture," but then neither did Gottfried von Kalmbach, the principal hero of the tale. We can sense, perhaps, in a letter written by Howard to Lovecraft in March 1933, at least some of the author's anxiety about the way in which these new characters were playing to his established audience: "I'm curious to know how the readers will like Gottfried ... I never created a character whose creation I enjoyed more. They may not seem real to the readers; but Gottfried and his mistress Red Sonya seem more real to me than any other character I've ever drawn."[3]

Another of Howard's female swashbucklers, Helen Tavrel, appeared in "The Isle of Pirate's Doom," but this story failed to find publication until long after the author's death. Howard also wrote three stories featuring Dark Agnes de Chastillon, all of which also went unpublished until Howard's fan-led recovery in the 1970s. "Sword Woman" tells the origin story for Agnes, a redheaded girl beaten by her father and forced into a loveless marriage that she avoids only by killing her would-be groom. On the run, Agnes meets up with Etienne Villiers, who initially tries to sell her into prostitution, and

Guiscard de Clisson, a mercenary who trains her to fight. A sequel, "Blades for France" sees Agnes and Etienne engaged in international intrigue with Cardinal Thomas Wolsey, while a third Agnes story, "Mistress of Death," was still only in draft form when Howard died in 1936.

Eric Davin's *Partners in Wonder: Women and the Birth of Science Fiction* has argued convincingly for the widespread presence of women in American pulp fiction during the 1920s and 1930s, both as creators and as characters, so Howard's inability to gain traction with his "she-devils" should not be reduced to arguments of patriarchal hegemony and a lack of audience appetite for these sorts of stories. Indeed, Howard was himself a fan of at least one female pulp writer, Catherine Moore, and in his correspondence with her we can glimpse a significant factor in the failure of his female creations to establish themselves in the public imagination.

Moore's own red-haired warrior woman, Jirel of Joiry, appeared in a story entitled "Black God's Kiss" in the October 1934 edition of *Weird Tales*. When the same magazine published a second Jirel story only two months later, Howard sent Moore a letter of congratulation with which he included a manuscript copy of "Sword Woman." In all, Jirel was to appear in five novellas, and Howard, sensing perhaps that he had failed to produce a female lead character with either Dark Agnes or Red Sonya, was keen to get some feedback from someone who had been successful in doing just that. Moore, for her part, was effervescent about Howard's female hero, writing, "My blessings! I can't tell you how much I enjoyed 'Sword-Woman.' It seemed such a pity to leave her just at the threshold of higher adventures. Your favorite trick of slamming the door on a burst of bugles! And leaving one to wonder what happened next and wanting so badly to know. Aren't there any more stories about Agnes?"[4]

Howard, of course, had created some memorable female characters that were finding fan approval, among them Valeria of the Red Brotherhood and Conan's lover Belit, but his untimely death only a year after this correspondence with Moore meant that Howard's efforts to expand on these successes were cut short. Significantly though, in the 1970s, when Roy Thomas searched around for a female character with which to follow up the Conan comics, he decided to amalgamate three of Howard's women into one.

Her presence at the siege of Vienna in 1529 places Red Sonya's birth at the very end of the European Middle Ages, but by losing her pistols and transporting her back to the age of Hyboria, Thomas transformed the postmedievalist Red Sonya, "Dog of War," into the thoroughly medievalist Red Sonja, "She-devil with a Sword." Thomas changed the spelling of her name to mark this transformation, thus Sonya became Sonja, and she began to take on some of the qualities of both Belit and Valeria as her interactions with Conan became both more frequent and more intense. Even Dark Agnes made an appearance, albeit unnoticed by any but the diehard Howard fans, when Thomas adapted "Mistress of Death" to become "Curse of the Undead-Man" in issue 1 of *The Savage Sword of Conan*.

This metamorphosis from an artifact of historical postmedievalism to one of medievalist fantasy is significant. The fact that comic book writers like Thomas were aware of both Red Sonya of Rogatino and Dark Agnes (and, no doubt, of Jirel of Joiry), but chose to translate these characters into mythical warrior women would seem to illuminate an interesting reality that underlies our engagement with the imagined past. Dystopian and utopian medievalisms seem to reach consensus on very few points, but on this much they agree—medieval women were disempowered by their gender.

For the dystopian medievalist, the dark ages of the premodern world offered little hope of equality for women—they were little more than oppressed chattels manipulated and controlled by an inherently patriarchal system. For the utopian medievalist, these women were either happy in their domestic duties as subservient members of the rural proletariat, or pampered princesses fortunate to be worshiped as objects of chivalric devotion. Feminism, it seems, has little place in either vision.

A character like Red Sonja, therefore, presents writers with a challenge. A historical Red Sonya challenges our ontologies of the past and undermines our consensus view of the present. A fantastical Red Sonja presents us with no such dilemmas. Before we progress to look at Red Sonja as a character, therefore, it will be necessary first to consider briefly these possibilities of historicity that we are so readily abandoning.

THE INVISIBLE WOMEN

In Howard's reimagining of ancient Europe, the steppes of (his) western Hyrkania were roughly analogous with the region of (our) modern Ukraine, an area that was inhabited by the Sarmatians between the fifth century BCE and the fourth century CE. Herodotus believed these Sarmatians to be the descendants of Scythian fathers and Amazon mothers, and Hippocrates asserted that Sarmatian women, who rode and fought alongside their men, could only marry once they had slain three enemies in battle.[5] It would be easy to dismiss such tales of warrior women were it not for an interesting correspondence in the archaeological record—of the Sarmatian "warrior graves" so far excavated on the lower Don and Volga Rivers, one in five contain "females dressed for battle as if they were men."⁶ So Thomas's refashioning of Red Sonya of Rogatino into Red Sonja of the steppes stayed true to Howard's greater mythos while at the same time providing the "She-devil" with a historically plausible backstory.

The world inhabited by Red Sonja—the armor she wears, the weapons she uses, the landscape she inhabits—is not a classical world. It is medieval. Analogies drawn, therefore, between Red Sonja and the Sarmatians, might seem irrelevant, except that, by positioning a female character within a medievalist world of swords and sorcery, the writers of *Red Sonja* are able to avail themselves of a considerable popular belief in the credibility of such a hero. This is a paradox of medievalism, whereby our temporal distance from the historical period magnifies its exoticism to such a point that anything might be possible. Indeed, it seems as if the projection of "self-evident" untruths back upon a subject serves to reduce our anxieties about engaging with it. With the possible exception of the "Viking Shield-maidens" of popular imagination, we "know" that women could not be warriors in the Middle Ages and so, by imagining a "fantasy" in which they might be, we feel less trepidation about emotionally engaging with that period. Except that, in this case at least, the projected belief is not the product of fantasy alone.

Although warfare in the European Middle Ages was primarily the domain of men, there were still a good many exemplars upon which a warrior-woman might be based. During the first decades of the tenth century, Æthelflæd of Mercia built fortresses and led her armies against the Welsh and the Danes. A century later, Guildinild of Catalonia was an equally active participant in the wars that plagued the Spanish peninsula, and, soon after that, *la Gran Contessa* Matilda of Tuscany was earning her title of the "Madonna of War" as the Investiture Crisis boiled over into an all-out conflagration between the Papacy and the Holy Roman Empire. In 1129, Sophia of Bavaria laid siege to the castle of Falkenstein while her brother, Henry the Proud, fought Agnes of Saarbrücken for the city of Speyer. The Empress Matilda of England, daughter of King Henry I of England, led armies during the Anarchy (1135–1153) and Ermengarde of Narbonne defended southern France against Matilda's son, Henry II.⁷

The Greek chronicler Niketas Choniates wrote about the German knights of the Second Crusade who numbered among their ranks women who sat astride their horses, "bearing lances and weapons as men do;

dressed in masculine garb ... more mannish than the Amazons."[8] Choniates refers to the leader of these women as "Goldfoot" and likens her to the Amazon leader Penthesilea. Although the identification remains disputed, both Steven Runciman and Philippe Contamine have identified this "Goldfoot" as Eleanor of Aquitaine, who pledged three hundred ladies to the crusade at Vézeley in 1147.[9]

Orderic Vitalis, in his *Ecclesiastical History*, paints a similar picture of Isabel of Conches, the daughter of Simon de Montfort. Isabel, we are told, "rode armed as a knight among the knights,"[10] and for a comparison, Orderic reaches back not to the Amazons, but to the *Aeneid*, likening Isabel to Virgil's Camilla, fierce leader of the Volscii.[11]

Where chronicles fall occasionally silent, we might look also to the clues found in medieval languages. The Order of the Blessed Virgin Mary was founded in Bologna in 1233 and achieved Papal approval under Alexander IV in 1261. The rules of this order included provision for *militissa*, or female knights. Medieval French attests two similar feminine nouns, but where *chevaleresse* would refer to the wife of a knight, *chevalière* can only mean a knight who is female. Subsequently, we find reference to the *chevalière*, and also to the similarly unambiguous *equitissa*, in knightly orders founded by women in the French Low Countries during the fifteenth century. Edward III, King of England, established the Order of the Garter in 1348. From the outset women participated in the ceremonies of the order and were permitted an associate role as *Dames de la Fraternité de Saint George*. Although two fifteenth-century funerary monuments depict women bearing the Garter on their left arms, female membership was eventually discouraged under the Tudors and virtually ceased by the early sixteenth century.[12] It is likely that women in all these orders, despite being recognized as knights or *militissa* or *chevalière*, never participated in combat, fought duels, or went to war. This does not mean, however, that all women knights eschewed such things.

The English antiquarian Elias Ashmole, citing an earlier Spanish source, wrote about the women of Tortosa in Catalonia who, in 1149, following their spirited defense of the town against a Moorish siege, were all made knights of a new order created specifically for them by Ramon Berenguer, count of Barcelona. The *militissa* of this order, the Order of the Hatchet, remained unnamed in Ashmole's retelling and the order presumably ceased upon the death of the last of the defenders.[13] These women, of course, became recognized as knights because of their actions, rather than the accident of their birth, and it is to be imagined that many lowborn women in medieval

Europe were forced to fight by the circumstances in which they found themselves. During the Third Crusade, for example, the crew of a Saracen ship captured at Acre was massacred by Christian women who severed the captive's heads with knives and then bore away their grisly trophies.[14]

The so-called *Tower Fechtbuch*, Tower of London manuscript I.33, was most probably published during the last decade of the thirteenth century and is, therefore, the oldest *Fechtbuch* preserved. Essentially a medieval martial arts manual, *Fechtbücher* such as this seem to have become increasingly popular in the fourteenth and fifteenth centuries as the knightly monopoly on combat was relaxed and as commoners, particularly urban commoners, became increasingly involved with disputes of honor and the business of the judicial duel. I.33 is a particularly puzzling artifact, however, as the fencing master would seem to be a monk employed to teach his young clients (the term *clientulum* is specifically used) and one of these clients is a woman.[15]

Fencing instruction in the *Tower Fechtbuch* is limited to the use of the sword and buckler only, the sort of weapons readily available to the urban merchant class and the sort of weapons we might expect to see them using in order to protect their property and their good name. The inclusion of a young woman as a student of such deadly arts, especially without comment within the text, would seem to indicate that such matters were also within the experience of at least some women during the European Middle Ages. Nor is I.33 the sole example of a *Fechtbuch* advising women. The *Fechtbuch* of Hans Talhoffer, first published in 1467, includes a number of plates offering tactical advice for women who are intending to defend themselves in judicial duels and for men intending to fight against such women.[16]

Evidence of women participating in the wars of the European Middle Ages is also to be found in the chronicles of the day. Jean Froissart describes the countess de Montfort, veteran of the bitter fighting in Brittany, who, armed and mounted on a warhorse, led sorties against the French and who, while directing the defense of Hennebont, "ordered the ladies and other women to unpave the streets, carry the stones to the ramparts, and throw them on their enemies."[17] We know also of a historical "Black Agnes," who, in 1338, defended Dunbar Castle in Scotland against Edward III, and Nichola la Hay, who held Lincoln Castle for Kings John and Henry III, and Jeanne Laisné, who earned her *nom de guerre* Jeanne Hachette (Jean the Hatchet) during her defense of Beauvais in 1472 against the forces of the Burgundian duke Charles the Bold. Moreover, there are, as James Blythe has written, all those "reports of brave fighters only . . . exposed as women after death in battle . . . accounts of low-born women dying in the ranks—especially in cases of rebellions against a king or lord" and the many women who "commanded troops in battle throughout the Middle Ages."[18]

This conception, then, of women warriors in the European medieval past seems more than just the projection of a modern wish-fantasy, and there seems to be a reasonable historical basis for challenging the received view of a martial world devoid of women. This inability to engage with the historical integrity of the Middle Ages lies at the heart of a number of contemporary discourses in medievalism. I have written elsewhere about the projection of an imagined past onto the historical Middle Ages by modern nationalists, about the projection of sexualized violence onto that era, and about the projection of preconceptions of torture.[19] In all cases, the key to challenging these misconceptions must necessarily lie in our capacity to contextualize and historicize our own experience of that engagement.

Perhaps Americans in the 1930s and 1940s were more able to imagine a world in which women warriors might exist, as evidenced in the pulp fiction so far surveyed, because that possibility more closely reflected their experience of the world, a world in which women's rights were finally burgeoning. If this is so, then the reception of heroes like Red Sonja can only be understood in the context of modern feminist discourse.

"I AM WOMAN"

This is not the appropriate place, of course, in which to offer a detailed analysis of the feminist movement. Nor is there any need to do so when so many other commentators have done, and continue to do, such important work in this field. A brief synopsis, however, of some key elements in the narrative of the struggle for gender equality will be necessary in order to contextualize our understanding of Red Sonja's place within that greater arc and, indeed, to locate the modern comic book itself within the history of the American Century.

The primary political objective of women in Europe and America at the outset of the twentieth century was enfranchisement. This "First Wave Feminism," as Marsha Lear famously referred to it in her 1968 *New York Times* article,[20] subsided as women gained the vote and as the world slid inexorably toward a second global war. America, largely spared the terror of combat on the home front, paid a terrible price nevertheless in men and materiel. Female personnel were also among the United States casualties, but, for the most part, American women served the war effort by replacing men in industry and agriculture, thereby increasing the pool of potential servicemen upon which the United States could draw. The success of these women in what had previously been considered a man's occupation fundamentally challenged a range of gender-delineated assumptions upon which Western civilization had based itself.

The level of female involvement in American industry during the war was phenomenal. By 1944 women constituted about 35 percent of the American labor force and, of these 19 million women, almost half had not had jobs before the war started.[21] Such women, many from middle-class backgrounds, demanded improvements in both the workplace environment and in workplace procedures, and this changed forever the face of American industry—prompting Doris Weatherford to comment that the "four years of American involvement in World War II may have done more to change the nature of modern employment than the previous forty years of worker activism had done."[22]

Although these changes remained after the war, women, for the most part, did not. As stated in chapter 2, the decade or so that followed the Second World War was, for America, a period of economic growth, population boom, suburban migration, and a return to the nostalgic comfort of a conservative, family-orientated lifestyle. It would not be until the 1960s that the next wave of feminism would begin.

In 1963 the report of the Presidential Commission on the Status of Women declared that discrimination against women was present in virtually every aspect of American life and outlined plans by which greater equality might be achieved. The specific recommendations of the report included the implementation of fair hiring practices, the provision of paid maternity leave and, in a return to the practices of the war years, the offer of affordable childcare. That same year the Equal Pay Act became law in the United States and Betty Friedan's landmark work, *The Feminine Mystique*, was published.[23] Friedan has drawn sharp criticism in recent decades for her oversimplification of the choices presented to women in postwar America, for her focus on white, middle-class women, and for her prejudice against homosexuality, but her work remains integral in the dissemination of feminist ideas into mainstream America.[24]

The year after *The Feminine Mystique* was published, the Civil Rights Act became law in the United States. Title VII of that act barred employment discrimination by any private employers, employment agencies, or unions on the grounds of race, color, religion, sex, or national origin. The Equal

Employment Opportunity Commission was also established in 1964 and, by 1969 it had received some 50,000 complaints of gender discrimination. By 1965 the term "sexism" had passed into the English language[25] and by 1966, twenty-eight women, among them Betty Friedan, had founded the National Organization for Women (NOW). Dismayed by failures to enforce the Civil Rights Act of 1964 and united by the thesis of *The Feminine Mystique*, NOW was committed to the advancement of women rights through legal and constitutional reforms.

Other groups, such as the New York Radical Women, were less interested in negotiating their rights, and in 1968 Robin Morgan led members of the New York Radical Women to protest the Miss America Pageant of 1968 bearing placards that read "Women's Liberation." Dramatic protests such as these garnered more attention and were possibly more in tune with the *zeitgeist* of the counterculture movement of the 1960s, a movement fast becoming associated with anticapitalist rioting and mass demonstrations against the war in Vietnam. In 1969, members of another radical women's group, the Redstockings, disrupted a hearing concerning abortion laws in the New York Legislature.

Feminist protesters also disrupted the Miss World contest in 1970 by pelting the contestants with flour, water, and foul-smelling substances. That same year, the fiftieth anniversary of women's suffrage in the United States, tens of thousands of women across America participated in the Women's Strike for Equality, organized by Betty Friedan, while other protesters occupied the offices of the *Ladies Home Journal* to highlight the sexism of women's magazines. Australian feminist Germaine Greer also published what was to become an international bestseller, *The Female Eunuch*, in 1970.

In 1971 the women's liberation movement gained an anthem with the release of *I Am Woman* by another Australian, Helen Reddy. Reddy has described her own indignation when, as a young woman, she found no empowering messages in the music she grew up with. Indeed, against the growing force of the women's movement, the record industry continued to release songs like Sandy Posey's 1966 hit *Born a Woman*. Posey's lyrics warned her audience that "if you're born a woman, you're born to be hurt, you're born to be stepped on, lied to, cheated on, and treated like dirt," but finished with the refrain "and I'm glad it happened that way."[26]

Nineteen seventy-one also saw the introduction of Women's Equality Day in America, an annual celebration and commemoration of the women's movement. American feminists Gloria Steinem and Letty Cottin Pogrebin cofounded *Ms.* magazine as a stand-alone publication the following year (the first issue featured Wonder Woman on the cover) and, in 1973, the Supreme Court of the United States ruled that laws prohibiting abortion were unconstitutional (*Roe v. Wade*). The right to abortion has been seen as fundamental to women's right to control their own destinies and, in 1974, these rights were further enhanced by the passage of the Women's Educational Equity Act (WEEA), which promoted educational equity for American girls and women, including those who suffered multiple discrimination based on gender, race, ethnicity, national origin, disability, or age. Finally, in 1975, *Time* magazine declared that feminism had "transcended the feminist movement," that it had "penetrated every layer of society, matured beyond ideology to a new status of general—and sometimes unconscious—acceptance" and that, in order to celebrate "the successes of the feminist movement" the magazine had decided to award its person of the year award to "American Women."[27]

With the publication of Susan Brownmiller's *Against Our Will* in 1975 and the advent of the first "Take Back the Night" march in Philadelphia that October, feminism found itself more heavily focused on the causes and nature of violence against women. Groups such as Women Against Violence Against Women (WAVAW) campaigned to shut down the 1976 slasher-film *Snuff* and to remove billboards promoting the Rolling Stones' *Black and Blue* album, which featured a distressed model Anita Russell, bound by band front man, Mick Jagger. Another group, Women Against Violence in Pornography and Media (WAVPM), organized the first national conference on pornography in San Francisco in 1978.

By the end of the 1970s it had become common to read feminist critiques of pornography and its role in the oppression of women. Andrea Dworkin, a founding member of WAVAW produced *Pornography: Men Possessing Women* in 1981, the same year that Robin Morgan released her documentary *Not a Love Story: A Film about Pornography*. Two years later Ann Snitow, Christine Stansell, and Sharon Thompson edited the influential *Powers of Desire: The Politics of Sexuality*. By this stage, however, the debate had become more opaque.

Antipornography feminists had been excluded from the planning committee of the ninth annual Scholar and Feminist Conference held at Barnard College in 1982. This decision prompted Women Against Pornography (WAP), a group led by Brownmiller, Dworkin, and Morgan, to picket the event. The subsequent actions of the picketers, the reactions of the public, and the acrimony of the debates within the conference itself, ushered in a divisive period within feminism that some have likened to a war.[28]

Opposing WAP were women such as Gayle Rubin, whose essay *Thinking Sex: Notes for a Radical Theory of the Politics of Sexuality* would find publication in 1984. Rubin had come out of the radical group Samois, a Lesbian-Feminist BDSM (Bondage, Domination, Sadism, and Masochism) organization that had been founded in 1978 and which took its name from the fictional estate of the dominatrix of Pauline Réage's *Histoire d'O*.

This, then, was the social and political climate into which *Red Sonja* emerged. This chapter is not claiming that the comic book hero was a product of the feminist movement, or that her entrance into the world of publishing in any way changed the direction of that discourse, but *Red Sonja* was not immune to the ideological vicissitudes of her time. Indeed, a close reading of the character's various iterations reveals a persistent tension between what her authors would make of her and what her audience wanted, or would accept—and in that, Sonja's modernity was very much at odds with her imposed medievalism.

WONDER WOMEN

Harvard-trained psychologist William Moulton Marston spent several decades attempting, admittedly with some success, to convince the world that he had invented the Systolic Blood-pressure Test for Lie Detection (the forerunner of today's polygraph test). He was subject to the surveillance of J. Edgar Hoover and the FBI, who kept a file on his claims and who solicited reports that indicated Marston was possibly more interested in publicity than scientific rigour.

In October 1940, Marston was interviewed for *Family Circle* magazine and the subsequent article, "Don't Laugh at the Comics," led Max "Charlie" Gaines to hire the psychologist as an "Educational Consultant" for his company, All-American Publications, which, as we have seen, would eventually become part of DC. Marston pitched his new superhero idea to Sheldon Mayer, editor of All-American, in February 1941. "Suprema the Wonder Woman" was to be a female crime fighter to offset all the musclemen. Mayer and Gaines eventually agreed, and Marston penned the stories under the pseudonym Charles Moulton, borrowing Gaines middle name and putting it with his own. "Wonder Woman" appeared for the first time in the December 1941 issue of *All Star Comics* and, by the middle of the following year, she had her own title series.

Marston and his supporters liked to make much of his innovation in the comic book industry, but it is important to note that Wonder Woman was not the only female to fight crime on the pages of wartime illustrated fiction, nor was she the first. That prize goes to "Fantomah," a supernatural hero from Pharaonic Egypt who fought crime in the modern world by changing herself into a skull-faced demon. Fantomah débuted in *Jungle Comics* issue 2 (February 1940) and was followed quickly by a succession of other female superheroes.

In March 1940, the "Woman in Red" appeared in *Thrilling Comics*, to be followed that June in *The Spirit Section* by "Lady Luck." That same month, "The Invisible Scarlet O'Neil" appeared in her own comic strip, while the antihero "Black Widow" débuted in August and "Red Tornado" in November. Nineteen forty-one saw four more female crime fighters added to the list: "Miss Fury" in April; "The Phantom Lady" and "Miss Victory" in August; and "The Black Cat" in September. Miss Fury started out as a Sunday comic strip, but soon expanded into her own eponymous magazine.

Of all these comic book heroes, Miss Fury was the only one scripted and drawn by a woman—June "Tarpé" Mills. Miss Fury's feline sidekick, "Perri-Pur," became a popular icon for allied soldiers during the Second World War and Mills quipped that Miss Fury had "donated" the kitten to the war effort. Mill's creation continued in syndication until 1952, although she had moved back to a comic strip by then, having lost her own series in 1947.

Successful as Miss Fury was, however, she was nowhere near as popular as Marston's creation. By the third installment of *Wonder Woman*, the comic book was selling a phenomenal half-million copies per issue.[29] It was a popularity that was to outlive Marston himself and see Wonder Woman in near continuous serialization until the present day.

One of the artists who later would work on the Wonder Woman series was Trina Robbins, and her transition from a creator of comics to a historian of the comic book industry has yielded some paradigm-shifting research. In *From Girls to Grrrlz*, for example, Robbins has argued convincingly that girls, rather than boys, were the major consumers of comic books from the early 1940s until late in the 1950s.[30]

As we have seen, American women moved into a vast range of industrial jobs during the Second World War and publishing companies were no less affected than those that produced munitions. Subsequently, the early 1940s also saw an enormous rise in the number of women employed to produce comic books, but, whereas women in factories gave up their jobs to returning servicemen after 1945, the same was not necessarily true of these female artists and writers. Indeed, the postwar years saw both a proliferation of women creators and the rise of comic books targeted specifically at young women—titles such as *Young Romance* (1947) and *My Life* (1948). By 1950 almost one-fifth of the comic books in production were romance titles.[31] Beyond this, women featured prominently in superhero and action titles, and there were even crossover comic books with titles like *Cowboy Love*, *Range Romances*, *Romantic Adventures*, and *True War Romances*.

Major producers such as Fiction House (who put out best-selling titles like *Fight Comics*, *Wings*, and *Jungle Comics*) were well known at this time for the number of women they employed and the quality of their employees' output. Fiction House stalwarts such as Ruth Atkinson, Fran Hopper, Lily Renée, and Marcia Snyder are still respected names within the industry and most of Fiction House's action stories, whether authored by men or women, "either starred or featured strong, beautiful, competent heroes. They were war nurses, aviatrixes, girl detectives, counterspies, and animal skin-clad jungle queens, and they were in command ... And they did not need rescuing."[32] This message of female empowerment was echoed in comic books produced by other companies as well—some issues of *The Black Cat* went as far as detailing self-defense techniques for women—but all this began to change during the mid-1950s.

The rising discontent of Middle America with comic books in general was at its high point by 1955, fueled by the criticisms of educationalists, church and civic groups, and the findings of the United States Senate Subcommittee Hearings into Juvenile Delinquency. The self-imposed censorship that comic book producers entered into at this time, which eventually coalesced into the Comics Code, forced the artists and writers to turn away from complex, adult concepts and storylines and to emphasise innocence and domesticity instead. Some publishing houses went even further, with Michael Uslan relating how, at DC in the 1950s, the "inclusion of females in stories" was "specifically discouraged" and how, when women were included in a comic book, it was stipulated that they "should be secondary in importance."[33] The result, according to Charlton and DC artist and editor Dick Giordano, was that girls "simply outgrew romance comics."[34]

Other authors were engaging the growing sophistication of the female audience, and as women turned toward the works of Betty Friedan and Germaine Greer, the allure of *Young Romance* began to dissipate. As a result, during the 1970s, female characters, both heroes and villains, saw a substantial increase in their numbers as the industry attempted to win back all those (female) readers that the patriarchal strictures of the 1950s and 1960s had lost.[35] Moreover, the storylines and general preoccupations of these Bronze Age comic books began to reflect the tensions of modern feminism.

Wonder Woman was still in production, of course, but she was the noticeable exception in DC's dearth of female titles so, from 1969, Supergirl became the lead feature in *Adventure Comics*, and by 1972 the editors at DC believed that she might be able to sustain her own series. *Supergirl* only ran as a series until 1974, however, and a second title, *The Daring New Adventures of Supergirl*, fared similarly, surviving from 1982 until 1984.

Batman's female equivalent, Batgirl, also suffered mixed fates during her various incarnations. By the end of the 1960s, fan-based reaction had determined that Barbara Gordon, the librarian daughter of Gotham city's police commissioner, was the definitive Batgirl. She debuted in issue 359 of *Detective Comics* in 1967, but never managed to convince DC of her worth. During the late 1960s and early 1970s she continued to appear as a supporting character in *Detective Comics*, as well as performing cameos in *Justice League of America*, *World's Finest Comics*, *The Brave and the Bold*, *Adventure Comics*, and *Superman*. Her appearances become less frequent over time, though, and her story in *Detective Comics* #424 (1972) was entitled "Batgirl's Last Case." By 1973, Batgirl was largely retired. DC had always been known for its conservatism, so these mixed responses in the face of a rising tide of feminism could not have been unexpected, but over at DC's main rival, Marvel, change was certainly in the air.

The Fantastic Four had always been the flagship of Marvel, although the *X-Men* series was gaining market share by the end of the 1960s. Sue Richards, known as the "Invisible Girl," was a foundation member of the Fantastic Four and was happily married to the team's leader Reed Richards. In a storyline that finished in issue 130 of *The Fantastic Four* (1973), Reed made a unilateral decision about the fate of their son. Sue, no longer willing to accept this patriarchal domination, left both the team and their marriage. They remained separated for the next eighteen months.

The X-Men experienced similar disruptions to their male-dominated world. In 1975 a new woman joined the squad with Ororo Monroe (Storm) providing a much-anticipated role model for both girls and African Americans (*Giant-Size X-Men* #1). Although Lorna Dane had been a member of the X-Men since the late 1960s, she appeared in the series only sporadically and lacked significant powers. That changed in early 1976 when she became the superhero Polaris (*X-Men* #97). A few months later, Marvel Girl, until then the weakest member of the team, transformed into the almost omnipotent Phoenix (*X-Men* #101). Finally, in early 1980, the X-Men received yet another female character in the form of Kitty Pryde (*Uncanny X-Men* #129).

In the meantime, Marvel had launched other titles with female leads, perhaps the most significant of which was the 1977 debut of Ms. Marvel. Gloria Steinem and Letty Cottin Pogrebin had founded their groundbreaking *Ms.* magazine in 1972 and now, only five years on, Marvel was launching their own liberated superhero—as the promos of the time said, "This female fights back!"

By 1982, Wasp, a foundation member of the other Marvel super team the Avengers, had also had enough. Having endured the verbal and mental abuse of her controlling superhero husband, Hank Pym,[36] Wasp drew the line at being physically beaten. She divorced Hank and then, rather than leaving the series, demanded that they vote for a new leader—an election that she won. Not too long after that, Sue Richards decided that she would no longer be known as the Invisible Girl. Having labored through three pregnancies and countless thwarted invasions of the earth by various intergalactic supervillains, Sue thought it was time she be known as the Invisible Woman. Sue also went on to lead the Fantastic Four.

The appearance of Red Sonja in her own comic book, then, is not unrelated to a greater picture. Not only were there significant changes happening for women in the real world at that time, these changes could already be seen affecting the comic book industry.

RED SONJA

Three years after transforming Conan from a cult icon into a comic book superstar, Roy Thomas was casting around for a suitable female equivalent. Feminism was in full swing, fans were ready to accept a woman warrior, and Marvel was, no doubt, keen to cash in on all those female readers who had been driven away from the medium by a decade of condescension. Thomas transplanted Howard's "Vulture," Mikhal Oglu, back into the mythical Hyboria, made him a servant to Yezdigerd, King of Turan, and set him on a collision course with Conan. The siege of Vienna became the siege of Makkalet, Gottfried von Kalmbach became Conan, and Red Sonya became a Hyrkanian "she-devil with a sword."

Red Sonja's appearance in two issues of *Conan the Barbarian* during 1973 was followed by two more in 1974, and another in 1975. She also appeared in the very first issue of the *Savage Sword of Conan* in 1974. In 1975 her origin story was featured in another Marvel sword and sorcery title, *Kull and the Barbarians*, in which it was revealed that her martial abilities were a gift from the Red-Goddess Scáthach, a gift that would be withdrawn if ever she lies with a man who is unable to best her in combat.

The fan response to Sonja was encouraging and Marvel decided to highlight the she-devil in a new title, *Marvel Feature*, in November 1975. She starred in the first seven issues of this bimonthly comic book while still making cameo appearances in *Conan the Barbarian*. By the beginning of 1977, Marvel felt enough confidence in their female fantasy character to launch a title series and the first *Red Sonja* was on sale that January.

This first volume of *Red Sonja* ran for only fifteen issues. Red Sonja was still turning up in *Savage Sword of Conan*, she featured in the 1978 *Marvel Super Special*, and, in early 1979, she teamed up with Spider-Man after her nemesis Kulan Gath possessed the body of Mary Jane Watson. Despite all this cross-title promotion, however, sales were not sufficient to induce Marvel to extend her title beyond May 1979.

This slump in sales did not necessarily mean that Sonja's fans had deserted her, of course. She still appeared sporadically in *Savage Sword of Conan* and she was, by this stage, a clear favorite with cosplayers—Red Sonja costumes featured heavily at comic conventions across the United States. Frank Thorne, who drew Sonja from 1976 until 1978, was often asked to judge these competitions and by the late 1970s Frank was appearing on stage with various cosplayers performing a show entitled "Red Sonja and the Wizard." Of the cosplayers who performed in these shows as Red Sonja, perhaps none was more famous than Wendy Pini.

Wendy's Red Sonja became a stalwart of the burgeoning convention scene and she even appeared, clad in her armor bikini, on national television. Like so many cosplayers of the time though, Wendy's devotion to comic books also included creating her own stories and, in 1978, she launched the title *Elfquest*. Following a disappointing first issue, Wendy and her husband Richard started their own company WaRP (Wendy and Richard Pini) and published a twenty-issue story-arc over the next few years. In 1985 Marvel began republishing this story in a 32-issue run, but WaRP retained their rights to the product, which meant that the Pinis were able to publish a 33-issue sequel themselves after Marvel passed on the option. In 2003 *Elfquest* was sold to DC, although the Pinis retained creative control.

Wendy's engagement with comic books as both writer, artist, and entrepreneur is remarkable in itself, but it seems all the more so given that she entered the industry at a time when women were not being sufficiently valued for their input, their intelligence, or their expertise. The transformation from cosplayer to successful comic book author is an intriguing one, and one integrally linked with the Red Sonja phenomenon.

By the early 1980s, at least some Red Sonja fans had moved from comic books to novels, as new adventures began to appear in paperback. Six Red Sonja novels were published between 1981 and 1983, all of them written by David C. Smith and the H. P. Lovecraft scholar Richard L. Tierney. The novels—*The Ring of Ikribu* (1981), *Demon Night* (1982), *When Hell Laughs* (1982), *Endithor's Daughter* (1982), *Against the Prince of Hell* (1983), and *Star of Doom* (1983)—were published by Ace paperbacks and featured covers by Boris Vallejo.

At about the time Sonja's run with Ace was coming to a close, Marvel attempted to relaunch her comic book title once again. There was an abortive two-issue attempt in February and March of 1983, followed quickly by a third volume that began in August of the same year. *Red Sonja* volume three fared even worse than volume one, lasting only thirteen issues. A two-issue comic book tie-in with a *Red Sonja* movie was released in 1985, and Sonja was seen briefly in a new Marvel series (*Conan the King*) that same year, but, by the end of 1986, *Red Sonja* had ceased as a title once more.

During the late 1980s and early 1990s it seemed that Marvel was unsure just what to do with their "she-devil." There were some eighteen issues of *Conan the Barbarian* that featured Sonja at this time and another twenty-five issues of *The Savage Sword of Conan* that did likewise, along with a graphic novel and the odd one-shot, but the company's interest had moved elsewhere.

Sonja was sold across to Blackthorne, and then to Cross Plains, before finally finding a home at Dynamite Comics in 2005. Her series at Dynamite, written by Michael Oeming, ran for eighty issues and only finished in 2013. During that run she also appeared in some two dozen limited series, annuals, one-shots, or crossovers swelling her back catalogue and expanding her fan base enormously. Nor has Dynamite finished with her yet, with the new series, authored by Gail Simone, having kicked off in 2013.

This, then, is an overview of Red Sonja's publication history. She has maintained a constant fan base for more than forty years and, during that time, has convinced publishers on several occasions to entrust her with her own title series. These series, in turn, have met with varying degrees of success. Yet it would be foolish to assert that Red Sonja's publication history was uniform in its approach or that the presentation of her character did not change over time. Indeed, when we compare Sonja's publication history to those broader issues of women's struggles for equality outlined above, we can see some particularly interesting correlations.

Sonja's trademark armor bikini is instantly recognizable to comic book fans and yet represents an obvious and, at times, self-consciously contested signifier. When Barry Windsor-Smith drew the original Red Sonja for her debut in *Conan the Barbarian*, he followed Robert E. Howard's description quite closely and drew her in a long-sleeved mail shirt with high boots and short pants of red silk. By the time Sonja was ready for her second foray into comic books, Esteban Maroto had abandoned this conservative garb for a revealing "bikini" made, apparently, of metal scales. Both Maroto and John Buscema drew Sonja this way for the first issue of *The Savage Sword of Conan*, and Buscema continued to do so in subsequent issues of *Conan the Barbarian*. When Dick Giordano drew Sonja for the first issue of *Marvel Feature* he did the same, as did Frank Thorne when he took over from issue 2. The bikini remained throughout the 1970s and was carried over into the cover art of Boris Vallejo when the Red Sonja novels appeared in the early 1980s.

By that stage, though, there was clearly some disagreement at the Marvel offices as to just how Red Sonja should be portrayed. An abortive relaunch of Red Sonja in 1983 lasted only two issues, but was the first to take the hero out of her metal bikini and put her in something slightly less revealing. Conan most often appeared in a fur loincloth, so now Sonja was drawn in a female version of the same outfit that covered her hips and midriff as well. This costume continued in the slightly longer-lived third series.

For the first time, too, volume three of *Red Sonja* saw the artwork taken over, for the most part, by a woman. Mary Wilshire, who had come to Marvel from the underground *comix* scene only three years before, drew ten of the thirteen issues of the new series and was the first since Windsor-Smith to draw the Hyrkanian swordswoman in something other than a scale-mail bikini. For most of the new series, the now less-busty Sonja was to wear the more conservative blue pelt, although Pat Broderick, who drew Sonja for issues 5 and 6, put her in an even less revealing blouse with full leggings.

Sonja's bikini had become something of an inside joke by this stage, it would seem. In issue 8 (April 1985) Sonja is seen rummaging through her saddlebag when she finds the impractical armor bikini. Passing them to a friend who wants to try the costume on she warns: "It's not too practical... and it chafes! You'll see! But ... I couldn't bear to throw it out!" This same joke would be revisited in a much later (2011) one-shot entitled "Blue."[37]

Wilshire's artwork on the series was highly technical and lineally precise. Even a passing glance serves to remind the reader of Hal Foster's work on *Prince Valiant*, particularly the brickwork, but the siege splash page in issue 3 (December 1983) and the octopus in issue 5 (January 1985) are directly referent to Foster's groundbreaking style.

From issue 8 *Red Sonja* was also written by a woman—Louise Simonson. By this stage Simonson had already established herself as a writer at Marvel with her new title *Power Pack*. The Power Pack were the first preteen superheroes in the Marvel universe and the only child superheroes in any comic book at that stage to operate without adult supervision. The series proved to be long lived and, despite the tender ages of the Power Pack themselves, Alex (12), Julie (10), Jack (7), and Katie (5) featured in stories that dealt with serious issues such as bullying, violence, drug abuse, kidnapping, and homelessness. Mary Wilshire later became an artist for *Power Pack* as well. Under Wilshire and Simonson, then, Sonja became a hero whom girls could look up to, rather than one whom boys simply looked at.

This is not to say that, by the 1980s, Red Sonja had become a feminist icon, but she was inhabiting the same bitterly contested territories in which the sex wars were being waged. And Sonja had suffered. Sonja's origin story, "The Day of the Sword," had appeared as early as September 1975 in *Kull and the Barbarians*. In July 1982, in the immediate wake of the Barnard Conference on Sexuality, this story was redrawn for issue 78 of *The Savage Sword of Conan*.

In "The Day of the Sword" we are witness to an attack by a band of mercenaries on a simple cottage in western Hyrkania. Sonja's house is burned down, her family is killed, and a young Sonja, unable to lift her brother's heavy sword, is raped. Sonja cries out for vengeance and her prayers are answered by the Red Goddess Scáthach, who gives her superhuman fighting skills on the condition that she will never lie with a man who cannot defeat her in fair combat. Howard's Sonya, then, a mercenary captain the equal, if not the better, of any man, is transformed into a fury, empowered by rage at the whim of a deity.

This became the dominant origin myth of Red Sonja. It was revisited in both the second and third series. It is central to the plot of her foray onto the silver screen in 1985 and, therefore, in the comic book tie-in to the movie. It was also repeated in flashbacks when Michael Oeming rebooted Red Sonja for Dynamite in 2005, but, confronting as this storyline might seem, especially for the CCA-approved comic books, worse was yet to come.

In 2010 Oeming decided to kill the title's eponymous swords-mistress altogether and continue the series with a new hero, a descendant and reincarnation of the original Red Sonja. With her husband slain by pirates and left for dead herself, this new character is nursed back to health by a warrior, Osin, who then teaches her martial arts. The new Sonja has inherited some of her namesake's abilities, but her powers are nowhere near as developed as they were under Scáthach's guidance, and so she is forced to be more cunning than combative. By the time this series wrapped up in 2013, not much was left of the original nature of Howard's she-devil.

Sonja's often-recalled rape and her eventual demise make for dramatic storylines, of course, and it is no surprise that bad things happen to characters, even important characters, in all forms of literature, but the nature and the extent of the violence perpetrated against female comic book characters in particular has led some to question the gender politics being played out within the industry. In 1999 a website was launched that began disseminating the long list of female comic book characters who had been maimed, killed, or depowered as a plot device. The project, *Women in Refrigerators*, took its name from an incident in a 1994 issue of *Green Lantern* in which the hero's girlfriend was murdered and her body stuffed into a refrigerator.

Gail Simone, Daniel Merlin Goodbrey, Rob Harris, and Beau Yarbrough began *Women in Refrigerators* as a way of actively engaging with the depiction of violence against women in comic books, violence they saw as disproportionate and often overtly sexualized. For Simone, a comic book artist and the principal contributor to the website, these attacks were more than just dramatic plot twists, they constituted a sustained, perhaps intentional, attack against female superheroes, the values they stood for, and the audiences that were attracted to them: "If you demolish most of the characters girls like," she wrote "then girls won't read comics."[38]

The original list compiled by Simone included more than 110 female comic book characters who had been "killed, raped, depowered, crippled, turned evil, maimed, tortured, contracted a disease or had other life-derailing tragedies befall" them. Considering that the list was published in 1999, at a time when superhero comic books were almost entirely marketed to children, it makes for somber reading.

At about the same time that Red Sonja's rape was being turned into a storyline, Gwen Stacy, Spider-Man's girlfriend, was being killed. The Flash lost his wife in 1979; Green Lantern's girlfriend was murdered in 1994; the Hulk's mother was killed by his abusive father in 1991, and his own wife died in 1998. Batwoman was killed in 1979; Batgirl was paralyzed in 1988; and

Stephanie Brown, the fourth Robin, was tortured to death in 2004. Stephanie's highly sexualized death in the crossover storyline *Batman: War Games* and DC's subsequent decision to exclude her memorialization in the ongoing series was controversial. Even more disturbing, though, Stephanie had been killed with a power drill and, following the release of *Batman: War Games*, DC marketed a toy version of the drill as a collectible.

Other female superheroes fared no better—both Supergirl and Aquagirl died during the 12-issue limited series *Crisis on Infinite Earths* released during 1985 and 1986. They lasted longer than the Black Canary, however, who was killed in 1983. By 1997, even Wonder Woman had died, although she did not stay dead for long.

Ms. Marvel may have begun in 1977 with a nod to Gloria Steinem's magazine, but by the early 1980s, she had suffered more than many superheroes that had been in print for decades. Brainwashed, kidnapped, and impregnated by rape, Ms. Marvel gave birth to a rapidly aging version of her abductor who transported her into another dimension. In later story arcs she had her powers stripped from her and ended up battling alcoholism. The treatment of Ms. Marvel, who should have been a rallying-point for Marvel's drive to recruit female readers, drew particular scorn from Carol Strickland in an essay entitled "The Rape of Ms. Marvel."[39] Interestingly, Jean Grey, who had been transformed into the almost godlike Phoenix at about the same time that *Ms. Marvel* began, also foundered in early 1980—Jean began to devolve into the Dark Phoenix and by the end of the year she too was dead.

As fans became increasingly disenchanted with the levels of violence meted out to female comic book characters, studies such as Strickland's became more common. *Women in Refrigerators* was a logical continuation of that commentary as was *Project Girl Wonder*, a website established by Mary Borsellino to protest against DC's treatment of Stephanie Brown. In an article that appeared initially on *Women in Refrigerators*, John Bartol has argued that even when male superheroes are killed or lose their powers, they are usually restored in a future storyline with very little alteration from their original condition. Women, on the other hand, are "never allowed, as male heroes usually are, the chance to return to their original heroic states."[40] More recently, Jeffrey Brown's *Dangerous Curves: Action Heroines, Gender, Fetishism, and Popular Culture* has demonstrated just how integral gender is as a defining factor in the incidence of comic book violence: "male heroes" he writes "tend to die heroically and are often commemorated" whereas women "are more likely to be casually, but irreparably, wounded"—moreover, "the violence against women is often overtly sexualized."[41]

Red Sonja's rape, then, and her later death, fit neatly within a recognized and much remarked upon phenomenon within the comic book industry. Sonja's latest incarnation, though, has made a substantial break from this gloomy and disempowering past.

In the newest *Red Sonja* series launched by Dynamite Comics in 2013, the original hero has returned with all her might and all her martial prowess, but, like Howard's original Red Sonya, this she-devil's capacities are entirely the product of her own effort, her own determination. Trained to fight as a gladiator by a fellow prisoner, this new Red Sonja has not been endowed by a goddess and, in place of the earlier rape scene, we are shown a younger Sonja who avenges her slain family by leading the bandits into the forest and killing them one by one. Sonja herself is not seriously injured, she is never raped, and she never makes a vow of conditional chastity.

This latest run of *Red Sonja* still occupies an ideological and intensely contested space within contemporary feminist thought. Sonja is powerful and self-assured, a thoroughly modern woman, but she is still wearing that bikini, that bikini so many young women still choose to wear at comic conventions. All the artists working on the new series are women as well, and in its brief run so far we have seen work from Nicola Scott, Colleen Doran, Jenny Frison, Fiona Staples, Amanda Conner, Stephanie Buscema, Nei Ruffino, Pia Guerra, Ming Doyle, Becky Cloonan, Jill Thompson, Amy Reeder, and Agnes Gabowska. And the author?

The author for this newest *Red Sonja* is Gail Simone.

CONCLUSION

Comic book characters like Red Sonja lie at the heart of this study's conceptualization of the relationship between reception and creation. To some extent the Hyrkanian she-devil is a creation of Roy Thomas. By transposing a fictional character from a relatively obscure, yet ostensibly historical, pulp-fiction story back into an imagined and fantastical world of sword and sorcery, it could be said that Roy Thomas changed Red Sonya of Rogatino so much that very little of her original character remained. Furthermore, this transposition placed Thomas's creation, Red Sonja, into a new world of hitherto unforeseen opportunities that enabled her to grow in ways that the historical Red Sonya never could.

Even so, Red Sonja was still received from the same author who created that alternative fantasy, and his fantasy was, in turn, received from an intense reading of the history available to him at the time. Creation and reception, it seems, can be difficult things to delineate. And, for the purposes of this study in particular, audience reactions are just as integral to this process of analysis.

The popular success of Red Sonja, like that of so many other comic book superheroes, is intrinsically connected to the reader's perception of social relevance and the capacity of the character to reflect key elements of the American Century, no matter how far removed from reality the storylines might be.

Prince Valiant is the icon of what has come to be known as the Greatest Generation. Just like them, he fought great wars then settled down to raise a family. Green Arrow finally emerged as a distinct archetype during the iconoclasm of the 1960s when his writers were able to bend the outlaw Robin Hood into the renegade green archer. The Mighty Thor burst onto the scene just as the grandchildren of a generation of northern immigrants were discovering their own place within the history of America.

Conan may well have come from a dark place in the American psyche, but Sonja is a demonstrable product of a contentiously gendered history. She rides a wave of reclamation that swelled in the aftermath of women's exclusion from comic books. Her storylines echoed the experiences of American women as they fought for equality, and as they debated among themselves as to just what form that equality should take. Sonja was brutalized by an industry that fought back against feminism, but, thanks to writers like Gail Simone, she has emerged with a new confidence and an increased self-reliance ready to face the new challenges of the twenty-first century. And she has maintained a fan base even in the face of all these challenges, a point that leads us into our next chapter.

Thus far we have looked only at the successes of medievalist comics in order to understand what it is that they might tell us about the American Century. In the next chapter, we turn our attention toward failure in order to understand what that might tell us about the sorts of medievalism that America would not embrace.

CHAPTER 6

Beowulf: Dragon Slayer (1975)

They set a gold banner high above his head, then gave him to the sea, let the ocean bear him on, and they were wretched in their hearts and mourned. No one alive, no wise man of the halls, no hero under heaven, can say in truth who it was that gathered in that precious cargo . . .

—*BEOWULF* (LL. 47–52)

At first glance, the mid-1970s comic book *Beowulf: Dragon Slayer* bears little resemblance to the West-Saxon poem one might imagine as its inspiration.[1] The series starts off conventionally enough with the eponymous Geat champion making his way to castle Hrothgar in "Daneland" to fight the monster Grendel, but a detour to the underworld sees Beowulf rescue a Scylfing amazon (Nan-Zee), before being sucked through a dimensional gateway that leads to adventures with a mysterious "Lost Tribe of Israel," Ulysses and his Achaean warriors, some human-hunting aliens that look like Egyptian deities, and the fabled city of Atlantis. To complicate matters further, a secondary plot sees Grendel mixed up in a dynastic conflict for control of Hell—originally enthroned as Satan's heir, Grendel is forced to fight with Dracula for control of the fiery realm.

Small wonder then, some might say, that the series only made it to six issues, but *Beowulf: Dragon Slayer* has earned a chapter in this study precisely because of its failure. In chapter 4 we witnessed the renaissance of Conan, resurrected from pulp-fiction obscurity by the medium of the comic book and buoyed along on a wave of fantasy literature that essentially started with Tolkien. In chapter 5 we saw that wave was large enough to carry Red Sonja with it and, in the process of telling and retelling her story, she was transformed from an adolescent male wish-fantasy into something now approaching a feminist icon. And yet, subsumed within that narrative of success for Conan and Red Sonja was a parallel history of failure for a good many Conan clones.

In *Beowulf: Dragon Slayer* we can see an obvious attempt to cash in on the cult of Robert E. Howard's Cimmerian. The comic book Beowulf, with his heavily muscled physique, fur loincloth, and shaggy mane, is Conan's *doppelganger*, and his companion, Nan-Zee, bears more than a passing similarity to Red Sonja. Why, then, at a time when America could not get enough of fantasy literature and barbarian heroes, did this series fail?

The traditional answer has been to locate this failure within a greater framework of rivalry between the two major players in the comic book industry. *Beowulf: Dragon Slayer* appeared at a critical moment in the history of the industry at which the balance of market domination swung for the first time away from DC Comics and toward Marvel, and the subsequent foundering of DC at this time has come to be known as the "Great DC Implosion." This chapter will demonstrate, however, that, whatever the truth of the DC Implosion, it had nothing to do with the demise of *Beowulf: Dragon Slayer*.

Another trajectory of argument has contended that the artistic and cultural distance between the comic book and the literature that it so clearly references justifies its failure,[2] but I am tempted to argue, as does Catherine Clarke,[3] that *Beowulf: Dragon Slayer* has more in common with the original poem that we now call *Beowulf* than some might think. A detailed comparison of the two texts illuminates a number of mutual resonances: transtemporal considerations of honor, loyalty, and masculinity abound; cultural ownership is contested and defined; and the relative values of popular literature are critically underscored in both. These are points I intend to elucidate in this chapter.

The abject failure of *Beowulf: Dragon Slayer* as a commercial entity belies the significance of its place within the narrative of the medievalist comic book. In fact, *Beowulf: Dragon Slayer* deserves a chapter in this study because its failure serves to support the underlying thesis of this work. Red Sonja, Conan, Thor, Green Arrow, and Prince Valiant all succeeded because of the groundwork laid for their reception by the generations of popular consumption that predated their comic book premieres. *Beowulf: Dragon Slayer*, on the other hand, was a poor imitation based on a scholarly text that had consistently failed to excite the public imagination and that had never taken root in the popular consciousness of America.

MICHAEL USLAN AND A NEW GRENDEL

The first issue of *Beowulf: Dragon Slayer* hit the shops in early 1975. The comic book was a bimonthly publication and so, when production ceased some twelve months later, the entire corpus ran to only six issues. All artwork was done by Peruvian-born Ricardo Villamonte and the writer on the series was a young Michael Uslan.

Uslan's original career focus was not on comic books, although he had always been an avid reader and collector. Having graduated from Indiana University, he began attending law school there, but spent a considerable amount of his time sending off resumes to film production companies. It was during this period that he also began to teach an accredited course that was eventually entitled "The Comic Book in Society," the first of its kind in an American university.

Press coverage of the course saw Uslan invited to other colleges and high schools as a guest lecturer, and he received invitations to appear on television and radio talk shows. In 1971, he published a textbook to support his course, *The Comic Book in America*, and, soon after that, he was approached by DC to write scripts.[4] Uslan's editor for *Beowulf: Dragon Slayer* was to be comic book heavyweight and regular guest speaker at Uslan's Indiana University course, Dennis O'Neil,[5] whose contribution to the saga of Green Arrow was detailed in chapter 2.

Media releases associated with the comic book's launch indicate an anxiety on the part of DC Comics that the new title would be perceived as educational: "An epic poem we've all had to read for junior high school English class! Don't tell me D.C. is doing 'Classics Illustrated?'"[6] It seemed a reasonable fear. Uslan was a university lecturer, after all, and in letters published within the comic book itself, he claimed influences as diverse as John Gardner's *Grendel*, William Golding's *Lord of the Flies*, Thornton Wilder's *Our Town*, and Shakespeare's *A Midsummer-Night's Dream*.[7] The influence of at least the first of these works is certainly clear in Uslan's script.

John Gardner's *Grendel* was published in 1971. A parallel text to the original poem, Gardner's novel retells the first half of the Beowulf legend from the viewpoint of the monster. Gardner's Grendel is a savage child questioning the world around him, a world that seems contradictory and brutal. Unable to communicate with either his own kind or the men that colonize his wilderness, this Grendel embraces an arbitrary and violent nihilism and is eventually murdered by an almost sociopathic Beowulf.[8] The Grendel of

Beowulf: Dragon Slayer exhibits the same mixed qualities of introspection, fear, and rage.

Grendel's rage is expressed at the outset of the comic book series. On page two of the first issue, the first storyline panel after the introductory "splash" on page one, Grendel rises up from his swamp to seek vengeance on mankind: "Shut them up! Tear their faces off! Make them stop!" This mindless hatred of humanity finds resonance in the original poem, and Grendel's Satanic motivation, hinted at in the original, is made transparent in the modern comic: "To the castle ... castle Hrothgar ... the mead-hall ... spill the blood! For Satan! For Grendel!"[9]

The original *Beowulf* survives in a manuscript designated London, British Library Cotton MS Vitellius A.15, which comprises five works in the West-Saxon vernacular inscribed around the year 1000, together with four twelfth-century texts, apparently first bound together by Sir Robert Cotton (1571–1631). The five West-Saxon pieces are collectively referred to as the *Nowell Codex*, or sometimes as the *Beowulf Manuscript*. The debate as to when the poem was first composed, or as to who might have composed it, or even where, is still very much undecided, but for the purpose of this chapter I shall be referring to the original *Beowulf* as a tenth-century poem because of general consensus on the inscription date of the sole surviving (but possibly only) copy.[10]

The diabolic nature of Grendel's origin is clear enough in the original West-Saxon poem. A descendant of Cain, the first fratricide, Grendel warred with God and was cast down. Uslan's vision of Grendel remains true to the poem, and during one of the comic book Grendel's many moments of introspection, his mother outlines this relationship with Cain and, indeed, with Satan:

> I tell you today, as I did yesterday and the day before ... when Cain killed his brother Abel ... it was the first crime against nature. From the heart of Cain sprang demons and spirits. And then came Grebnel![11]

Grendel's ontology is not particularly important in the original *Beowulf*, and little words are wasted in establishing his motivation beyond malice and spite. Although the moment in which fear enters his heart during the final battle with Beowulf is a powerful image in the poem, we never reach this scene in *Beowulf: Dragon Slayer*. That moment was never realized, partly because of the comic book's limited production run, but partly also because Uslan's desire to flesh out the character of Grendel engendered subsequent distortions to the original storyline. Whereas the West-Saxon Grendel exists only as a foil to the hero of the poem, Uslan's Grendel, like Gardner's, was meant to be much more developed. In keeping with this vision, the monster of *Beowulf: Dragon Slayer* takes on a role no medieval poet could have imagined for him—he becomes overlord of Hell.

Issue four of *Beowulf: Dragon Slayer* sees the Geatish champion dispatch a strangely Ottoman-looking Count Dracula. Satan, overjoyed to find a human as utterly evil as himself, nominates Dracula as his heir to the kingdom of the underworld. It takes Grendel a further two issues to find this out, but when he does he is far from happy—Satan had promised that inheritance to him. In issue 6, the swamp dweller catches Satan dispatching the vampire to castle Hrothgar, there to feast on the Danish king's men: "You will even be a better blood-beast than Grendel!" says Satan.[12] Grendel is overcome with rage at this betrayal and kills Satan, and "as the murderous Grendel ascends the throne of evil, he prepares himself for the unholy vengeance of Dracula!"[13]

Uslan's desire to salvage the primary monster of the Beowulf poem, to flesh out Grendel's character and lead us toward an understanding of his motivations, is no doubt, like Gardner's, an aesthetic born from Deconstruction. It is both modern and modernist, but how might the original audience of the West-Saxon poem have reacted to this reclamation? The answer might seem surprising, but the resonances between the tenth-century exemplar and its animated descendant are more numerous and more profound than an initial glance might lead us to believe.

The Grendel of *Beowulf: Dragon Slayer* first stirs from his mire to "shut up" the residents of castle Hrothgar. It is worth remembering that it is in the exact same context that we first meet the monster in the original poem: "Then the fierce spirit who dwelt in darkness endured torture, hearing each day that joy loud in the hall" (ll. 86–89).[14] Just like the comic book Grendel, this "fierce spirit" is irrepressibly savage: "fierce and greedy . . . savage and furious" (ll. 154–58). Both versions of the monster refuse the usual offers of settlement and compensation (ll. 154–58), and both versions eke out a lonely existence on the limens of human society: literally a *sceadugenga* (l. 703: shadow-walker) and a *mearcstapa* (ll. 103 and 1348: edge-prowler). Nor would the satanic subscript of the comic book have seemed out of character for a West-Saxon audience.

Grendel's association with the underworld is quite explicit in the original poem—he is an "enemy from Hell," a "captive of Hell," and a "Hell-spirit" (ll. 101, 788, and 1274). He is referred to in much the same way as Satan himself, as "God's adversary" (l. 786). Indeed, in order to still the murderous hand of Grendel, the Danes look not to Christ, but to the Devil for assistance, for they "sacrificed to idols then, called out at heathen altars, implored the Slayer of Souls to bring help to the suffering people" (ll. 175–78).

Even the comic book subplot of Grendel's rebellion against Satan finds textual resonance in the original. Grendel, of course, is the offspring of Cain and so rebellion is part of his genetic coda. He is a member of that race of giants that warred against Heaven, "God's Adversary" by name and nature, but possibly no friend to Satan either—did the Danes pray to the *Gastbona* to control his beast, or to aid them in a fight against a common enemy? And do the regicidal ambitions attributed to Grendel in the poem foreshadow for us the possibility of the comic book Grendel's war against his infernal lord: "And so he prevailed. Against righteousness he fought, one against all, until the best of houses stood empty."[15] The inherent evil enunciated in this last line might be lost on modern audiences, especially those audiences acculturated with contemporary notions of individuality and personal freedom, but there were few traits more invidious to Anglo-Saxon sensibilities than selfishness and disloyalty.[16] To fight against righteousness, one against all, was a damning criticism in early medieval Wessex.

Uslan's modern Grendel, then, shares some remarkably medieval qualities with his West-Saxon progenitor, and if his position of prime antagonist is somewhat lessened by the inclusion of a bevy of subsidiary enemies (minor dragons, giant snakes, swamp men, pygmy head-hunters, minotaurs, laser-wielding aliens and, of course, Dracula) it is something that the original *Nowell Codex*, with its preoccupation with strange monsters and fabulous beasts, should have prepared us for. What might seem less anticipated is the role of *wyrd* in the comic book version of the story and the presence of "the Shaper."

THE SHAPER AND THE *WYRD*

The Shaper was clearly set to become a principal character in *Beowulf: Dragon Slayer*. He appears early in issue 1, brought to Beowulf as the victorious Geat surveys the battlefield upon which he has just vanquished the Franks.[17] It is the Shaper who sets Beowulf on his quest to vanquish Grendel by telling him of the attacks on castle Hrothgar.

The demonic nature of the Shaper is commented upon immediately by one of Beowulf's hearth-troop and seems to be confirmed when the Shaper later magically appears at Hrothgar's court before the Geats have arrived.[18] In a later issue we actually witness the Shaper vanishing before the eyes of another group of confused captors, possibly rematerializing on the isle of Crete as the one-eyed and decidedly malevolent "Peeper."[19]

Uslan claimed that his inspiration for the Shaper had three primary sources: the Master of Ceremonies from the musical *Cabaret*; Puck from *A Midsummer-Night's Dream*; and Batman's nemesis, the Joker.[20] No such character is named in the original *Beowulf*, of course, although that is not to say that he is entirely absent from the poem.

Gardner's novel also has a Shaper, the name given to Hrothgar's court poet by Grendel. A literal translation of the West-Saxon *scop*, the Shaper elicits violent emotion in Grendel as the monster listens to the songs from within his dark fastness. Uslan continues the deconstruction of the original poem by further elaborating upon the character of the Shaper and by crediting him with superhuman powers. It is a particularly modern elaboration and one that seeks to make transparent the multiple *loci* of authority within the transmission of the poem itself. The naming of this previously unnamed character elucidates the trace of the poet within the text, substantially transmogrifying the reader's experience. No longer an authoritative record passed on from a collective past, the poem becomes an authorial work whose veracity is contingent upon subjective analyses. Surely an interpretation so modern could have no textual basis in a tenth-century poem?

The *Scop* is mentioned specifically three times in the original *Beowulf*. It is his singing that brings Grendel's wrath down upon Hrothgar's hall when first we meet the monster. The subsequent return of the *Scop* to this hall is enabled only by the coming of Beowulf. Finally, the song of Hengest's revenge, sung by the *Scop*, foreshadows the bloody assault of Grendel's mother (ll. 90, 496 and 1066). It should be pointed out, however, that our experience of the poem is entirely textual, a written script read silently to ourselves. This would not have been the case for West-Saxon audiences. They would have experienced such poetry as recitation, the presence of the *Scop* made manifest by the very act of its performance, and there are clear textual indicators that the role of the audience was not meant to be a passive one.

The very first verb to be encountered in *Beowulf* is *gefrunon*, the first-person plural form of *(ge)frignan*, to learn by inquiry, to hear of. An unnamed poet tells us from the outset that we have learned of the Spear-Dane's might in the days of old—"we" have learned. We find ourselves in the act of learning what "s/he" (the *Scop*) has already learned, but because s/

he has learned it already, then so too have we. Gardner and Uslan might be deconstructing the text of *Beowulf*, but it is not a process devoid of textual authority. This textual authority is augmented, too, when we look further into the motivation of Uslan's Shaper and his service to the Wyrd.

The power of the Wyrd is represented both textually and visually in *Beowulf: Dragon Slayer*. A full-page "splash" in issue 3 sees the Shaper summoning Wyrd:

> The omnipotent god of Fate, known by countless names throughout time—an all-seeing spirit neither good nor evil, neither just nor merciless, who does what must be done and insures that which is, is that which must be! He is the path of life and death! He is destiny![21]

How would this vision sit with a West-Saxon audience?

Wyrd is an undoubtedly ancient word. In *The Well and the Tree*, Paul Bauschatz argued that the Anglo-Saxon feminine noun *wyrd* could trace its origins to the Indo-European root **uert-* which denoted a turning, spinning, or rotating motion. It is from this same root that we derive the Old Indian *vártate* [revolve], Latin *vertere* [to turn], and Old Slavic *vratiti* [to turn].[22] Among the Germanic languages, this concept evolved from one of "turning around" to one of "turning into" and so the Gothic *wairþan*, Old High German *werdan*, Old Saxon *werðan*, Old Frisian *wertha*, Old Icelandic *verða*, and Old English *weorðan* all carried the same sense of "to turn into" or "to become." The nouns construed from these verbs—Gothic *uburt*, Old High German *wurt*, Old Saxon *wurd*, Old Icelandic *urðr*, and Old English *wyrd*—subsequently carried with them connotations of "that which has become" or "that which is to become"—connotations that were, from the very outset, aligned to the concept of fate. In the Old Norse *Edda*, for example, the roots of the world-tree *Yggdrasill* rise from the spring of *urðr*, the Old Norse cognate of *wyrd*.

Christian authors among the early Anglo-Saxons were not disposed to relate matters concerning the idolatry of their ancestors, and references to ancient beliefs and practices are correspondingly few. We can discern, however, via etymologies, a certain linguistic nexus connecting *wyrd* with traditional customs. The closely related noun *wyrt*, which became "wort" in modern English, was used both as a general term to describe efficacious herbs gathered for medicinal purposes and as a specific term to designate the brew made from such gatherings. Beer and mead were also decanted from a *wyrt*.

However opaque these beginnings, it is certain that *wyrd* had become an integral concept in Anglo-Saxon ontologies by the time of their conversion to Christianity. The compilers of the eighth-century *Epinal Glossary* may have possessed no native words for "giant,"[23] but they employed the term *condicionem id wyd* to translate *sortem*[24] (oracular response) and *wyrdae* to translate *parcae*[25] (The Fates). Originally personal deities, the Parcae had been transformed upon Roman contact with Greek culture to take on many of the qualities of the Hellenistic Fates, the *Moirai*.

The primacy of fate necessarily precludes the authority of the Christian God, of course, for if God cannot alter fate, then God must be subject to it. This concept was clearly unacceptable to the early church. Isidore of Seville discussed both the Parcae and *fatum* (fate) in his *Etymologiae*, but, always the orthodox Christian, Isidore delineated the function of *fatum* and of the Parcae as being subordinate to that of God. The reduction of fate to an agency of God, however, as evident in Isidore's theology, leaves little room for the intervention of saints and, to some extent, can be seen to negate the obligation of the individual to piety. God and fate, therefore, could not easily coexist, but in some West-Saxon literature they obviously did.

This belief in the subjugation of *Wyrd* to the will of God is also explicit in the West-Saxon redaction of Boethius's *De Consolatione Philosophiae*, where *wyrd* is used to translate the Latin *Fortuna* (personified, and deified, Fortune). The West-Saxon redactors of Boethius were consistent in their use of this term and applied it only to the personification of Fortune (*Fortuna*), never the results of her actions (*fortuna*). These events were translated using the native term *sælð* (happiness, prosperity, a blessing). This redaction also replaced Boethius's universe, held together by the *foedus perpetuum* (eternal alliance) of *amor* (love) and overseen by classical deities such as Phoebus, Phoebe, and Hesperus,[26] with "God Almighty," who is the "one creator beyond all doubt, and he is also the ruler of heaven and earth and all creation, the seen and also the unseen."[27] Nor is the West-Saxon *Consolatio* any less explicit about the relationship of *wyrd* to God: "Some things in this world are subject to *wyrd*, some are not in any way subject to it; but *wyrd* and all the things that are subject to it are subject to divine consideration."[28] Dorothy Whitelock wrote that it

> is often held that Anglo-Saxon poetry is permeated by a strong belief in the power of fate, inherited from heathen times, and some have even seen a conflict between a faith in an omnipotent Christian God and a trust in a blind, inexorable fate. To me, this view seems exaggerated . . . I doubt if these [passages

concerning fate] are more than figures of speech by the time the poems were composed.[29]

Whitelock's position was informed by the earlier work of B. J. Timmer[30] and was echoed in an article by Ida Gordon in which concepts such as *wyrd* were described as "the linguistic remains of outmoded ideas."[31] Morton Bloomfield concurred with both Whitelock and Gordon, believing that "the widespread tendency to use the word 'wyrd' as evidence of Germanic Paganism seems to be dangerously simplistic."[32] More recently, Joseph Trahern Jr. went as far as to conjecture that when Anglo-Saxon poets employed terms such as *wyrd seo swiðe* and *wyrd seo mære* (Fate the mighty, Fate the excellent), they were merely utilizing "a dead epithet."[33] Secure in the support of Whitelock, Gordon, and Bloomfield—and claiming also the support of authorities such as Fred Robinson, Eric Stanley, and Gerd Weber—Trahern presented his view as being "the prevalent one in contemporary Old English scholarship."[34] Even so, Trahern conceded that the alternate view was still "not without adherents" and readily acknowledged a number of his own "nagging doubts" as to the significance of such concepts as *wyrd* in Anglo-Saxon literature.[35] Such anxiety is well founded.

It would indeed be easy to imagine the conflict between God and Fate as an entirely modern creation, were it not for the evidence of Late West-Saxon literature. I have argued in more detail on this matter elsewhere,[36] but it would be valuable at this point to summarize, however briefly, just how integral to Anglo-Saxon thought this issue of fate was, especially in its relationship to *Beowulf* in particular.

Kevin Wanner posits God as the dominant force in the first two-thirds of *Beowulf*, but argues that this situation would seem to be reversed in the last third of the poem.[37] A close reading of the epic would seem to confound this argument. In his first formal speech before Hrothgar, Beowulf declares his lineage and his intentions in Denmark—to win fame or to die. This speech finishes with the caveat that "*wyrd* goes always as it must" (l. 455). Here Beowulf speaks with the resignation of a man who knows that nothing he can do will alter the hour of his death, a point made again a few lines later when he reiterates that "*wyrd* often saves the undoomed man when his courage serves" (ll. 572–73). Wanner correctly points out that Beowulf's later speeches continue to avow the power of *wyrd*,[38] but argues that the voice of Christian orthodoxy is still to be heard in the final section of the poem. In reality, the individual voices in *Beowulf* show consistency throughout the poem and it is the listener, or for us the reader, who is left to decide who they must believe—the fatalistic hero or the Christian narrator.

The centrality of this fatalism in the Anglo-Saxon ontology is encountered throughout the corpus of their poetry—the thematic power of the Gnomic verses of the Cotton Manuscript, *Deor*, *The Fates of Men*, *The Ruin*, and *The Wanderer* all derive from this complex, and essentially unchristian, preoccupation. An orthodox Christian ontology necessarily obviates any engagement with fatalism. The Christian God benevolently grants absolute freedom of will and humans are obliged, but not forced, to follow the divine laws as revealed in the Bible. Fatalism is antithetical to this belief, but the "nagging doubts" remain because if this orthodoxy was universally understood, then why were clerics throughout the tenth century still urging the faithful to abandon their belief in *wyrd*? If *wyrd* had become merely a dead epithet by this time, why did Ælfric continue to preach against it in his homilies using such strenuous terms as *forðan ðe gewyrd nis nan ðing buton leas wena ne nan ðing soðlice be gewyrde ne gewyrð ac ealle ðing þurh Godes dom beoð geendebyrde*[39] (for *wyrd* is nothing but lying fancy—nothing truly happens through *wyrd*, but all things are ordered according to the will of God).

It seems hard to imagine that Ælfric felt it necessary to deploy double and triple negatives to denounce an idea that had no currency. Double negatives in West-Saxon, of course, do not cancel themselves out as they do in standard modern English, and so we witness the vehemence of Ælfric's criticism of fatalism in phrases such as *nis nan ðing* (literally "not nothing") and *ne nan ðing soðlice be gewyrde ne gewyrð* (literally "not nothing truly by *wyrd* does not happen"), phrases utilized in order to indicate the absolute negation of a concept.

We must acknowledge, also, that Ælfric's intended audience was not exclusively a secular one. This homily would have been promulgated, no doubt, to those lay individuals who resided within Ælfric's literary circle, but it must have been composed for, and initially delivered to, a clerical, monastic congregation. That Ælfric should have to employ such forceful rhetoric to turn the minds of clergymen against a belief in *wyrd* must indicate just how pervasive this conviction must have been among ordinary Anglo-Saxons. Uslan's Shaper, then, would seem to be an authentically medieval element in his medievalist comic.

SELLING *BEOWULF*

The final point of similarity to be discussed here, between the comic book and the West-Saxon poem, is that of its popularity—or lack thereof. For all the hype that DC put into selling the new series, for all the grand designs of a university lecturer to popularize a medieval classic, *Beowulf: Dragon Slayer* failed utterly. It would be tempting to blame that failure on the so-called DC Implosion, the near collapse of the company that forced the discontinuation of more than two dozen titles in the late 1970s, but this is not the case.

The DC Implosion occurred during the bleak northern winter of late 1977 and early 1978. The post–Vietnam War recession was steadily worsening in America, and there was less money for luxuries like comic books. When blizzards started to ground flights and seal trucks into their terminals, DC lost the ability to distribute their product. This combination of a reduced market coupled with distribution failure was almost fatal. As it was, DC could only hope to continue by cutting titles, which it did, but that was in late 1977, at the earliest, and by then *Beowulf: Dragon Slayer* was already almost two years dead.

The cover date for the final issue of *Beowulf: Dragon Slayer* is March 1976, but a cover date is not the same as a date of publication. More typically, cover dates represent "pull dates," the dates at which unsold issues can be removed (pulled) from newsstands and disposed of—either returned to the publishers or thrown away. The publishing date inside the cover indicates that issue 6 of *Beowulf: Dragon Slayer* was for sale during February and March 1976, which would give a publication date of late January that year, a full two years before the blizzards that marked the beginning of the DC Implosion.

If not the Implosion, then, what caused the death of the series? A close reading of the comic books themselves, gives a clue as to the nature of their demise.

Bronze Age comic books such as *Beowulf: Dragon Slayer* existed to fulfill a commercial purpose. The 25-cent cover price did little to cover the costs of publication, let alone the wages of scriptwriters and artists, and so real revenue and, therefore, series sustainability was reliant upon advertising. Less literature than platforms for ads, a quick perusal through a Bronze Age comic book reveals just how important this sponsorship was.

The standard Bronze Age comic book format comprised thirty-four printed pages each issue, including the covers. Eighteen pages were reserved for the story, one page for letters, and one page for the cover. This left sixteen pages, 47 percent of each edition, for advertising. This advertising can be divided into three main types: in-house advertising for the parent company; advertising directed at children; and advertising directed at adult readers, usually young men.

These adult men constituted a significant demographic in comic book consumption throughout the 1960s, 1970s, and 1980s. Large companies like DC and Marvel had contracts with the United States military to provide comics to service personnel, and they were frequently commissioned to produce simplified script versions of popular series to help with literacy training. Comic book advertising from businesses specializing in post-service training aggressively targeted both active and recently decommissioned service personnel. Learn-by-mail courses in plumbing, locksmithing, car detailing, and drafting vied with high schools and colleges offering a second chance for former dropouts. These ads were typically large, often full page, and guaranteed the publisher both the revenue of the advertisement itself and the promise of an adult audience. Adults, after all, spent their own money, whereas children had to convince their, often skeptical, parents as to the value of reading comic books.

Beowulf: Dragon Slayer was obviously pitched at this adult audience. The first issue saw 35 percent of its advertising space, five and a half pages, taken up with promotions targeting young men. By issue 5 this had been reduced to less than 5 percent, or only half a page. Obviously, the sponsors had withdrawn their support, perhaps after poor sales. Worse still, the advertising shortfall was being filled not with companies selling to children, but by in-house marketing. More than 40 percent of the available space in issue 5 was taken up with revenue-neutral in-house ads, and this failure to generate advertising income would have been a crucial factor in deciding to discontinue the series.

Presumably the inclusion of the scantily dressed amazon Nan-Zee was also part of DC's plan to recruit adult readers to the series. Uslan named his female lead after his wife, Nancy, and Nan-Zee, like Red Sonja, and apparently unaffected by the cold of Scandinavia, deported herself in a series of bikinis. Nan-Zee's relationship with Beowulf is explicitly sexual from the outset—we see their naked silhouettes in issue two as Nan-Zee teaches the barbarian the "art of softness without weakness"[40]—and it would seem that DC was aiming for the sort of adult audience that was still happy to read CAA-approved publications. This might seem like a contradiction in terms, but it should be remembered that Marvel's original Conan series, *Conan the Barbarian*, was also CAA approved.

The decision to axe *Beowulf: Dragon Slayer* must have been made with some speed, if the storyline of issue 6 is anything to go by. There is no announcement in the letters page and the very last panel on the last page sees our hero making a promise to his companion—"we must make our way back to Daneland at once for my battle-to-the-death with Grendel!"—before a hastily addended and barely visible "The End" pops up in the bottom corner. It would seem that the series was not a popular one and, after a year of trying to make it sell, DC just let it go.

The failure of *Beowulf: Dragon Slayer* helps to illuminate a theme that runs through this study, that the success of a comic is contingent on far more than the strength of its script and the power of its art. If Howard Pyle and Wyeth Newell had not laid the groundwork for Hal Foster's *Prince Valiant*, if they had not illustrated the tales that Francis Child had resurrected in preparation for the various Robin Hood analogues, then none of these early series would have caught hold in the public imagination. Similarly, the success of Conan and the spin-off Red Sonja, found its genesis in the long history of American pulp fiction and on the primacy of Robert E. Howard within that world.

Beowulf: Dragon Slayer could have been a success. It was part of a clearly identifiable fantasy genre that was, by 1975, moving into a long-term publishing boom. In the two lead characters, Beowulf and Nan-Zee, we see identifiable archetypes that were popular in other series—DC's answer to Conan and Red Sonja. The artwork was well executed and the storyline not dissimilar to material that was elsewhere being bought, plus it paid at least some lip service to a recognizable classic, a classic that lay at the heart of Tolkien's scholarship, a classic that was being taught at universities by the same scholars who were teaching the *Eddas*. But Beowulf was not Conan and Nan-Zee was not Red Sonja and, perhaps most important, the DC readership was not the same as Marvel's.

Interestingly, the publication success of the original poem bears a striking similarity to that of the comic book when it is considered in context. *Beowulf* survives in a single medieval manuscript. No other copy of *Beowulf* exists from before its rediscovery in the nineteenth century. Not one. *Beowulf* apologists put this lack of textual plurality down to the Vikings, of course, or the weather—two bibliotechnical calamities that destroyed the libraries of England. Multiple recensions of the *Anglo-Saxon Chronicle* survived, though, and Bede's *Historia ecclesiastica gentis Anglorum* fared even better. We still have more than 250 medieval exemplars of Bede's opus, five of them from the eighth century, but no other *Beowulf*.

No epic concerning the tragedy of Ingeld has come down to us, but reference to the tale in *Beowulf* and in *Widsith* illuminates for the modern reader Alcuin's remonstration of the monks at Lindisfarne: "What has Ingeld to do with Christ?"[41] *The Fight at Finnsburh* is only a fragment, as is *Waldere*, but we find mention of the former in the *Anglo-Saxon Chronicles*, and a number of continental analogues survive for the latter. The popularity of the legends of Sigemund and Sigurd, alluded to in *Beowulf* and represented in Anglo-Saxon art, need not be demonstrated here again—suffice it to say that their forms are myriad across the Germanic-speaking lands.

In *Beowulf*, however, we have a single monolithic work, the longest extent poem in the Anglo-Saxon corpus, the hero of which is nowhere else attested. We have no extant continental source, no Norse corollary, no mention in any historical source, and no representation in art of any aspect of the Beowulf legend. Unless the poem is a late creation, composed in the twilight of the Anglo-Saxon epoch just before their language ceased to be a language of power, then we have in *Beowulf* a poem that throughout its long history made no impact on its audience—and some commentators would have us believe that *Beowulf* existed in written form for some three hundred years before the *Nowell Codex* was commissioned.

The unpopularity of *Beowulf: Dragon Slayer* may well have brought about its early demise as a comic book series, but it would seem that in that lack of popularity it was doing little more than following in the footsteps of its illustrious forebear. Which is not to imply, of course, any sort of correlation between popularity and artistic merit. *Beowulf* remains one of the great literary masterpieces of the English language, albeit in a dialect variant that few modern speakers of English can now understand.

Even if Uslan's vision of Beowulf had been better imagined, however, more literary in its execution, more engrossing in its design, it would still have struggled against the resistance that audiences have persistently demonstrated to the underlying story. The manifest unpopularity of the original poem has been mirrored by modern audiences since Grímur Thorkelin's first print edition appeared in 1815, and before the twentieth century it was seldom used except as an historical tool or as a nationalistic centerpiece.

For the United States, although the epic poem might have figured in a shared cultural history, there was never the popular acceptance that went with the stories of Arthur, or Robin Hood, or even the Norse gods. The American composer Howard Hanson produced his opus 25, *The Lament for Beowulf*, in 1925, using the translation published by William Morris and

Alfred John Wyatt some thirty years earlier. In 1974 Victor Davies and Betty Jane Wylie produced the rock opera *Beowulf: A Musical Epic.*

Prior to Gardener's *Grendel*, only one adult novel had engaged with the original poem. This was *The Ring-givers*, by English author William Canaway, which was published in 1958. Rosemary Sutcliffe produced her book *Beowulf: Dragonslayer* two years after that, in 1961. Illustrated by Charles Keeping, Sutcliffe's storybook was aimed at a much younger audience, although the close resemblance of the mid-1970s comic book title with this earlier children's book does seem to indicate at least some borrowing on the part of Uslan.

In 1976 Michael Crichton published *Eaters of the Dead*, which stitched together elements of *Beowulf* with the ethnographical writings of the tenth-century Arab traveler Ahmad ibn Fadlan, and this book was eventually made into a movie, *The 13th Warrior*, in 1999. These scant efforts aside, we do not witness a long and complex reception history for *Beowulf* of the sort revealed in earlier chapters for other cultural icons. Whether or not the early English audiences embraced the poem, certainly modern audiences have not.

CONCLUSION

In his 1936 lecture, "*Beowulf:* The Monsters and the Critics," Tolkien warned against the dangers of using medieval poetry for the purposes of decontextualized analysis. By the early twentieth century, facile historicism was in danger of strip-mining Anglo-Saxon literature into a wasteland, its poetry harvested for historical facts, its artistry discarded as worthless. Dragons could not exist, Grendel could not exist, and this manifest nonexistence rendered such aberrations unworthy of serious study. It was Tolkien's address that awakened a new generation of Anglo-Saxon scholars to the literary merits of early pan-Germanic poetry in general, and *Beowulf* in particular.

Remaindered to the unhappy position of cultural relic, *Beowulf* had been plundered for historical references and utilized as a primer for Old English language classes, but it had seldom been enjoyed for its own sake. Tolkien's address to the British Academy sought to redress this, but the poem has been a long time making its way out of academia and into popular fiction.

There has been no Wagner to proselytize for Beowulf. Edwardian children's books enumerated the Norse heroes, but did not look to the legends of Wessex. Gardner's *Grendel* was a literary reworking of the poem, rather than a popularization. No movies were made, no television series were aired. Even as late as 2005, attempts by the director Sturla Gunnarsson to envisage a modern representation of the poem met with critical success, but commercial failure—his *Beowulf and Grendel* faced limited release and proved to be a box office disappointment.

The one success in this long history of failure, however, has also been the most recent. During the weekend of its debut in late 2007, Robert Zemeckis's *Beowulf* ranked first in the United States and Canadian box offices. Within six months of its release, it had grossed almost $200 million. Filmed in performance capture animation, the film was scripted by Neil Gaiman.

Gaiman was mentioned in chapter 3 in relation to his work on the *Sandman* series. His literary successes include the Hugo Award, the Nebula Award, the Bram Stoker Award, the Newbury Medal and, in 2010, the prestigious Carnegie Medal in Literature, but, despite all this work in text fiction, Gaiman is still best known for his work in comic books and graphic novels, a career that started with DC in the late 1980s—too late, unfortunately, to breath some life back into *Beowulf: Dragon Slayer*.

For whatever reason, Beowulf, in all his manifestations, failed to become a major part of the American Century. Perhaps the utilization of the original poem as a national epic rendered the character too implacably British at a time that America was seeking to self-consciously distance itself from its parent country. The contested and convoluted reception history of the Arthurian legends enabled them to transcend simple chauvinism, and Robin Hood, egalitarian and rebellious from the outset, made for a natural immigrant. Thor excited in the American imagination what the scholarly Beowulf could not, and Conan, together with Red Sonja, rode the ranges of a distant, yet familiar, landscape.

Being a medievalist comic, even at a time when medievalist comics were so clearly in fashion, was not enough. In many ways, *Beowulf: Dragon Slayer* stayed too true to its birthplace—it failed to embrace the American Century, and America, in turn, refused to embrace it.

CHAPTER 7

Northlanders (2007)

Flames from one log leap to another, fire kindles fire—a man learns from the minds of others, a fool prefers his own.
—*HÁVAMÁL* (V. 57)

Although medievalist comics have been in constant production throughout the American Century, a quick glance back at the chronology of our chapters will evidence some broad trends. We have witnessed an initial surge during the Golden Age with *Prince Valiant* and *Green Arrow*, consolidation during the Silver Age with *The Mighty Thor*, and a deluge of sword and sorcery titles during the Bronze Age. Our focus now shifts forward to 2007 and the publication of the first issue of *Northlanders*, but this should not be read to imply that there were no medievalist comics produced during the more than thirty-year gap between this series and *Beowulf: Dragon Slayer*.

All the major titles looked at so far continued to find production in one form or another throughout the 1980s and 1990s. Prince Valiant, Green Arrow, Thor, Conan the Barbarian, and Red Sonja continued to appear in comic books, in motion pictures, in live-action television shows, and in cartoons, but neither DC nor Marvel seemed interested in pursuing a new medievalist product.

Mike Barr managed to sell a space-age King Arthur to DC, although it took some years to convince them. *Camelot 3000* launched as a 12-issue limited series in December 1982, wrapping up in April 1985. Brian Bolland drew the adventures of Arthur, Merlin, and the Knights of the Round Table, reincarnated into an overpopulated future Earth on the eve of an alien invasion orchestrated by Morgan Le Fay. The series has been credited with introducing the first transgendered character to a mainstream comics audience—Sir

Tristan returns as a woman, in which form he is forced to deal with his preconceptions of gender and his own sexually violent past. *Camelot 3000* also deals explicitly with the issue of incest, a powerful theme in the earliest of the Arthurian cycles, and portrays homosexuality in a positive manner.

The series was one of the first directly marketed runs produced by DC, and these subscription sales allowed the company to bypass both newsstand distributors and, more importantly, the CCA. There is much yet to be written about *Camelot 3000*, but the nature of its distribution makes it less applicable to the thesis at hand, which seeks to contextualize broad consumer trends through widely distributed and popular titles.

Toward the end of the 1990s another significant medievalist comic began production in France. *Donjon* began as a series of graphic albums released by the French publishing house Delcourt in 1998. The series creators were Joann Sfar and Lewis Trondheim, the latter of whom was also involved in establishing the influential publishing company L'Association, one of the most important firms to emerge from the new wave of Franco-Belgian comics in the 1990s. Another L'Association founder, Jean-Christophe Menu, has also worked on *Donjon*.

The series is a parody of the sword and sorcery genre, with the eponymous dungeon serving as a deadly business establishment in which various heroes come to prove themselves and, usually, to die. The parody extends to specific elements of the genre as well—*Dungeons and Dragons*, for example, would seem to be the target of particular ridicule—as well as the comic book medium itself. The central hero of the early issues is Herbert the Duck, an anthropomorphic avian more than a little reminiscent of Marvel's Howard the Duck. The dungeon at the heart of the series also serves to illustrate a range of allegorical truths as well, and the comic book is probably best seen as satire that uses common tropes of medievalism rather than as a medievalist work.

Nantier Beall Minoustchine Publishing (NBM) Anglicized the series title to *Dungeon* and began releasing the French comic in the United States in 2002, where it remains in distribution at the time of writing. Significant as the comic is, though, it remains ostensibly European in its outlook. It may well serve another author to analyze this series in terms of medievalist discourse in France, but it cannot readily be applied to this study.

So it seems fitting to finish this excursus with a look at the *Northlanders* series, written by Brian Wood and published by Vertigo between 2007 and 2012. Vertigo is an imprint of DC Comics and was founded in the early 1990s so that DC could produce comic books for a more adult readership without compromising the CCA approval of their most popular lines. From its very genesis, therefore, *Northlanders* was destined to be a viscerally bloody romp through the early Middle Ages. What strikes the reader as significant about the series, however, is not its use of medievalism, but, rather, its steadfast refusal to engage with medievalism at all. Where every other comic book examined in these pages has been a product of an historicized use, or reuse, or even abuse, of a real or imagined medieval past, *Northlanders* is almost entirely removed from any such concern. Rather than reinterpreting old stories for a new audience, *Northlanders* projects modern stories onto an epoch so ill defined and nebulous as to be almost ahistorical. *Northlanders* is, in short, an "unmedievalist" comic book.

This monograph began with an assertion that comic books are "intrinsically modernist and undeniably American," but *Northlanders* challenges that paradigm. Finding publication during the early years of the twenty-first century, this series provides a postmodern counterpoint to the titles looked at so far, and demonstrates an artistic sensibility more in keeping with the "Asian Century" than the American. As such, it reveals a more culturally diverse America than that which gave us *Prince Valiant* or Green Arrow, and an America less infatuated with its past than it was when *The Mighty Thor* first hit the newsstands. Moreover, although both *Conan the Barbarian* and *Red Sonja* demonstrate an eclectic and somewhat de-historicized relationship with the European Middle Ages, *Northlanders* presents the reader with a medievalism even more indicative of a postmodern approach to history—an approach that is sometimes coupled with the adjective "throwaway."

Richard Bauckham and Trevor Hart have argued that "contemporary Western society" is characterized by this "throwaway culture" and that the phenomenon itself is fundamentally linked to prevalent concepts of periodization: "whereas pre-modern (traditional) societies gave priority to the past and modern (progressive) society gave priority to the future, with the decline of the idea of progress a postmodern society is emerging in which priority is given to the present."[1] This prioritized present is also a dominant aesthetic in *Northlanders*.

NORTHLANDERS

In the very first issue of *Northlanders*, Brian Wood set out in a letter to his readers exactly what it was that he hoped to achieve with the new series. It had to be more than just "badasses in fur and horns, watched over by scary gods of thunder and death, lissome shield maidens at their sides, all stalking the frozen northlands"—it had to be "something more," something with "maturity and sophistication." In the end, Wood opted for a "nihilistic crime saga set in A.D. 870," creating a series about not only "millennial fears, clash of cultures ... the death of the pagan way of life and the relentless march of progress," but also "identity, location, politics, war, people in love and lives in flux."[2]

From the outset, Wood was eager to distance *Northlanders* from the other historical comic book series that would naturally invite comparison. Andy Khouri of *Comic Book Resources* was quick to point out in an early review that *Northlanders* was unlike epics such as *Age of Bronze* (Eric Shanower's retelling of the Trojan War) and *300* (Frank Miller's meditation on the battle of Thermopylae) in "a number of pronouncedly modern ways," noticeably featuring "compelling, modern characters" and "foregoing the occasionally wearisome language that some readers may associate with literary depictions of the era."[3] Informing Wood's interpretation of the Viking Age was his underlying belief that the Vikings "pulled Europe out of its dark ages and changed the world,"[4] that they "were forcing change on Europe, opening it up to trade and settlement ... albeit at the point of a sword."[5] Distanced as *Northlanders* might be, therefore, from the medievalist comics so far surveyed in this work, we can still see at play here at least some of the themes outlined in Luce's editorial—optimism in the face of change, the intrinsic worth of modernization, and a valuing of entrepreneurial trade no matter the personal or cultural costs.

The series was never intended to demonstrate a narrative continuity—characters would appear in single story arcs and then be retired. Some of the storylines ran for a substantial number of issues, essentially forming limited mini-series within the title. *Sven the Returned* ran in issues 1 through 8; *The Cross and the Hammer* issues 11 through 16; *The Plague Widow* issues 21 through 28; *Metal* issues 30 through 34; *The Siege of Paris* issues 37 through 39; and *The Icelandic Trilogy* issues 42 through 50. These longer stories were, in turn, separated by brief single- or double-issue arcs such as *Lindisfarne* (issues 9 and 10); *The Viking Art of Single Combat* (issue 17); *The Shield Maidens* (issues 18 and 19); *Sven, The Immortal* (issue 20); *The Sea Road* (issue 29); *The Girl in the Ice* (issues 35 and 36); *The Hunt* (issue 40); and *Thor's Daughter* (issue 41).

The modernity of the series is ever-present and often invasive. One early commentator described Wood's depiction of Constantinople as the "11th century's answer to Las Vegas."[6] The "occasionally wearisome language" of

Wood's competitors is replaced with intrusively contemporary patter—"Do I need to remind yeh this's an invasion?" says a Saxon warrior during a raid on the Orkneys, "Like with pointy swords and people dying and shit?"[7] Christians are depicted throughout the series as venal and self-serving, although pagans are also sometimes portrayed as backward and superstitious. Nihilism would seem to be the ideology of choice for most of Wood's heroes—a gritty, neo-noir refusal to believe in anything beyond the cruelty of existence and the inevitability of death. Indeed, issue 40, *The Hunt*, is a protracted exploration of just this ontology, and one in which the final image resonates with a sad and desperate hopelessness all too familiar to modern audiences, but one largely unknown, I would suggest, to their medieval counterparts.

In *The Cross and the Hammer* we are witness to an eleventh-century forensic detective.[8] His rule threatened by the murderous rampage of a serial killer, King Sygtrygg dispatches this sleuth, Ragnar Ragnarsson, to hunt the "perp" down. Aided by men of the "King's Forest Guard North (Special Detachment)," Ragnar utilizes his "college" training to examine "splatter patterns" and footprints, to read maps, to write down notes, and to organize dragnets. The tense psychological contest that ensues is part Sherlock Holmes, part *Sin City*, and in no way medieval.

Indeed, much of what we have come to regard as standard within the genre of medievalist comics is missing in *Northlanders*. Although the series ran for fifty issues, we at no time see torture or torture devices, and plague features in only one story arc (*The Plague Widow*), where it is treated as an unfortunate accident rather than a natural byproduct of a less hygienic age. Readers of *The Plague Widow* could also be forgiven for seeing the pestilence that strikes the Viking outpost in early Russia as a thoroughly modern one—the graphics would seem to depict zombies rather than plague victims.

Pagans in *Northlanders* may engage in sorcery, but, with a single exception, such sorcery is always depicted as backward nonsense. That single exception is encountered in the *Metal* storyline, which features the Germanic goddess Hulda as a deity of ambiguous motivation, and pits the hero of the storyline, Erik, against a *draugr*, or undead spirit. Erik, a blacksmith by trade, is also skilled at making charcoal, so the association might be, also, with the Norse Huldra—the forest spirits who were thought to be the special friends of charcoal burners. Erik is an emotionally and psychologically unstable character, though, and his initial meeting with Hulda follows his ingestion of what would appear to be *amanita muscaria* (fly agaric mushrooms), so perhaps the supernatural elements of this story arc are meant to be, in fact, the hallucinations of the central characters.

The Shield Maidens storyline does allude to the Norse legends of the Norns, mythical female beings believed by pagan Scandinavians to rule the destiny of the living. In Snorri Sturluson's interpretation of the ancient poem *Völuspá*, the three most important Norns (Urðr, Verðandi, and Skuld) spin the fates of gods and men, and in Wood's *The Shield Maidens* we see three Norse women (Thyra, Lif, and Grettr, also weavers), as they try to survive a Saxon counterattack on their Nordic colony in England. Wood's script even indulges us with a quote from the *Völuspá*, but the shield maidens in the *Northlanders* story are palpably real, flesh-and-blood women, with no supernatural powers and little hope for survival.

As it turns out, Thyra, Lif, and Grettr do manage to survive and eventually make it back to Jutland where they become successful merchants. Their escape from the Saxon forces initially surrounding them is achieved with the use of some psychotropic mushrooms and a good deal of violence. The question of Norse women participating in actual battles is one that has waxed and waned in recent decades, but recent research by Shane McLeod would seem to indicate that this idea is far less fanciful than previously perceived.[9]

Old Norse texts are quoted elsewhere in *Northlanders* as well. The one-shot *Viking Art of Single Combat* encompasses quotes from the *Orkneyinga Saga*, the *Vopnfirðinga Saga*, the *Hávamál*, and one of Harald Sigurdsson's poems recorded in the *Heimskringla*, but, for the most part, such medieval artifacts do not surface in the series and the stories remain steadfastly modern in their focus.

A good deal of this focus seems to be fixed on dysfunctional relationships between fathers and their children. Mads, the hero of *The Siege of Paris*, remarks casually on his inability to do anything other than kill: "What else can a man like me possibly be good for? A husband? A father? Give me a fucking break!"[10]

This sentiment, men ruined by the cruelty they have seen or the carnage they have caused, is carried throughout the series. The first three storylines (*Sven the Returned*, *The Cross and the Hammer*, and *Lindisfarne*) all revolve around the cruelty of fathers and the effect this cruelty has on their offspring. This theme is returned to later in the series in both *Thor's Daughter* and *The Icelandic Trilogy*. In fact, more than half of all the issues of *Northlanders* (twenty-seven out of fifty issues) use this device to power their narrative.

Freud, of course, was one of the great philosophers of modernity and so it comes as no surprise to encounter his theories in a text as contemporary as *Northlanders*. Indeed, the stage is set for Freud's intrusion into *Northlanders* very early when, in issue 3, we are informed that a "famous philosopher talked of the link between sex and death. One drives the other, moving in a circle." Psychological disorder, then, becomes a mainstay of *Northlanders*, be it the cognitive disassociation of Magnus in *The Cross and the Hammer*, the Ahab-like madness of Dag in *The Sea Road*, or the manic aggression of the appropriately named Mads in *The Siege of Paris*. Even Sven, one of the few characters who find some sort of redemption through their adventures, is portrayed in a thoroughly modern way: "a self-loathing Viking, a guy in the middle of a massive identity crisis."[11]

All this, of course, serves to illustrate just how far the series diverges from texts such as *Prince Valiant*, or even *Conan the Barbarian*. The deracinated medievalism of *Northlanders* is indicative of a postmodern and problematized reading of history, and yet such interpretations are not without value and, certainly, not without purpose. Kathleen Berry has argued that the

> dramatic arts that consider reconstruction of the historical consciousness . . . throw up obstacles to the historical process. These obstacles such as memories of the past serve to illuminate not only what is but what could be. The question remains not so much an insertion or change of the historical consciousness but a problem of what to keep and what to throw away in our historical sensibilities.[12]

It is precisely this "reconstruction of the historical consciousness" that can be witnessed on the pages of *Northlanders*.

BRIAN WOOD

Any text, of course, is the product of its author or authors. So the postmodernism of *Northlanders* must, logically, be the product of its primary creator, Brian Wood. Wood famously began his artistic career as a designer for Rockstar Games. *Grand Theft Auto*, *Max Payne*, *Midnight Club*, and the controversial *Manhunt* are among the titles that he worked on for Rockstar and, when he made his move into the world of full-time professional comic book writing in 2003, he brought with him the same neo-noir sensibilities.

Wood initially worked with artist Becky Cloonan to produce *Demo*, a twelve-issue limited series that was published by AiT/Planet Lar during 2003 and 2004. The series consisted of twelve stand-alone stories each involving young people with supernatural powers, although, as the series progressed, these powers were less central to the storylines and the focus shifted to the characters, their emotions, and their relationships with others. A second, six-issue limited series, *Demo: Volume 2*, appeared in 2010.[13]

In 2005, Wood began publishing *DMZ* through DC Comics under their Vertigo imprint. With artwork by both Wood and Riccardo Burchielli, *DMZ* is set in a dystopian near future where the demilitarized zone (DMZ) of Manhattan serves as a buffer between the forces of the United States and the secessionist Free States in a second American Civil War.[14] As such, *DMZ* is somewhat reminiscent of Wood's first professional comic book, the five-issue *Channel Zero*, which is also set in a near-future New York and meditates on themes of freedom and oppression. *Channel Zero*, eventually published by Image Comics, was created in 1997 as part of a final graduation project while Wood was studying illustration at the prestigious Parsons School of Design.

Both *Demo* and *DMZ* were successful comic books, well regarded within the industry and well subscribed. Wood worked on a number of other projects besides these, however, and soon became a stalwart at DC/Vertigo.

Will Dennis, editor at the DC-owned Vertigo Comics, approached Wood urging him to work outside his "comfort zone"[15] at about the same time that Steve Wacker, then an editor at DC head office, also sounded Wood out on the concept of reworking the Silver Age character of Jon, the Viking Prince—a hero we have already met elsewhere in this study. The Viking Prince enjoyed a four-year run in the late 1950s as a regular character in DC Comic's *The Brave and the Bold*, and in 1966 was revived (literally, from a block of ice) for a two-issue story arc in *Our Army at War*, only to die fighting the Nazis. It was in *Our Army at War* that Jon, the Viking Prince, was retconned, having been banished from Valhalla by Odin because of his love for a Valkyrie.

DC, who owned the rights to the Viking Prince, evidently never gave up hope of resurrecting him yet again, and he continued to appear sporadically in the years after 1966. Death, of course, is no barrier to continuity within comic books, especially once a character is retconned, and it soon became clear that, although Jon had certainly died during the Second World War he had not been imprisoned in an ice flow since the Middle Ages. The Viking Prince had, in fact, traveled through time to set himself into the block of ice that Sergeant Rock found, and this meant that, although Jon had died (and would always die) fighting the Nazis, he had also lived a full and productive life across multiple time zones before that fixed event took place. Thus freed from the constraints of a linear history, the Viking Prince began to appear in a number of surprising adventures.

In 1978, another two-issue story arc, this time in *The Justice League of America*, pitted five time travelers assembled by the Lord of Time against modern-day superheroes. The Viking Prince teamed up with Black Pirate, Miss Liberty, Jonah Hex, and Enemy Ace to battle the Justice League and bring about the Lord of Time's conquest of the universe, but the time travelers eventually realized that they were being used and the world was saved.[16]

Four years later, DC again tried to resuscitate the Viking Prince in a four-part story, "Frozen Hell for a Viking," that appeared as a backup section in *Arak, Son of Thunder*.[17] *Legends of the Dark Knight* briefly attempted the same thing in 1992 with Batman encountering a modern-day descendant of Jon. This chance meeting permitted the retelling of an ancient legend concerning an encounter between the original Viking Prince and a Viking Batman.[18]

A 2001 story in *Birds of Prey* saw Black Canary, Green Arrow's sometime love interest, transported back to twelfth-century America where she met the Viking Prince during his exploration of Vinland. After a brief relationship Black Canary returned to the twenty-first century, leaving Jon to mourn "a love lost to time."[19]

Even as late as 2004, the Viking Prince was appearing, albeit briefly, in Darwyn Cooke's award-winning limited series *DC: The New Frontier* and, in 2008, Jon teamed up with the Golden Gladiator, his old *Brave and the Bold* comrade, to fight Enemy Ace, Firehair, and Tomahawk in Bruce Jones's *The War That Time Forgot*.[20] Thus, when the DC editors approached Brian Wood about rebooting the Viking Prince, it was part of a long and ongoing strategy to reuse old characters, maintain a working copyright, and reward brand loyalty.

Wood, however, was not interested in working with DC's Viking star. All of his projects to that point had been uncompromisingly modern, and he seemed reluctant to abandon his postmodern sensibilities. Wood recalled that after the meeting with Dennis he sat "slowly turning in my office chair, scanning my bookshelves" until his eyes came to rest "on the DVD set *The Yakuza Papers*."[21]

THE YAKUZA PAPERS

The motion picture *Jingi Naki Tatakai* was released in 1973. Directed by Kinji Fukasaku, the film was adapted from a series of articles written by journalist and former gang member Kōichi Iiboshi. These articles were, in turn, based on the prison diaries of Kōzō Minō, an underworld stalwart in postwar Hiroshima.[22] The criminal cartels operating in Japan at that time came to be called *yakuza*, although the Japanese police still refer to them as *bōryokudan* (violent gangs), while the gangs themselves prefer the term *ninkyō dantai* (chivalrous organizations). Subsequently, *Jingi Naki Tatakai* and its sequels were eventually marketed to an overseas audience as *The Yakuza Papers*.

The title of the first film in this series refers to battles that lack *jingi*. *Jingi* is a difficult concept to translate into a single English word and so *Jingi Naki Tatakai* was marketed in translation as *Battles Without Honor and Humanity*—although it was also occasionally sold as *The Yakuza Papers, War Without a Code*, or, in Australia, as *Tarnished Code of Yakuza*. The film, which chronicles the bleak journey of a disillusioned Japanese soldier, Shozo Hirono (played by Bunta Sugawara), as he is compelled to rise through the ranks of the *yakuza*, was revolutionary in both its nihilistic theme and its violent, documentary-style presentation. It was an outstanding success at the 1974 Kinema Junpo Awards, beating out all competition for Best Film, Best Actor, and Best Screenplay.

Buoyed by this success, Fukasaku quickly followed up with no less than seven sequels in the next three years: *Hiroshima Deathmatch* (1973); *Proxy War* (1973); *Police Tactics* (1974); the ironically misnamed *Final Episode* (1974); *New Battles Without Honor and Humanity* (1974); *The Boss's Head* (1975); and *The Boss's Last Days* (1976). In 1979, Eiichi Kudo was asked to direct an eighth sequel, *Aftermath of Battles Without Honor and Humanity*. As further testament to the ongoing popularity of the series, Junji Sakamoto was hired to direct yet another sequel, *New Battles Without Honor and Humanity: Another Battle*, in 2000 and, two years later, *New Battles Without Honor and Humanity: Conspiracy* was directed by Hajime Hashimoto.

In 2004 the first five films in the series were compiled as a DVD set and released onto the international market as *The Yakuza Papers*, although by this stage Western audiences had imbibed much of Fukasaku's innovation through the interpretation (some might say plagiarism) of his work by any number of Hollywood directors. Brian Wood must have been influenced by Fukasaku long before the five DVD set of *The Yakuza Papers* was ever released, nevertheless, it was upon this set that his gaze drifted to after his meeting with Will Dennis.

Even a casual viewing of *Battles Without Honor and Humanity* indicates just how much of Wood's initial vision for *Northlanders* was indebted to Fukasaku's pioneering direction. Nor should this come as any surprise to comic book readers for, in many ways, these *yakuza* films were readily translatable into graphic novels. Fukasaku made constant use of freeze-framing to identify key characters in his movies, to emphasize drama and to heighten tension. Comic books, by their very nature, use sequential images arranged in such a way as to connote movement and give the illusion of action. For a comic book reader, then, Fukasaku's films demonstrate an innately illustrative aesthetic.

The action sequences in the initial story arc of the *Northlanders* series, *Sven the Returned*,[23] are drawn with the characters taking up most of the panels. The artist here is Davide Gianfelice, who has also worked on modern retellings of classical Greek myths through Vertigo's *Greek Street*, but the direction in *Northlanders* is that of Wood. The implied movement is frenetic and the emphasis tends to be on long rectangular panels that frequently crop the characters' heads and lower limbs. This framing adds to the feelings of closeness and claustrophobia, but also mimics exactly the framing Fukasaku uses in *Battles Without Honor and Humanity*.

Early in this first film, Fukasaku shocks his audience with the severing of limbs and gravity-defying sprays of blood. Against the muted palette of postwar Hiroshima, where everything is indistinguishably gray and drab, these jets of bright-red blood are all the more visceral. Similarly, *Sven the Returned* begins with egregious splatters of blood, black against a predominantly red background, returning to a far more somber color scheme once Sven journeys to his Orkney homeland—and where Fukasaku gives his audience severed limbs, Wood and Gianfelice are quick to give us severed heads, disembodied spines, and desiccated corpses.

Wood, by his own admission far happier in the world of the present or the near future, must have taken some solace from the fact that the initial crimes in *Battles Without Honor and Humanity* make use of a sword, and it is at the conclusion of the first of these critical scenes, where Shozo kills his first gang member, that we see a clear parallel between *Northlanders* and the Japanese master. Having killed the *yakuza* swordsman, Shozo is seen in a tilt-frame, standing triumphant, left of center. This is exactly the same way that Sven is shown in the splash page of the first issue of *Northlanders*.

In *Battles Without Honor and Humanity*, Shozo returns to the ruin of his hometown Hiroshima, to find his people starving and living in squalor. The Americans occupy Japan and do as they please—the film starts out with two GIs raping a local woman. When Sven returns to his hometown of Grimness, he is met by similar scenes. Thugs working for Sven's uncle enforce their own tough (in)justice and one of Sven's childhood friends, Thora, is now a sexual plaything passed between them. The islanders have been disposed of their property, houses have been destroyed, farms have been left fallow. "This is worse than I remember," says Sven, "Grimness was hardly beautiful, but it was never a sewer."

Having killed the sword-wielding gangster in *Battles Without Honor and Humanity*, Shozo is put into prison. These scenes are initially shot from overhead with only enough lighting to illuminate Shozo and his companion against the inky blackness of the cell around them. So, too, when Sven is first captured by his uncle, the backgrounds are reduced to a solid black panel and the action is viewed from above.

Later in Wood's story arc, Thora becomes a passing love interest for Sven and, on several occasions, the two are depicted having sex. Interestingly, Wood chose to stage his sex scenes in exactly the same way as Fukasaku. Not only does Sven appear in the same positions as Shozo, but, in issue 2 of *Northlanders*, the wounded Sven appears naked but for a bandage swathed across his back, a bandage that occupies exactly the same portion of his back as the enormous fish tattoo that Shozo sports in *Battles Without Honor and Humanity*.

Finally, just as Shozo becomes blood-brothers with a member of a rival *yakuza* clan while imprisoned, a friendship which becomes problematic upon their release, so too Sven eventually forms a grudging admiration, and then reluctant friendship, with Hakkar, the head enforcer of his uncle's malevolent band. *Sven the Returned*, in fact, concludes with Sven ceding to Hakkar his right to rule the Orkneys.

It should be pointed out that, derivative as *Sven the Returned* might be, the idea of recasting a *yakuza* war into tenth-century Scotland is still a fresh one and, as the *Northlanders* series progresses, the influence of *Battles Without Honor and Humanity* becomes far less pronounced. The Vikings continue to act like gangsters, of course, and family disputes do tend to take on the appearance of cartel takeovers, but there is a lot of originality in the storylines as well. Moreover, it has to be said that Fukasaku's directorial vision owes much, in turn, to the American gangster films of the 1940s and 1950s that must have similarly influenced Wood.

With the final installment of the *Northlanders* series—the nine-part *Icelandic Trilogy*—Wood returned his comic book to its *yakuza* roots. The *Icelandic Trilogy* is, strictly speaking, a trilogy of trilogies, hence the nine issues, which deals with several centuries of conflict between two families, the Hauksons and the Belgarsons. Essentially two crime syndicates, these families battle each other for power, honor, and the lucrative seaborne trade that comes out of Iceland. Just as Fukasaku ended his series with the gradual rise of a revitalized police force and the subsequent demise of the criminal cartels, so, too, Wood injects the Catholic Church into the last phases of the Haukson-Belgarson war, as the Vikings themselves become little more than bit-players on a far bigger stage.

The Icelandic Trilogy is also significant in that it makes constant use of title boxes, small inserts that tell the audience who or what it is that we are seeing. Wood uses these throughout the series, but, in *The Icelandic Trilogy*, they are used extensively to enable readers to keep track of a burgeoning cast of characters. Fukasaku uses the same technique in *Battles Without Honor and Humanity*, where characters are frozen briefly as they are introduced and titles appear telling the audience who they are. *Northlanders* finishes, therefore, just as it started, with obvious reference to a cinematic pioneer and a return to the crime genre from which it was spawned.

That Wood should model his Viking epics on Fukasaku's cinema is significant within the immediate context of this study. For some commentators, the last few decades have marked a gradual shift away from an American Century and toward an Asian one, and the effects of this transition are particularly apparent within the comic book industry.

We have seen already that the work of Yoshitaka (Henry) Kiyama was foundational to the establishment of comic books in the United States, but, from the 1980s, American readers were increasingly exposed to Japanese-style comic books (manga) and animated features (anime) as these art forms began to filter in to the US mainland. Lisa Katayama has argued that Japanese exports such as manga and anime have embedded themselves as core components of US "geek culture," as she calls it, and that while bookstores "are going down, with people reading stuff online . . . the manga section is growing."[24]

This view is supported by hard evidence as well—while Japan's total export revenue increased some 21 percent between 1992 and 2002, the value of its *cultural* exports more than tripled, increasing from about $4 billion to more than $12 billion during the same period.[25] This shift in cultural credibility has led Douglas McGray to claim that Japan's "Gross National Cool" is "re-inventing superpower":

> Japan has made deep inroads into American culture . . . Bestselling Sony Playstation and Nintendo home video games draw heavily on Japanese anime and manga for inspiration . . . Japanese anime-style cartoons currently fill the majority of time slots in the after-school and Saturday morning schedules on U.S. cable television. The cartoon and video game franchise Pokémon—broadcast in 65 countries and translated into more than 30 languages—even made the cover of *Time* magazine.[26]

Northlanders, then, constitutes a graphic representation of an intellectual evolution from modernity toward postmodernity, and a fracturing of cultural hegemony to facilitate the inclusion of the East. It may not be a medievalist comic book in the truest sense, but it does, nevertheless, evidence an underlying axiom of this study—that comic books, as artifacts of popular culture, serve to illustrate truths about the societies that create them.

CONCLUSION

Northlanders concludes our survey of medievalist comics by providing us with an antithesis. The presence of swords or armor or knights or Vikings is not enough to make the art form in which they appear medievalist. Without that essential devotion to, or acceptance of, the ideas, beliefs, customs, or practices of the medieval period, the mere presence of medieval signifiers is not enough to substantiate a demonstrable engagement with this system that has, over the last two centuries, become so integral to our understanding of ourselves and our imagined past.

Northlanders may be set in a medieval world, but its characters, its storylines, its themes, its ontology, its very essence, is entirely modern—a neo-noir gangster saga that finds itself, largely for reasons of product security, translated into a Norse tableau. This is not meant to be a criticism of the series, of course, its value must be assessed on other criteria, but, for the purpose of this study, *Northlanders* exists as a cautionary exemplar for those who might wish to read medievalism into every tangential text. It also serves to contextualize a greater debate, that of the origins and use of medievalism, and that debate will be explored further in the final chapter of this volume.

CONCLUSION

The Stories Upon Which We Agree

What then is, generally speaking, the truth of history? A fable agreed upon.
—NAPOLEON BONAPARTE, *MÉMORIAL DE SAINTE HÉLÈNE* (1816)

At the outset of this study I posited that medievalist resonances worked to integrate various realities into our contemporary experience, while challenging the inherent limitations of problematic schema such as "the medieval" and "the Middle Ages." The previous seven chapters have demonstrated the myriad ways in which those integrations have occurred, and so, in this final chapter, we turn our focus toward the ways in which our understanding of the past, and the present, is limited by such apparently simple descriptors as "medieval."

As a temporal indicator, and used in a purely historical sense, the adjective medieval is relatively benign—it situates the associated object within a broad time frame, typically somewhere between the sixth and the sixteenth centuries of the Common Era. Yet, as we saw in the introductory chapter, such terms are also indissolubly linked to ontological structures, both utopian and dystopian, and it is this reality, in part, that makes medievalism so difficult as a system of inquiry.

I have used "the Middle Ages" as a complex noun throughout this monograph, and medieval as an adjective, and I have used them consistently in a purely temporal sense. Even using them in this way is not entirely straightforward, however, for, when we look at the circumstances in which these terms were first created, as we did in the introduction, we are witness to the exercise of various political, religious, and nationalist agenda. I want to conclude this work, therefore, by challenging the very terms that I have used throughout it, in order to divorce them as much as possible from discursive error, and I want to begin this process by elucidating the historiographical connections between the somewhat problematic "medieval" and the highly problematic "feudal."

I wrote at the outset of this work that the medievalism of the United States is inextricably linked with that of allied cultures, particularly Great Britain and France. The medievalist comics that have constituted the bulk of this study have provided a space in which to explore the interrelationship of American and British medievalism, but the reception histories of American medievalism with those of France have not been covered in such great depth.

The history of Revolutionary France, of course, was closely tied to that of Revolutionary America, and the cross-Atlantic correspondence between the two nations included a great deal of discourse on philosophy and cultural theory. Where British and American writers might denounce antiquated practices as medieval, however, French *philosophes* were more inclined to use the pejorative feudal. These two terms, medieval and feudal, are far from unrelated in the ontologies that inform our discourse, and so this final analysis of cross-cultural medievalism will serve, therefore, to contextualize arguments within a more inclusive ideology.

FEUDALISM

On the night of August 4, 1789, the National Constituent Assembly of France agreed to abolish feudalism. It was a night of miracles and magic. Writing a half century later, Thomas Carlyle famously set the scene when, "fired suddenly by an almost preternatural enthusiasm," the nascent Assembly worked feverishly, "through whole masses of work in one night." Carlyle's prose, idiosyncratic in its use of the present tense, draws his readers into the unfolding tableau:

> Peers, Archbishops, Parlement-Presidents, each outdoing the other in patriotic devotedness, come successively to throw their (untenable) possessions on the "altar of the fatherland." With louder and louder vivats . . . they abolish Tithes, Seignorial Dues, Gabelle, excessive Preservation of Game; nay Privilege, Immunity, Feudalism root and branch.[1]

There was raucous cheering and applause. A *Te Deum* was sung. Finally, at about three in the morning, the emotional representatives stumbled out into the gardens of Versailles, "striking the stars with their sublime heads." Carlyle's vision, however, of this "new night of Pentecost," was not a perspective shared by most French historians of his day.

The Marquis de Ferrières had been witness to these "excesses," as he called them. His memoirs, first published in 1821, enunciated the cynicism with which post-Napoleonic France interpreted the August Decrees: "Imperious directives hurried on those who still wavered—a feeling of hatred and a blind desire for vengeance, and not the love of what is right, seemed to animate them."[2] For the Marquis, like so many notables of the Bourbon restoration, the night of August 4 marked the ruin of the French constitution. The Assembly behaved like "a pack of drunkards," he wrote, "set loose in a store full of valuable furniture, they shatter and smash everything that comes to hand."[3] Other witnesses were no less scathing.

Mirabeau denounced the session as a "nocturnal orgy." Dumont likened it to the actions of a dying man making his will in too much haste: "each member gave away what did not belong to him and prided himself on his generosity at the expense of others." Rivarol also utilized images of death in his summation of the event: "The representatives of the nobility and the clergy," he said, "sought, like Japanese, their honor in public suicide."[4]

So which of these two schools of thought is the more defensible? Does the democratic idealism of Carlyle fatally compromise his interpretation? Or is the scathing critique by Restoration gentry too obviously self-serving? Two centuries of debate have not served to reconcile Ferrières's understanding with that of Carlyle. Nor has interest in the question receded.

The anarchist prince, Peter Kropotkin, noted the revolutionary enthusiasm of the Assembly, but also the fatal vagueness of their legislation.[5] Georges Lefebvre similarly interpreted the night in terms of "enthusiasm" and "magic."[6] For Timothy Tackett the deputies had been united by a "curious combination of idealism, anxiety, and the feelings of fraternity."[7] Michael Fitzsimmons has also championed the idealism of the Assembly in the face of historical skepticism:

> However contrived or premeditated the initial renunciations of that evening may have been, they electrified the Assembly. A wave of emotion overtook the deputies and launched them into an unrelenting condemnation of privilege, producing a new ideal of a polity that could be sublime—a belief that the nation should henceforth be a source of equity and the focus for the highest ideals and conduct of its members.[8]

Against such positive readings of the events of August 4, however, there have been a number of historians who view the motivations of the Assembly as confused, self-interested, or difficult to construe.

"If 'feudalism' in 1789 did not mean seigniorial rights," wrote Alfred Cobban, "it meant nothing,"[9] and for Cobban, the abolition of seignorial dues was "the work of the peasantry, unwillingly accepted by the men who drew up the town and *bailliage cahiers*, and forced on the National Assembly through the fear inspired by a peasant revolt."[10] John Markoff is similarly doubtful as to the power of ideals in the face of economic and social imperatives.[11] Most recently, Jon Elster has highlighted the inherent difficulties in attempting to deduce the motivations of a diverse group of representatives who are now so historically distant from us. "It is hard to tell," he warns, "whether the behavior was due to the fear of being (seen as) sacrificing less than others, to the vainglorious desire of being (seen as) sacrificing more, or to genuine enthusiasm."[12]

If the historiography of the "Abolition of Feudalism" offers little consensus as to the driving forces behind the legislation, the same is not true when it comes to explaining just what the August Decrees achieved. Most historians now agree that the act of abolition accomplished very little at all.

Both Tackett and Fitzsimmons assert that the power of the August Decrees lay, not so much in their legislative capacity, but rather in their potential as revolutionary signifiers. In a less complimentary vein, William Doyle has pointed out that the legislation enacted a week after the meeting on August 4 served only to "lay down that most feudal dues were redeemable, and should continue to be collected until compensation was paid."[13] Paul Hanson suggests that there was not much to legislate against anyway: "to be accurate, feudalism properly speaking survived only in the Franche-Comté and parts of Burgundy, and even there mainly in the institution of *mainmorte*."[14] In Hanson's view, therefore, the decrees themselves were almost empty rhetoric. In *The Abolition of Feudalism*, Markoff established that the Third Estate saw feudalism as synonymous with seignorial rights, but argued, also, that "in the period preceding the Revolution, one finds the use of 'feudal' instruments of domination for purposes that are not archaic in the least."[15] For Markoff, revolutionary change "was to consist in renaming things" rather than "altering the material content of the obligations of the rural population to those claims upon them."[16] Cobban's reading of the August Decrees, however, is even more damning.

Cobban's seminal revisionist text, *The Social Interpretation of the French Revolution*, emphasized the limiting nature of the abolition of feudalism.

Rather than a force for social progress, Cobban saw the reforms as part of a "capitalist offensive" that eventually destroyed the traditional village community.[17] Cobban argued that a great many of the seignorial rights had been appropriated, over the course of the eighteenth century, by the urban bourgeoisie. In Cobban's thesis, even *mainmorte* (the practice whereby land passed back into the possession of the "feudal" lord in the absence of a legitimate male heir) was criticized by the rising Third Estate deputies not because it was a relic of an antiquated past, but because such legal entanglements discouraged land speculation and made property difficult to resell.[18]

As a result of this general consensus among historians, it is now unfashionable to refer to the August Decrees as the "Abolition of Feudalism," and yet the deputies who met on the night of August 4 clearly thought that it was precisely this that they were doing. When the decrees were promulgated a week later, they were to begin with the grand injunction:

> The National Assembly entirely destroys the feudal system. It decrees that, among the rights and duties, both feudal and *censuel*, those relating to *mainmorte* either real or personal, and personal servitude, and everything pertaining to them, are abolished without compensation. All other dues are declared redeemable, and the National Assembly will determine the price and mode of redemption. Those rights that are not extinguished by this decree shall nevertheless continue to be collected until indemnified.[19]

The purpose of the decree was apparently straightforward. Even its title, the *Décret portant abolition du régime féodal*, seems unambiguous. If not feudalism, what then did those representatives think they had abolished? Is it all a matter of semantics and pedantry, or is there something important to be illuminated here?

In reference to the revolutionary concept of feudalism itself, Markoff wrote that there are "few terms on which scholars so intensely insist on the necessity of proper usage and on which there is so little actual consensus as to what that proper usage might be."[20] For Markoff, the term is ultimately little more than a signifier: "The revolutionary leadership in Paris tirelessly announced to themselves and to others the existence of a clear rupture with the past, a past that was frequently associated with the term feudal."[21] Against the obstructive social accretions of the "dark ages" then, against the "feudal" and the "medieval," the new leaders of France were utilizing the radiance of a human intellect unfettered by the shackles of church and caste.

Feudalism, in short, was the antithesis of the Enlightenment. In reality, as Markoff has demonstrated, very little of what the Assembly brought to an end with the August Decrees was medieval, and almost none of it was feudal.

Taxation was a central issue underlying the French Revolution, of course. Taxes deemed as feudal were abolished on the night of August 4, only to be indemnified by the Decree of August 11. It took another seven months for the Assembly to distinguish clearly between what was meant by abolition and indemnification, and a further four months from that for rates of indemnification to be set. Unable to finance such indemnification, it was a full four years before the ideals of August 4 became a reality, and only then under the shadow of a rising terror. Even so, the taxes abolished were not actually feudal.

Surprisingly perhaps, the most universally hated of the indirect taxes, the one most frequently denounced in the *cahiers*, was the *droit de contrôle*—a royal, and relatively modern, tax on the official registration of documents.[22] Other taxes that came in for criticism were equally new. The *vingtième* had been introduced in 1749, the *dixième* in 1710, and the *capitation* in 1695. Only the *taille* (1439) and the *gabelle* (first levied in 1286, but not permanent before the 1370s) were actual medieval, but still not feudal, taxes. The *aides* were certainly perceived as feudal taxes by the deputies, and their association with rural produce would certainly reinforce that misconception, but a misconception it remains.[23] These taxes then, so hated by the peasants, were, for the most part, products of a centralized Bourbon monarchy—an extension of privilege that was both modern and royal, rather than feudal. Moreover, as Markoff has shown, it was not even the exercise of this royal privilege that drove the French peasants to the despair of the Great Fear, but rather it was the appropriation of these taxation rights by a burgeoning, and urban, middle class. This was also possibly why peasants on estates where the seignorial lords were in residence rarely participated in revolutionary activity—not because they were cowed by the nobles, but because these landowners had not relinquished their seignorial obligations to town-based merchants.

In fact, taxation would not seem to be the major grievance of the legislators who passed the *Decree for the Abolition of Feudalism*. Having begun their document with the grand gesture of destroying the régime féodal, the next two articles detail rights relating to the hunting and husbandry of pigeons and rabbits. It is not until article five that the deputies turn their attention to the question of taxation and when they do so it is with tentative vagueness. Even more puzzling than this vexatious imprecision, though, are the inexplicable absences. Surely no institution could be more inimical to democracy, more feudal, than the abuse of the *lettres de cachet*, but in the *Decree for the Abolition of Feudalism*, they are nowhere mentioned.

The lonely prisoner chained in a dungeon, held forever on a *lettre de cachet*, was an image promulgated and exploited by the revolutionaries. The Bastille was imagined as a repository for such martyrs, and the people's assault on this ancient fortress signaled the start of the revolution proper. The *lettres de cachet* signified the junction of feudalism and absolutism, terms that were often conflated in revolutionary France, but the institution itself was very modern.

A review of a book on the subject of the *lettres* that was published during the reign of Louis XVI stated "their denomination is not very ancient, as it is said to have been employed, for the first time, in the *Ordinance* of Orleans, anno 1560."[24] The *Lettres de Cachet et des Prisons d'État* was published anonymously, but it was widely read and must certainly have been known to the revolutionaries, if for no other reason than because its author was the Comte de Mirabeau.

Mirabeau had written the book while being held on a *lettre de cachet* in the Château de Vincennes and his denunciation of the *lettres* was no innovation. The Cour des Aides had demanded the suppression of *lettres de cachet* in 1779. On the eve of the revolution, in 1788, the *parlement* of Paris made similar demands. The institution itself, however, was not formally abolished until early 1790, although the final few prisoners held on the royal prerogative, among them the Marquis de Sade, were not actually released until several months later. That revolutionaries like Mirabeau could denounce the *lettres de cachet* as both feudal and absolutist highlights both the imprecision of revolutionary language and the conceptual difficulties intrinsic to the concept of feudalism per se.

Feudalism, as Markoff has noted, has never been an easy term to define. Historians have long used the word as a kind of academic shorthand, but the word itself has bled into the public consciousness with injurious results. The thesis underlying Marc Bloch's monumental *La Société Féodale* has often been oversimplified by those who wanted to universalize the system.[25] Indeed, few conceptual models have been so egregiously misapplied as Bloch's feudalism—it is commonplace to read not only of feudal Europe, but also of feudal Japan, feudal India, feudal China, even feudal Africa.

Writing soon after Bloch, François-Louis Ganshof enumerated some of the problems inherent in the model and concluded that the term "lends itself to confusion."[26] This confusion led, in turn, to an active discussion among historians as to the "proper definition and delimitation" of feudalism, until Frederic Cheyette's seminal article irrevocably altered the course of the debate. Discussions on feudalism, Cheyette noted, "remind one of nothing so much as a group of medieval tapestry weavers debating the proper shape of the unicorn's head."[27] More recently, publications by Elizabeth Brown,[28] Bernard Bachrach,[29] and Susan Reynolds[30] have led many historians to question the usefulness, even the validity, of feudalism as a paradigm.

This is not the place to rehearse those arguments in any depth, for the present focus is on the origins of the word itself and the place it occupied within the historiography of the French Revolution, but it should be apparent that "feudal" enjoyed much the same contested position within that historiography that "medieval" did in the historical ontology of the English-speaking world. It should also come as no surprise that no one in the feudal era, if such a thing ever existed, would have used this term to describe their society. Although the term *feodal* is extant in French legal documents of the seventeenth century (but no earlier than that), it was not until the eighteenth century that its use became widespread.

Montesquieu is credited with the creation of the concept in his *De l'esprit des lois* first published in 1748, although Henri de Boulainville's *Histoire des anciens parlements de France*, which predates *De l'esprit des lois* by eleven years, used the same term. Either way, the term feudalism, as a cypher for retrograde and deleterious systems of government, was coined by French *philosophes* as a proposed antithesis to their neoclassical, often democratic, models. The idea gained traction and moved quickly into the philosophy of other nations, hence its appearance in Adam Smith's *Wealth of Nations*, first published in 1776.

The adjective feudal, therefore, employed in this manner, predated the pejorative use of the term medieval by a considerable period of time, even in English. Moreover, when medievalism as a concept did enter English in the middle of the nineteenth century, these earlier, continental associations must have informed the reception of the word.

By the advent of the French Revolution, the modern construct of feudalism, like the similarly modern constructs of onerous taxation and the *lettres de cachet*, were widely accepted as vestiges of a backward, medieval regime, as was the ancient custom known as the *droit du seigneur*. The *droit du seigneur* (right of the lord) is the term used to describe the putative legal right of a feudal estate owner to take the virginity of his vassal's daughters. Also referred to as the *droit de jambage* (right of the leg), the *droit de cuissage* (right of the thigh), or in Latin as the *jus primae noctis* (law of the first night), it remains today a popular medievalist fiction.

Although Herodotus mentions the custom as practiced by some tribes in ancient Libya (4.168), the right was nowhere else mentioned in Europe until the sixteenth century. Its use at that time was restricted to the support of critiques against other times or other peoples—the imagined crimes of distant enemies. By the eighteenth century, the lie had been so often repeated that Voltaire reported the practice as authentic in his *Dictionnaire philosophique*. It had by this stage passed into the popular imagination, a place from where it has never been dislodged.[31]

In *Nineteen Eighty-Four*, George Orwell has his character Winston Smith question the nature of history through the agency of, among other things, the *jus primae noctis*: "There was also something called the *jus primae noctis*," Smith tells the reader, "which would probably not be mentioned in a textbook for children. It was the law by which every capitalist had the right to sleep with any woman working in one of his factories."[32] Smith, employed to remove unwanted facts from the history of the totalitarian regime in which he lives, soon achieves a moment of clarity in which he realizes that:

> It might very well be that literally every word in the history books, even the things that one accepted without question, was pure fantasy. For all he knew there might never have been any such law as the *jus primae noctis*, or any such creature as a capitalist, or any such garment as a top hat.[33]

Smith's despair in the face of such maddening opacity is the natural byproduct of profound insight. If history is indeed the stories upon which we are agreed, what, then, is left of truth?

THE MIDDLE AGES

The feudalism denounced by the French revolutionaries did not exist. For the most part, the regime they imagined as feudal—the taxes, the *lettres de cachet*, the outrageous abuses of the *droit du seigneur*—were either out-and-out fictions, or modern products of the absolutist Bourbons. They were collective nightmares validated and amplified by projection onto the dark geography of the *Moyen Âge*. Few landscapes can serve so well to elaborate modern fears.

Even today, the Middle Age, as it is known on the continent, or the Middle Ages, in Anglophone countries, serves to epitomize retrogression and violence. When Slobodan Milošević faced trial in 2002 for crimes against humanity, the chief prosecutor Carla Del Ponte declared that his actions "revealed an almost medieval savagery."[34] In 2008, a popular blog site dedicated to political reform in Iran changed its name from "Stop the Mullahs" to "Stop the Medieval Cruelty in Iran."[35] Former Oxford professor Richard Dawkins has stated as recently as 2010 that the "Medieval mindset" of modern Islam makes it dangerous, malicious, and malign,[36] a turn of phrase repeated in 2014 by United States secretary of state John Kerry, when he declared the execution of American journalists by members of the so-called Islamic State an "act of medieval savagery."[37] It seems that, as feudalism has retreated from academic discourse, the Middle Ages have emerged to take its place. It must be understood, though, that the Middle Ages are every bit as illusory as feudalism.

Professors of medieval history routinely remind their students that no one living during the Middle Ages would have been aware of the transitory nature of the era in which they found themselves. This is the force behind the humor of Sellar and Yeatman's classic observation: "Noticing suddenly that the Middle Ages were coming to an end, the Barons now made a stupendous effort to revive the old Feudal amenities of Sackage, Carnage, and Wreckage."[38] Petrarch, of course, may well be the single exception to this observation.

It is to Petrarch, the "Father of Humanism," that we owe our modern conception of the periodization of history. It is Petrarch who made us modern. But Petrarch did not seem to see himself as located within that modernity. Rather, Petrarch saw himself existing in the quiet darkness of a fallen age, waiting for a cultural dawn that he would probably never see.

European scholars before Petrarch had engaged with their classical forebears with some misgivings. For them the elegance and artistry of Roman literature was tainted by its pagan origins. Alcuin, the genius behind Charlemagne's renaissance, loved to read Virgil, but he felt great shame and guilt in doing so. Thomas Aquinas worked unceasingly to reconcile the sophistry of Aristotle with the testaments of Christ and, in doing so, often ran afoul of the Church of Rome. Petrarch was no less a Christian than Alcuin or Aquinas, and he was no less dismayed by the paganism of the Latin texts, but he was also aware of their brilliance. He refused to judge harshly these men who had lived before "the true sun of justice had dawned." "Amidst the errors," he wrote, "genius shone forth. No less alive were their eyes, though darkness and dense cloud surrounded them. Thus they should not be hated for their errors, but rather pitied for an undeserved fate."[39]

Petrarch saw himself as living in a "Middle Age," and we have agreed with him ever since. Defining that Middle Age in general terms seems a simple enough task. The Middle Age lay between the Classical Age and the Modern. Historians will debate, of course, just when the Classical Age ended and the Modern began, but the Middle Age remains both defined and limited by its relationship to these two greater epochs.

Typically, the Classical world ends with the fall of Rome sometime during the fifth century of the Common Era—perhaps when Alaric the Goth sacked the city (410) or perhaps when the last emperor was deposed (476). When the Modern Age began depends largely on the nationality of the historian telling the fable.

Some English historians imagine the modern world began on the field of Bosworth (1485) when Henry Tudor defeated Richard III, last of the Plantagenets. French historians would prefer to date the Modern Age from the succession of Louis XII, "Father of the People," to the throne in 1498. For Spanish historians the deaths of Isabella I (1504) or Ferdinand II (1516) usher in the Modern Age. These kings and queens are integral to political histories not just as markers, but because their reigns demonstrate such a tangible shift in governance—the advent of modern absolutism and the diminution of premodern feudalism.

Social historians might be less interested in the life cycles of the elite and more inclined to see greater significance in the fall of Constantinople to the Ottoman Turks (1453), the fall of Granada to the Spanish (1492), the first voyage of Christopher Columbus to the New World (1492), or the promulgation of Luther's 95 theses (1517) as possible dates for the birth of modernity. Ultimately, though, the debate seems to range between a fairly tight cluster of dates, and most academics have no difficulty in dating the Middle Ages as having lasted from (about) 500 until (about) 1500. A thousand years, give or take. Such round numbers, of course, should be worrying to any historian.

THE STORIES UPON WHICH WE AGREE

If all the dates for the end of the Middle Ages (and, therefore, the beginning of the Modern Age) seem to congregate around 1500, might it not be that we are projecting rather than discovering? Why is Henry VII seen as more modern a monarch than his son Henry VIII, or his granddaughter Elizabeth? Why is the fall of Constantinople in 1453, by which time the city was a pitiful and isolated shadow of its former glory, more significant than the fall of Christian Jerusalem in 1187, or the final destruction of the Christian Levant in 1303? Why is the Christian conquest of Muslim Granada in 1492 more significant than the Portuguese conquest of Moorish Ceuta in 1415? Why are Columbus's journeys to the Caribbean more significant than the Viking settlements in Greenland and America? Why are Luther's protests against the Catholic Church more significant than those of his Hussite predecessors? The answer lies in Napoleon's cynical observation—that history is a set of stories agreed upon.

Petrarch may have seen himself as benighted in a transitional period of stagnation and gloom—certainly he looked back to the glory of ancient Rome and hoped one day for its renewal[40]—but the generation of intellectuals that followed him were in no doubt that renewal, indeed rebirth, had come with Petrarch. Leonardo Bruni published his *Historiarum florentini populi* (History of the Florentine People) in 1442 and was among the first of the new Humanist historians to use a tripartite periodization based on Petrarch's observation. Bruni equated the end of the Classical period with the deposition of the last Roman emperor, Augustulus, by the Germanic mercenary Odoacer in 476. A "New" (*Nova*) period began during the late eleventh century with the urban revival in Italy, which led to the demise of the Holy Roman Empire as a force in Italian politics by the middle of the thirteenth century. Bruni's Middle Ages, therefore, had finished by about 1250.[41]

Flavio Biondi adopted a similar periodization in his *Historiarum ab inclination Romanorum Imperii decades* (History of the Decades from the Decline of the Roman Empire) that was written between 1439 and 1453, but which remained unpublished until 1493. For Biondi, the decline of Rome had begun with its sacking in 410, and the New Age had only begun at the beginning of the fifteenth century with the consolidation of the Humanists. Biondi was a full generation younger than Bruni and arguably less interested than his senior colleague in the contributions of poets such as Dante and Petrarch—Bruni had also written his *Vite de Dante e del Petrarca* about the same time as his Florentine history—nevertheless, Biondi's use of the same periodization indicates just how pervasive this ontology was becoming in fifteenth-century historiography.

The dark, middle period envisaged by Bruni and Biondi, the epoch between the grandeur of ancient Rome and its modern rebirth, was, as it had been for Petrarch, scarcely worthy of a name, let alone study. In 1469, Giovanni Bussi published his edition of Pliny's *Naturalis Historia* (Natural History) and, in his foreword, used the term *media tempestas* (middle season) to refer to the period between the Classical age and the New. The Middle Ages were born.

This tripartite periodization is now ubiquitous. Academics rarely address the origins of the terms and even less frequently question its implicit ontology. A brief discussion of the system of periodization it replaced, however, does illuminate some interesting points.

Before Petrarch, Christian scholars had used two dominant *schemata* to classify periods of history—the Six Ages of the World and the Four (or Five) Monarchies. The Six Ages of the World (*sex aetates mundi*) were described by Augustine in his *De catechizandis rudibus* (Concerning the Catechism of the Uninstructed) written around the year 400.[42] For Augustine, the world had passed through six ages already: the Age before the Flood; the Age from the Flood until Abraham; the Age from Abraham until the rule of David; the Age from David until the Babylonian Captivity; the Age from the Captivity until the coming of Christ. With Christ's advent, the world had passed into its sixth and final age.

Writing around the same time as Augustine, Jerome had favored a periodization of history drawn directly from the scriptures. In the Book of Daniel, the Babylonian king Nebuchadnezzar relates a dream he has in which he saw a statue. The head of the statue was made of gold, its chest and arms were made of silver, its belly and thighs were made of bronze, its legs were made of iron, and its feet were made of clay mixed with iron.[43] A rock that struck the feet, toppling the statue, then expanded and filled the entire world. Daniel, advising the king, interprets the dream as relating to a series of monarchies that are to succeed him. As the Book of Daniel had probably reached its present form by about 165 BCE, scholars of the Torah usually identify the kingdoms as those of the Babylonians (gold), the Medes (silver), the Persians (bronze), and the Greeks (iron). The fifth kingdom, the rock that fills the world, is seen, in this analysis, as referring to the kingdom of the Maccabees, then at war with the Seleucid successor state.

For Christian scholars like Jerome, the rock that filled the world could only have meant Christ, and so the monarchies were altered. In Jerome's commentary on Daniel, the kingdom of the Medes was merged with that of the Persians so that Rome might be added as the fourth kingdom.[44] Both Jerome's Four Monarchies and Augustine's Six Ages placed Christ at the historical apex of the schema. Both envisioned a world history, therefore, that had come to fruition and, much like the later Italian Humanists who abandoned these periodizations, earlier Christian historians such as Bede saw themselves as living in a New Age. Even Petrarch, who saw flashes of brilliance in the literature of his pagan ancestors, counted himself lucky for having lived after Christ's birth. Petrarch might well have mourned the waning of Roman imperium, but it would seem that any such loss was far outweighed in his mind by the advantages of Christ's redemptive powers.

This Patrician view excluded non-Christians from the story in any but an oppositional role, but it also excluded nations. Rather than focusing on Europe, both the Four Monarchies and the Six Ages place the northern continent at the periphery of world history and deny the relevance of tribe or nation or people. There is only one people, the followers of Christ, and one language, Latin. In the fracturing world of the fifteenth century, this was not seen as a useful paradigm.

For Italian Humanists like Bruni, Biondi, and Bussi, an Italian renaissance could translate into a cultural imperium that meant real power in fifteenth-century Europe, so it is easy to understand why they might want to place Rome, rather than Christ, at the alpha and the omega of time. What seems less straightforward is how this idea spread through Europe. What did non-Italians get from being children of the empire?

In Jerome's interpretation, Rome was the last and the greatest of the world empires. Rome conquered the whole world, but Rome was conquered, in turn, by the majesty of Christ. In the millennium that followed the Roman conversion to Christianity, European political legitimacy was essentially a question of imperium—that is, which polity possessed the strongest claim as successors to the Roman Empire.

From the second half of the fourth century, with the decline of Roman Imperial authority in the West, the Papacy began to emerge as a credible contender for secular imperium as well as spiritual leadership. The power of the Roman popes, however, was challenged, initially, by the Roman emperors of the East—the Byzantines as Montesquieu eventually termed them—and then later by warlords in the West who styled themselves as emperors of Rome. In 1157, Frederick I Barbarossa was the first of these emperors to refer to his dominion as the Holy Empire and, by the middle of the thirteenth century, it had become common to combine the two terms and speak of the Holy *Roman* Empire.

In part, this nomenclature was used by the German princes to bolster their territorial claims to former Imperial provinces, especially in Italy, and thus the Italian reassertion of Roman cultural imperium served to undermine the legitimacy of German aggression. The Italians, however, were not the only people facing German threats.

By the end of the fifteenth century, France had emerged victorious from a protracted series of wars with England and Burgundy. When Ferdinand I died in 1494, Charles VIII of France seized the opportunity to press his Angevin claim to the throne of Naples. The subsequent wars in Italy eventually brought France into direct opposition with the Holy Roman Empire.

Jean Bodin (1530–1596) was born into a France recently at war with both the Holy Roman Empire and the Papacy, and his writings reflect those political realities. Bodin, in whose political manifestos many have seen the beginnings of the "Divine Right" of kings, was dismissive of the Four Monarchies model precisely because it empowered the enemies of his country.[45] The newer tripartite periodization enfranchised both the Italian Humanists and their philosophical heirs, in this case France, while simultaneously marginalizing medieval rulers like France's Hapsburg enemies. Like the earlier humanists, Bodin saw himself as living in a New Age, an age of steady political centralization and growing nationalism, but it was also a period of intense religious upheaval in Europe.

Bodin was frequently critical of the Papacy, though he remained a nominal Catholic throughout his life. His criticism may have been politically motivated, a product of French disputes with the secular authority of the popes, but it may be also that Bodin's philosophy was more in tune with that of the French Huguenots—Bodin was suspected of Huguenot sympathies during the Third War of Religion and was imprisoned in Paris in 1569. After the Saint Bartholomew's Day massacre, Bodin became an intimate of François d'Alençon, a prince of known Protestant association, and it was while accompanying the prince to England in 1581 that Bodin refused requests for help from English Catholics.[46]

Protestant writers were naturally attracted to the tripartite periodization because it denied primacy to both the Holy Roman Empire and the Papacy. Both the Four Monarchies model and the Six Ages of the World placed Rome at the evolutionary apex of world politics and left the Hapsburgs and the Pope arguing for supremacy. The new Humanist periodization posited Rome as a fallen state whose imperium was recoverable by any prince of integrity and intellect. Machiavelli had adopted the periodization and possibly influenced Bodin to do the same. Bodin's contemporary and one-time Huguenot Pierre Pithou (1539–1596) referred to the period between the Classical world and the New as a Moyen Âge, but Pithou's histories, like those of his non-abjuring brother Nicolas, were overtly and specifically anti-Catholic.[47] Englishman William Camden (1551–1623) similarly spoke of a *middle time*, a time before the light of Martin Luther. As the sixteenth century progressed then, the tripartite periodization became more common, but it also became more political.

Where Italian Humanists had seen luminaries such as Dante, Giotto, and Petrarch as integral in establishing this new world, and even Biondi was sure that the Middle Age was in retreat from 1400, Protestant writers of the sixteenth century were far more likely to see Luther as the man who ushered in the new age. The Middle Ages, therefore, became increasingly linked to that most medieval of institutions, the Church of Rome. This interpretation was then standardized by the publication of Christophe Cellarius's *Historia Universalis in Antiquam, et Medii Aevi ac Novam Divisa* (Universal History Divided into Ancient, Medieval and New Periods) in 1683.[48] Cellarius further divided each age into named centuries: the fifteenth was the *Hussitisones saec.* (Hussite century), for example; the sixteenth the *Reformations saec.* (Century of Reformation). For Cellarius, and for most European historians after him, the Middle Ages ended with the posting of the ninety-five theses to the door of All Saints' Church in Wittenberg.

Few historians today would want to associate themselves with a periodization so obviously sectarian or, indeed, so Eurocentric. And yet we do. In maintaining a model that incorporates a medieval period, we elevate Rome to a position of world (rather than just European) domination. In maintaining a model that incorporates a medieval period, we maintain a historiography that sees European changes in politics and religion as pre-eminent, we create a world in which Europeans alone have ushered in a New Age, in which Europeans alone have constructed modernity.

When casting about for dates to delineate the beginning of the Middle Ages, we tend not to look too far from the barbarian incursions into Italy. When casting about for dates to delineate the end of those Middle Ages, we tend not to look too far from Luther's protest. The Middle Ages, then, remain essentially European in our imagining, anarchic in their politics, ignorant and superstitious in their outlook. It is not too difficult to see in our envisioning of these Middle Ages the same backwardness and abuses that the French deputies sought to overturn on that August night in 1789. But it should not be too difficult, either, to acknowledge that we share with those deputies the same deluded prejudices and politicized misconceptions.

History is not a series of distinct periods. It is a continuous and interconnected narrative from which any given generation will harvest what seems relevant to their needs and to their experience of the contemporary world.

CONCLUSION

This book has looked at the place of the medievalist comic in the American Century. For some, the concept of American medievalism can seem incongruous simply because America, as a nation existing wholly within the modern period, has no medieval past. From such a perspective, any American engagement with the medieval risks being seen as quaint, at best, or at worst, delusional. For others, American medievalism can be seen as opportunistic and imperialist—foreigners laying claim to something that does not belong to them—but, in a very real sense, no nation has experienced a Middle Age.

Both "feudal" and "medieval" exist as descriptors of imagined historical eras, that is, eras that come into existence only once we imagine them. They function, therefore, as cultural constructs to be employed, rejected, abused, or disavowed by anyone seeking to adopt them.

This study has focused almost entirely upon comics produced and consumed within the United States. That is partly because of the physical location within which the bulk of my research was conducted—I was fortunate to be afforded a fellowship at the Library of Congress in Washington, an institution that houses the largest collection of books ever assembled, among which is the largest corpus of comic books in the world today. But the sheer scale of comic book production in America, the scale of their consumption, and the immensity of the American contribution to the history of the medium, means that any such study would have been drawn back inevitably into the orbit of the United States anyway.

It has not been possible to write here in any detail of the impact of these comics on the culture of other countries, but such research promises to be rewarding, especially in light of the monumental impact of American culture upon Europe following the surrender of the Axis powers, and the special distaste shown for American comics by authorities in Great Britain,

France, Germany, and Italy, all of whom struggled to keep the "Yankee menace" at bay. Nor has the scope of this study been broad enough to examine, to any great extent, expressions of medievalism in comics produced within those countries. Given the substantial history of comic book production in France, Belgium, and Great Britain, and given the contribution of British writers and artists to the American comic book industry, such research seems vital.

Still, this study has contributed to the process of historicizing American comics and placing them within a contextualized narrative of the creation, transmission, reception, and interpretation of medieval literature. The tendency among scholars of sequential graphic storytelling has been to focus on a largely literary and artistic analysis, but, unfortunately for many comics, this method of evaluation often finds them lacking in literary merit. As a result, academic criticism has tended to focus on the more erudite graphic novels. Moreover, such an approach would seem predicated upon the assumption that the work in question is the discrete product of an identifiable author, but this fails to acknowledge the production realities of a good many comics.

As we have seen, comics are more often the product of a number of authorial sources, and it is common for these sources to be in conflict with each other. The intention of the writer, the vision of the artist, the capacity of the colorist, the limitations of the editors, the imperatives of the company, the demands of society, and the expectations of the audience all merge to form a single, compromised product. Such products do not exist outside the coalescence of those authorial sources, and it is less than optimal to judge them as if they did.

Whereas this reality may present considerable, at times insurmountable, obstacles to literary criticism of the comic book, it does not pose the same difficulties for the historian. Indeed, assaying the nature of competing intentions and rationalizing the outcomes thereof is the historian's stock in trade. Comics are, by the contested nature of their production and their survival, ideal historical sources.

The purpose of this study has been to look critically at those sources in an attempt to celebrate the intricate, multidimensional lacework of their reception history. We have encountered a number of energetic, creative souls who produced these artifacts, and a great many more who enjoyed them. At times, hidden beneath this narrative of invention and craft, we have heard the resonance of deeper ideologies, or witnessed the conscious deployment of utopias and dystopias in order to promote nationalism or to denigrate it, to bring about change or to forestall it, to empower the masses or to render them powerless.

Such commentary is valuable and relatively easy to achieve, but the attribution of intent to the actors whose works we have observed is far more difficult to ascribe. The influences here are so multifaceted, and the accomplices so many, that motivation is difficult to establish. Nevertheless, those difficulties should not preclude for us the very real capacity of such humble objects to affect our world.

NOTES

INTRODUCTION

1. Henry Luce, "The American Century," reprinted in *The Ambiguous Legacy: U.S. Foreign Relations in the "American Century,"* ed. Michael J. Hogan (Cambridge: Cambridge University Press, 1999), 11–29, 29.
2. Aldo Regalado, "Modernity, Race and the American Superhero," in *Comics as Philosophy*, ed. Jeff McLaughlin (Jackson: University Press of Mississippi, 2005), 84–99, 85; but see also Aldo Regalado, *Bending Steel: Modernity and the American Superhero* (Jackson: University Press of Mississippi, 2015).
3. A more comprehensive, and very recent, definition of medievalism has been afforded by David Matthews's *Medievalism: A Critical History* (Woodbridge: D. S. Brewer, 2015).
4. *British Churchman* (August 1844): 291.
5. *The Southern Literary Messenger* (Richmond: White, 1849), 15:626.
6. Dante Gabriel Rossetti, *Letters* (London: Oxford University Press, 1965), 1:104, and John Ruskin, *Lectures on Architecture and Painting* (London: Smith Elder, 1854), 4:194.
7. See, for example, Hedley Bull, *The Anarchical Society: A Study of Order in World Politics* (New York: Columbia University Press, 1977), 254–66; Ole Wæver, "After Neo-Medievalism: Imperial Metaphors for European Security," in *Cultural Politics and Political Culture in Postmodern Europe*, ed. J. Peter Burge (Amsterdam: Rodopi, 1997), 321–64; Stephen Kobrin, "Back to the Future: Neomedievalism and the Postmodern Digital World Economy," *Journal of International Affairs* 51, no. 2 (1998): 362–86; and N. J. Rennger, "European Communities in a Neo-medieval Global Polity: The Dilemmas of Fairyland?" in *International Relations Theory and the Politics of European Integration: Power, Security and Community*, ed. Morten Kelstrup and Michael Williams (London: Routledge, 2000), 50–63.
8. Will Durant, *The Age of Faith* (New York: Simon and Schuster, 1950).
9. Nigel Yates, *Liturgical Space: Christian Worship and Church Buildings in Western Europe 1500–2000* (Aldershot: Ashgate Publishing, 2008), 114.
10. John D. Rosenberg, *The Darkening Glass: A Portrait of Ruskin's Genius* (New York: Columbia University Press, 1980), 50.
11. John Ruskin, *The Seven Lamps of Architecture* (New York: Dover Publications, 1880), 196.

12. Marian Moffett, Michael Fazio, and Lawrence Wodehouse, *A World History of Architecture* (London: Laurence King, 2003), 431.
13. James and Dorothy Volo, *The Antebellum Period* (Westport, CT: Greenwood, 2004), 131.
14. Umberto Eco, "Dreaming the Middle Ages," in *Travels in Hyperreality,* trans. W. Weaver (New York: Harcourt Brace, 1986), 61–72, and Isaiah Berlin, *The Hedgehog and the Fox: An Essay on Tolstoy's View of History* (London: Weidenfeld & Nicolson, 1953), esp. 76.
15. Justin Kaplan, *Mr. Clemens and Mark Twain: A Biography* (New York: Simon and Schuster, 1966), 171.
16. Eco, "Dreaming the Middle Ages," 61–72.
17. Kim Selling, "Fantastic Neomedievalism: The Image of the Middle Ages in Popular Fantasy," in *Flashes of the Fantastic,* ed. David Ketterer (Westport, CT: Praeger, 2004), 211–18; Cary Lenehan, *Post-Modern Medievalism: A Sociological Study of the Society for Creative Anachronism* (Unpublished Bachelor's Thesis, University of Tasmania, 1994).
18. Bull, *The Anarchical Society*, 254–55.
19. Kobrin, "Back to the Future," 362–86.
20. Karl Fugelso, ed., *Studies in Medievalism XVII: Defining Medievalism(s)* (Suffolk, UK: D. S. Brewer, 2009); Karl Fugelso, ed., *Studies in Medievalism XVIII: Defining Medievalism(s) II* (Woodbridge: D. S. Brewer, 2009); Karl Fugelso, ed., *Studies in Medievalism XIX: Defining Neomedievalism(s)* (Woodbridge: D. S. Brewer, 2010); and Karl Fugelso, ed., *Studies in Medievalism XX: Defining Neomedievalism(s) II* (Woodbridge: D. S. Brewer, 2011).
21. *Bible of Stephen Harding*, Dijon BM MS.14, Bibliothèque Municipale, Dijon.
22. See Frederik Schodt, *Dreamland Japan: Writings on Modern Manga* (Berkeley: Stone Bridge Press, 1996); Kinko Ito, "Growing up Japanese Reading Manga," *International Journal of Comic Art* 6 (2004): 392–401; and Adam Kern, *Manga from the Floating World: Comicbook Culture and the Kibyoshi of Edo Japan* (Cambridge, MA: Harvard University Press, 2006).
23. Wendy Siuyi Wong, *Hong Kong Comics: A History of Manhua* (New York: Princeton Architectural Press, 2001).
24. Republished in 1998 by Frederik L. Schodt as *The Four Immigrants Manga: A Japanese Experience in San Francisco, 1904–1924* (Berkeley: Stone Bridge Press, 1998).
25. Using Peter Coogan's working definition of superhero; see Peter Coogan, *Superhero: The Secret Origin of a Genre* (Austin: MonkeyBrain Books, 2006), 30–60.
26. Geoffrey Bunn, *The Truth Machine: A Social History of the Lie Detector* (Baltimore: Johns Hopkins University Press, 2012).
27. Fredric Wertham, *Seduction of the Innocent* (New York: Rinehart & Company, 1954).
28. The code is detailed in David Hadju's *The Ten-Cent Plague: The Great Comic Book Scare and How It Changed America* (New York: Picador, 2008).
29. Sean Howe, *Marvel Comics: The Untold Story* (New York: Harper, 2012).
30. The same medievalism is detailed in Kim Moreland, *The Medievalist Impulse in American Literature: Twain, Adams, Fitzgerald, and Hemingway* (Charlottesville: University Press of Virginia, 1996).

CHAPTER 1

1. Kenneth Whyte, *The Uncrowned King: The Sensational Rise of William Randolph Hearst* (Berkeley: Counterpoint, 2009), 465–66.
2. Arn Saba, "Hal Foster: Drawing Upon History," *Comics Journal* 102 (September 1985): 61–84, 84.
3. Brian Kane, *Hal Foster: Prince of Illustrators—Father of the Adventure Strip* (Lebanon, NJ: Vanguard Productions, 2001), 52.
4. Kane, *Hal Foster*, 80.
5. Oliver Carlson and Ernest Sutherland Bates, *Hearst: Lord of San Simeon* (Westport, CT: Greenwood Press, 1936), 305.
6. Carlson and Bates, *Hearst*, 304.
7. Mary Levkoff, *Hearst the Collector* (New York: Abrams, 2008), 91.
8. Levkoff, *Hearst the Collector*, 107.
9. Whyte, *The Uncrowned King*, 187.
10. Bill Blackbeard, ed., *R. F. Outcault's The Yellow Kid: A Centennial Celebration of the Kid Who Started the* Comics (Northampton: Kitchen Sink Press, 1995), 33.
11. Whyte, *The Uncrowned King*, 187–88.
12. Association, of course, is not the same as origin; for a more detailed discussion of the origins of the term *yellow journalism,* see W. Joseph Campbell, *Yellow Journalism: Puncturing the Myths, Defining the Legacies* (Westport, CT: Praeger, 2001), 25–49.
13. Whyte, *The Uncrowned King*, 27.
14. Whyte, *The Uncrowned King*, 63.
15. Ben Procter, *William Randolph Hearst: The Early Years, 1863–1910* (New York: Oxford University Press, 1998), 84–87.
16. Procter, *William Randolph Hearst*, 101.
17. Patrick McDonnell, Karen O'Connell, and Georgia Riley de Havenon, *Krazy Kat: The Comic Art of George Herriman* (New York: Harry N. Abrams, 1986), 57–58.
18. Gilbert Seldes, "The Krazy Kat That Walks by Himself," *The Seven Lively Arts* (New York: Harper and Brothers, 1924), 231.
19. George Herriman, *Krazy Kat* (New York: Madison Square Press, 1969).
20. McDonnell, O'Connell, and Riley de Havenon, *Krazy Kat*, 82.
21. McDonnell, O'Connell, and Riley de Havenon, *Krazy Kat*, 68.
22. Saba, "Hal Foster: Drawing Upon History," 62 and 70.
23. Saba, "Hal Foster: Drawing Upon History," 62.
24. Jill and Robert May, *Howard Pyle: Imagining an American School of Art* (Urbana: University of Illinois Press, 2011), 139–40.
25. James H. Duff, ed., *An American Vision: Three Generations of Wyeth Art* (Boston: Little, Brown and Company, 1987), 18.
26. May and May, *Howard Pyle*, 198–99.
27. Duff, *An American Vision.*
28. May and May, *Howard Pyle*, 45.
29. May and May, *Howard Pyle*, 119.

30. Andrew Lynch, "*Le Morte Darthur* for Children: Malory's Third Tradition," in *Adapting the Arthurian Legends for Children: Essays on Arthurian Juvenilia*, ed. Barbara Gepa Lupack (New York: Palgrave Macmillan, 2004), 3.
31. Kane, *Hal Foster*, 95–96.
32. Saba, "Hal Foster," 62.
33. Saba, "Hal Foster," 70.
34. Saba, "Hal Foster," 66–67.
35. Carlson and Bates, *Hearst*, 95.
36. Carlson and Bates, *Hearst*, 303.
37. Procter, *William Randolph Hearst*, 20–25.
38. Procter, *William Randolph Hearst*, 165.
39. Procter, *William Randolph Hearst*, 19.
40. Hasia Diner, *Erin's Daughters in America: Irish Immigrant Women in the Nineteenth Century* (Baltimore: Johns Hopkins University Press, 1983), xiv.
41. Procter, *William Randolph Hearst*, 12.
42. Carlson and Bates, *Hearst*, 28.
43. David Nasaw, *The Patriarch: The Remarkable Life and Turbulent Times of Joseph P. Kennedy* (New York: Penguin, 2012), 182.
44. Michael O'Brien, *John F. Kennedy: A Biography* (New York: St. Martin's Press, 2005), 180.
45. O'Brien, *John F. Kennedy*, 270.
46. John F. Kennedy Presidential Library and Museum, *Papers of John F. Kennedy. Presidential Papers, President's Office Files, 2 May 1945–13 December 1957* (Digital Identifier JFKPOF-129-003).
47. Nathan Bevan, "Lydia Hearst Is Queen of the Castle," *Wales on Sunday* (August 3, 2008).
48. Rose Fitzgerald Kennedy, *Times to Remember* (New York: Doubleday, 1974), 12.
49. Roberta Davidson, "The 'Reel' Arthur: Politics and Truth Claims in 'Camelot, Excalibur, and King Arthur,'" *Arthuriana* 17, no. 2 (2007): 62–84, 63.
50. Davidson, "The 'Reel' Arthur," 63.
51. *Prince Valiant* #276 (May 24, 1942).
52. Despite the works of such luminaries as Kim Moreland, see *The Medievalist Impulse in American Literature: Twain, Adams, Fitzgerald, and Hemingway* (Charlottesville: University Press of Virginia, 1996).
53. T. S. Eliot, *The Waste Land*, ll. 423–25.
54. William Faulkner, *Absalom, Absalom!* (New York: Random House, 1936), 160.
55. Alan Lupack and Barbara Tepa Lupack, *King Arthur in America* (Cambridge: D. S. Brewer, 1999), 183.
56. Davidson, "The 'Reel' Arthur," 63.
57. *Prince Valiant* #628 (February 20, 1949).
58. *Prince Valiant* #10 (April 17, 1937).
59. *Prince Valiant* #57 (March 12, 1938).
60. *Prince Valiant* #62 (April 16, 1938).
61. *Prince Valiant* #44 (December 11, 1937).
62. *Prince Valiant* #1123–#1126 (August 17, 1958–September 7, 1958).

63. *Prince Valiant* #1177 (August 30, 1959).
64. *Prince Valiant* #116 (April 30, 1939).
65. *Prince Valiant* #238–#243 (August 31, 1941–October 5, 1941).
66. *Prince Valiant* #1187–#1217 (November 8, 1959–June 5, 1960).
67. *Prince Valiant* #628 (February 20, 1949).
68. Barbara Tepa Lupack, *Illustrating Camelot* (Cambridge: D. S. Brewer, 2008), 188.
69. *Prince Valiant* #3 (February 27, 1937).
70. *Prince Valiant* #4 (March 6, 1937).
71. *Prince Valiant* #12 (May 1, 1937).
72. *Prince Valiant* #218 (April 13, 1941).
73. *Prince Valiant* #918–#931 (September 12, 1954–December 12, 1954).
74. *Prince Valiant* #1435–#1442 (August 9, 1964–September 27, 1964).
75. Saba, "Hal Foster," 70.
76. *Prince Valiant* #932 (December 19, 1954).
77. Louis Dublin, "Look at the Bright Side of Marriage: Some Facts and Figures Concerning American Family Life," *Parents' Magazine* 23 (December 1948), 11, 68–70, 68.
78. *Prince Valiant* #470 (February 10, 1946).
79. *Prince Valiant* #520–#594 (January 26, 1947–April 18, 1948).
80. *Prince Valiant* #782 (February 3, 1952).
81. *Prince Valiant* #1455–#1532 (December 27, 1964–June 19, 1966).
82. Thomas Andrae, *Carl Barks and the Disney Comic Book: Unmasking the Myth of Modernity* (Jackson: University Press of Mississippi, 2006), 149.
83. Gary Groth, "Jack Kirby," *Comics Journal* 134 (February 1990): 57–89, 91–99, 64.
84. Compare *Prince Valiant* #46–#48 (December 25, 1937–January 8, 1938) to *The Demon* #1 (DC Comics, August 1972).
85. Saba, "Hal Foster."
86. *Harold R. (Hal) Foster Papers*, Special Collections Research Center, Syracuse University Library, boxes 1–2.
87. Gary Groth, "Joe Kubert Interview," *Comics Journal* 172 (November 1994): 58–105, 60, and Gary Groth, "John Severin," *Comics Journal* 215 (August 1999): 46–93, 50.
88. Kane, *Hal Foster*, 90–94.
89. *Prince Valiant* #6–#11 (March 20, 1937–April 24, 1937).
90. "*streunenden Kindern in die Hände fielen*"; "*im Gepäck von fremden Soldaten*"; "*die Beutetaschen des weiblichen gefolges*" in *Allgemeine Deutsche Lehrerzeitung* 18 (October 15, 1952): 248.
91. Kane, *Hal Foster*, 83.

CHAPTER 2

1. Commentators tend to divide the history of American comic books into "ages." These ages can be broadly defined as the Golden Age (1938–1950), the Silver Age (1956–1970), the Bronze Age (1970–1985), and the Modern Age (1985–present). The interregnum during the early 1950s is sometimes referred to as the Genre Age. This taxonomy, of course, is

not universally agreed upon—see, for example, Ken Quattro, *The New Ages: Rethinking Comic Book History* (2004) http://www.comicartville.com/newages.htm.
2. Nick Groom, *The Making of Percy's Reliques* (Clarendon: Oxford University Press, 1999), 6.
3. Irving L. Churchill, "William Shenstone's Share in the Preparation of Percy's Reliques," *PMLA* 51, no. 4 (December 1936): 960–74.
4. Groom, *The Making of Percy's Reliques*, 106.
5. Groom, *The Making of Percy's Reliques*, 111.
6. James Boswell, *The Life of Samuel Johnson* (New York: Sturgis & Walton, 1909), 1:292.
7. Walter William Skeat, ed., *Piers Plowman* (Clarendon: Oxford University Press, 1886), sec. 8, l. 402.
8. Stephen Knight, *Robin Hood: A Complete Study of the English Outlaw* (Oxford: Blackwell, 1994), 32.
9. John Matthews, "The Games of Robin Hood," in *Robin Hood: An Anthology of Scholarship and Criticism*, ed. Stephen Knight (Cambridge: D. S. Brewer, 1999), 393–410, 396.
10. John Major, *Historia Maioris Britanniae*, trans. Archibald Constable (Edinburgh: Edinburgh University Press, 1892), 156–57.
11. Richard Grafton, *Grafton's Chronicle* (London: G. Woodfall, 1809), 1:221–22.
12. Joseph Ritson, ed., *Robin Hood: A Collection of all the Ancient Poems, Songs and Ballads, now extant, relative to that celebrated Outlaw* (Whitehall: T. Egerton, 1795).
13. William John Thoms, *Early English Prose Romances with Bibliographical and Historical Introductions* (London: Nattali and Bond, 1858), v.
14. Alice Chandler, "Sir Walter Scott and the Medieval Revival," in *Nineteenth-Century Fiction* 19, no. 4 (March 1965): 315–32, 332.
15. Chandler, "Sir Walter Scott and the Medieval Revival," 332.
16. See, for example, Sten Bodvar Liljegren's *The Revolt against Romanticism in American Literature as Evidenced in the Works of S. L. Clemens* (New York: Haskell House, 1970); and, more recently, Robert McParland's *Mark Twain's Audience: A Critical Analysis of Reader Responses to the Writings of Mark Twain* (Lanham, MD: Lexington Books, 2014).
17. Mark Twain, *Life on the Mississippi* (New York: P. F. Collier, 1917), 375.
18. Pierce Egan, *Robin Hood and Little John, or the merry men of Sherwood forest* (London: Forster and Hextall, 1840).
19. *Wat Tyler* (1841, republished in 1851); *Bell, Clym o' the Cleugh, and William of Cloudeslie* (1842); and *Paul Jones, the privateer* (1842).
20. Joachim Hayward Stocqueler, *Maid Marian: The Forest Queen* (London: George Peirce, 1849).
21. Mary Ellen Brown, *Child's Unfinished Masterpiece: The English and Scottish Popular Ballads* (Urbana: University of Illinois Press, 2011), 10–11.
22. "Jonathan Ingersoll Bowditch," *Proceedings of the American Academy of Arts and Sciences* 24 (May 1888–May 1889): 435–37, 435.
23. Brown, *Child's Unfinished Masterpiece*, 12.
24. Charles Eliot Norton, "Francis James Child," *Proceedings of the American Academy of Arts and Sciences* 32, no. 17 (July 1897): 333–39, 333.

25. James C. Turner, *The Liberal Education of Charles Eliot Norton* (Baltimore: Johns Hopkins University Press, 2002), 50.
26. Francis James Child, *Four Old Plays* (Cambridge, MA: G. Nichols, 1848).
27. Turner, *The Liberal Education of Charles Eliot Norton*, 63.
28. Brown, *Child's Unfinished Masterpiece*, 18.
29. Turner, *The Liberal Education of Charles Eliot Norton*, 26.
30. Turner, *The Liberal Education of Charles Eliot Norton*, 105.
31. See, for example, Stith Thompson, "The Indian Legend of Hiawatha," *Periodical of the Modern Languages Associaition of America* 37 (1922), 128–40; Chase S. and Stellanova Osborn, *Schoolcraft—Longfellow—Hiawatha* (Lancaster, PA: Jaques Cattell Press, 1942); Ernest John Moyne, *Hiawatha and Kalevala: A Study of the Relationship between Longfellow's "Indian Edda" and the Finnish Epic* (Helsinki: Suomen Tiedeakatemia, 1963); William M. Clements, "Schoolcraft as Textmaker," *Journal of American Folklore* 103 (1990): 177–90; and Mentor L. Williams, ed., *Schoolcraft's Indian Legends* (East Lansing: Michigan State University Press, 1956).
32. Hans Rudolf von Schröter, *Finnische Runen* (Upsala: Palmblad & Co., 1819).
33. Brown, *Child's Unfinished Masterpiece*, 12.
34. Brown, *Child's Unfinished Masterpiece*, 79.
35. Francis James Child, *English and Scottish Ballads* (Boston: Little, Brown and Company, 1858), vii.
36. Francis James Child, "Robin Hood," *Atlantic Monthly* 1, no. 2 (December 1857): 156–66.
37. Child, "Robin Hood," 166.
38. Brown, *Child's Unfinished Masterpiece*, 97.
39. Moreland, *The Medievalist Impulse in American Literature*, 4.
40. Tom Cheesman and Sigrid Rieuwerts, "Introduction: Child Who?" in *Ballads into Books: The Legacies of Francis James Child*, ed. Tom Cheesman and Sigrid Rieuwerts (Bern: Peter Lang, 1997), 9–18, 10.
41. Irving L. Churchill, "Shenstone's Billets," *PMLA* 52, no. 1 (March 1937): 114–21, 116.
42. Stephanie Barczewski, *Myth and National Identity in Nineteenth-Century Britain: The Legends of King Arthur and Robin Hood* (London: Oxford University Press, 2000), 89.
43. Barczewski, *Myth and National Identity in Nineteenth-Century Britain*, 77.
44. May and May, *Howard Pyle*, 31.
45. Emanuel Swedenborg, *True Christian Religion*, trans. John C. Ager (New York: Swedenborg Foundation, 1853), 102.
46. Delaware Art Museum, *Howard Pyle: The Artist and His Legacy* (Wilmington: Delaware Art Museum, 1987), 9.
47. *Classified Catalogue of the Public Library of Fitchburg, Massachusetts* (Fitchburg, MA: Blanchard and Brown, 1886), 310.
48. Tom Dewe Matthews, "The Outlaws," *Guardian* (October 7, 2006).
49. Gary Groth, "Look out Batman! It's the Jerry Robinson Interview," *Comics Journal* 271 (October 2005): 73–112, 83.
50. *More Fun Comics* #73–107 (November 1941–January 1946) and *Adventure Comics* #103–269 (April 1946–February 1960).

51. *World's Finest Comics* #7–140 (Fall 1942–March 1964).
52. *World's Finest Comics* #113 (November 1960); #118 (June 1961); and #134 (June 1963).
53. Retcon: to revise a storyline retrospectively in order to create a new continuity, a RETrospective CONtinuity.
54. Green Arrow's first origin story is given in *More Fun Comics* #89 (March 1943), but this is changed in *Adventure Comics* #256 (January 1959).
55. *Adventure Comics* #268 (January 1960).
56. *Adventure Comics* #262 (July 1959).
57. *Adventure Comics* #269 (February 1960).
58. Michael McAvennie, "1970s," in *DC Comics Year by Year: A Visual Chronicle*, ed. Michael McAvennie and Hannah Dolan (London: Dorling Kindersley, 2010), 143.
59. Dennis O'Neil, "Green Thoughts," in *Green Lantern/Green Arrow: Hard Travelling Heroes* (New York: DC Comics, 1992), i–ii, i.
60. *Green Lantern* #76 (April 1970).
61. Bradford Wright, *Comic Book Nation* (Baltimore: Johns Hopkins University Press, 2001), 239.
62. *The Flash* #217–19 (September 1972–January 1973).
63. *Green Lantern* #90 (August 1976).
64. *Green Arrow* #1–4 (May 1983–August 1983).
65. *Secret Origins* #38 (March 1986).
66. *Green Arrow: The Longbow Hunters* (1987).

CHAPTER 3

1. Carol Clover and John Lindow, *Old Norse-Icelandic Literature: A Critical Guide* (Toronto: University of Toronto Press, 2005), 74.
2. Margaret Clunies Ross, *A History of Old Norse Poetry and Poetics* (Cambridge: D. S. Brewer, 2005), 1.
3. In addition to Clover and Lindow's *Old Norse-Icelandic Literature* and Clunies Ross's *A History of Old Norse Poetry and Poetics*, see also Andrew Wawn, *Northern Antiquity: The Post-Medieval Reception of Edda and Saga* (Enfield Lock: Hisarlik Press, 1994), and Martin Arnold, *Thor: Myth to Marvel* (London: Continuum International, 2011).
4. Amos Simon Cottle, trans., *Icelandic Poetry or the Edda of Saemund* (Bristol: N. Biggs, 1797).
5. Árni Björnsson has argued convincingly that, of these sources, *Völsunga Saga* was by far the greatest influence on the Ring cycle; see Árni Björnsson, *Wagner and the Volsungs: Icelandic Sources of* Der Ring des Nibelungen (Exeter: Short Run Press, 2003).
6. La Verne Rippley, *The German Americans* (Lanham, MD: University Press of America, 1984), 164.
7. Lieselotte Overvold, "Wagner's American Centennial March: Genesis and Reception," *Monatshefte* 68, no. 2 (Summer 1976): 179–87, 179.
8. Albert Bernhardt Faust, *The German Element in the United States* (Boston: Houghton Mifflin Company, 1909), 524.

9. Faust, *The German Element in the United States*, 523 and 582.
10. Rasmus Anderson and Albert Barton, *Life Story of Rasmus B. Anderson* (Madison, Wisconsin, 1915), 141.
11. Anderson and Barton, *Life Story of Rasmus B. Anderson*, 142.
12. Anderson and Barton, *Life Story of Rasmus B. Anderson*, 143.
13. Arnold, *Thor*, 139.
14. James Baldwin, *In my youth: From the posthumous papers of Robert Dudley* (Indianapolis: Bobbs-Merrill, 1914), 32.
15. Peter J. L. Fisher and Sheila Shapiro, "James Baldwin (1841–1925): A Man Who Loved Stories," *History of Reading News* 27, no. 1 (Fall 1993).
16. American Book Company, *Books by James Baldwin* (New York: American Book Company, 1920), 1.
17. Arnold, *Thor*, 139–45.
18. Stan Lee and George Mair, *Excelsior! The Amazing Life of Stan Lee* (New York: Boxtree, 2002), 157.
19. Lee and Mair, *Excelsior!*, 157–58.
20. Sean Howe, *Marvel Comics: The Untold Story* (New York: HarperCollins, 2012), 63.
21. Howe, *Marvel Comics*, 279.
22. Lee and Mair, *Excelsior!*, 158.
23. Robert Frank, "The Invention of the Viking Horned Helmet," in *International Scandinavian and Medieval Studies in Memory of Gerd Wolfgang Weber*, ed. Michael Dallapiazza, Olaf Hansen, Preden Sørensen, and Yvonne Bonnetain (Trieste: Edizioni Parnaso, 2000), 199–208, 199.
24. Neil Gaiman, *American Gods* (New York: William Morrow, 2001).
25. *Our Army at War* #162 and 163 (January and February 1966).
26. James Baldwin, *The Story of Siegfried* (New York: Charles Scribner's Sons, 1882), *frontispiece*, 62, 94, 180, and 282.
27. *Journey into Mystery* #83 (August, 1962).
28. Casey Carlson, "KC: LOC" in *WoW* (Westfield Comics, September 2008).
29. *Journey into Mystery* #109 (October 1964) and #122 (November 1965)
30. *Journey into Mystery* #88 (January 1963), #91 (April 1963) and #92 (May 1963).
31. *Journey into Mystery* #114 (March 1965), #118 (July 1965) and *The Mighty Thor* #148 (January 1968).
32. *Thor Annual* #1 (1965).
33. *The Mighty Thor* #126–30 (March–July 1966).
34. *The Mighty Thor* #131–35 (August–December 1966).
35. *Journey into Mystery* #101 (February 1964), #113 (February 1965), and *The Mighty Thor* #145 (October 1967).
36. *The Mighty Thor* #136 (January 1967).
37. *The Mighty Thor* #137–39 (February–April 1967).
38. *The Mighty Thor* #143–44 (August–September 1967).
39. *The Mighty Thor* #154–57 (July–October 1968).
40. *The Mighty Thor* #160–62 (January–March 1969), #168–69 (September–October 1969).

41. *The Mighty Thor* #165–66 (June–July 1969).
42. *The Mighty Thor* #176–77 (May–June 1970).
43. *Marvel Spotlight* #30 (October 1976) and *Marvel Fanfare* #13 (March 1984).
44. *Balder the Brave* #1–4 (November 1985 to May 1986).
45. Roy Thomas and Gil Kane, *The Ring of the Nibelung* (New York: DC Comics, 1989–1990).

CHAPTER 4

1. Charlotte Laughlin, "Howard, Robert Ervin," in *Handbook of Texas Online* (Texas State Historical Association, 2013).
2. Ben Indick, "The Western Fiction of Robert E. Howard," in *The Dark Barbarian: The Writings of Robert E. Howard, A Critical Anthology,* ed. Don Herron (Westport, CT: Greenwood Press, 1984), 99–116, 99.
3. Mark Finn, *Blood & Thunder: The Life and Art of Robert E. Howard* (Austin: MonkeyBrain Books, 2006), 16–17.
4. Robert Howard, "On Reading—And Writing," in *The Last Celt: A Bio-Bibliography of Robert Ervin Howard,* ed. Glenn Lord (West Kingston: Donald M. Grant, 1976), 41–60, 44–45.
5. Lin Carter, "Chronicles of the Sword," *Savage Sword of Conan* #2 (October 1974), 42–45, 43.
6. Robert Howard, "A Touch of Trivia," in *The Last Celt,* ed. Lord, 31–36, 33.
7. Howard, "On Reading—And Writing," 53.
8. Leon Nielsen, *Robert E. Howard: A Collector's Descriptive Bibliography of American and British Hardcover, Paperback, Magazine, Special and Amateur Editions, with a Bibliography* (Jefferson, NC: McFarland and Company, 2007), 27.
9. George Scott-Elliot, *Romance of Early British Life: From the Earliest Times to the Coming of the Danes* (London: Seeley and Company, 1909).
10. Nithin Koshy made a similar observation in an article for the New Indian Express some years ago. See Nithin D. Koshy, "The Cowboy of Ancient Times Comes Alive," *The New Indian Express* (January 24, 2009).
11. This is Richard Slatta's description of Owen Wister's 1902 *The Virginian*—for many the archetypal cowboy novel. See Richard W. Slatta, *Cowboys of the Americas* (New Haven, CT: Yale University Press, 1990), 205.
12. Jennifer Moskowitz, "The Cultural Myth of the Cowboy, or, How the West Was Won," *Americana: The Journal of American Popular Culture (1900–present)* 5, no. 1 (Spring 2006).
13. "The Cowboy," *The Daily Times* (Deadwood, South Dakota) (July 6, 1884), 2.
14. "Knights of the Lariat," *North Adams Evening Transcript* (August 25, 1899), 4.
15. David Herbert Lawrence, *Studies in Classic American Literature,* ed. Ezra Greenspan, Lindeth Vasey, and John Worthen (Cambridge: Cambridge University Press, 2003), 65.
16. Luce, "The American Century," 28.
17. Luce, "The American Century," 25.
18. Luce, "The American Century," 28.

19. E. Hoffmann Price, "Introduction," in *The Last Celt*, ed. Lord, 9–16, 13.
20. Paul Sammon, *Conan the Phenomenon: The Legacy of Robert E. Howard's Fantasy Icon* (Milwaukee: Dark Horse Books, 2007), 29.
21. Sammon, *Conan the Phenomenon*, 31.
22. Price, "Introduction," 12.
23. Humphrey Carpenter, *Tolkien: A Biography* (New York: Ballantine Books, 1977), 211 ff.
24. Letter 109 to Stanley Unwin, July 31, 1947, quoted in Pat Reynolds, *The Lord of the Rings: The Tale of a Text* (Online: The Tolkien Society, 2003), 3.
25. W. H. Auden and Paul B. Taylor, trans., *The Elder Edda: A Selection* (London: Faber and Faber, 1969).
26. W. H. Auden, "At the End of the Quest, Victory," *New York Times* (January 22, 1956).
27. C. S. Lewis, "Tolkien's 'The Lord of the Rings,'" reprinted in *The Chesterton Review* 28, no. 1/2 (February/May 2002): 73–77, 73.
28. Reynolds, *The Lord of the Rings*, 2.
29. Joseph Ripp, *Middle America Meets Middle-Earth: American Publication and Discussion of J. R. R. Tolkien's Lord of the Rings, 1954–1969* (Master's thesis, University of North Carolina, Chapel Hill, 2003), 41.
30. Ripp, *Middle America Meets Middle-Earth*, 35–36.
31. Obituary: "J. R. R. Tolkien Dead at 81; Wrote 'The Lord of the Rings,'" *New York Times* (September 3, 1973).
32. Ripp, *Middle America Meets Middle-Earth*, 40.
33. All enrollment statistics in this paragraph taken from Thomas D. Snyder, ed., *120 Years of American Education: A Statistical Portrait* (Washington, DC: National Center for Education Statistics, 1993), 18.
34. Rosemary Jackson, *Fantasy: The Literature of Subversion* (London: Methuen and Company, 1981), 5.
35. Martin Croucher, "Latter-Day Knights Battle for Imaginary Kingdoms," *Epoch Times* (March 17, 2008).
36. Michael Cramer, *Medieval Fantasy as Performance: The Society for Creative Anachronism and the Current Middle Ages* (Lanham, MD: Scarecrow Press, 2010), 1.
37. Michael Moorcock, *Stormbringer* (London: Herbert Jenkins, 1965).
38. Fritz Leiber, *Swords in the Mist* (New York: Ace Books, 1968).
39. Ursula Le Guin, *A Wizard of Earthsea* (Julian, CA: Parnassus, 1968).
40. Sammon, *Conan the Phenomenon*, 42.
41. Sammon, *Conan the Phenomenon*, 45.
42. Marc Cerasini and Charles Hoffman, *Robert E. Howard: Starmont Reader's Guide #35* (Mercer Island: Starmont House, 1987), 14.
43. Tzvetan Todorov, *The Fantastic: A Structural Approach to a Literary Genre* (Ithaca, NY: Cornell University Press, 1975), although it appeared in French as early as 1970.
44. Shaun Manning, "C2E2: Roy Thomas Reunited with Conan," *Comic Book Resources* (April 17, 2010).
45. Sammon, *Conan the Phenomenon*, 63.
46. Roy Thomas, "The Hyborian Page," *Conan the Barbarian* #6 (June 1971).

47. *Savage Sword of Conan* #7 (August 1975), 73.
48. *Savage Tales* #2 (October 1973), 27.
49. *Savage Tales* #5 (July 1974), 63.
50. "The Hyborian Page" in *Conan the Barbarian* #8 (August 1971) in a response to a reader's inquiry.
51. *Conan the Barbarian* #14–15 (March–May 1972).
52. *Creatures on the Loose* #22–29 (March 1974–May 1974).
53. *Dagar the Invincible* #1–19 (October 1972–December 1976 and April 1982).
54. *Sword of Sorcery* #1–5 (March/April–November/December 1973); *Claw the Unconquered* #1–12 (May/June 1975–September 1978); *Stalker* #1–4 (June/July 1975–December/January 1976); *The Warlord* #1–133 (January/February 1976–Winter 1988).
55. *Ironjaw* #1–4 (January–July 1975); *Wulf the Barbarian* #1–4 (February–September 1975); *Elfquest* (WaRP Graphics 1978–2003; Marvel Epic August 1985–March 1988; DC 2003–2007).
56. Compare "The Frost Giant's Daughter" in *Savage Sword of Conan* #1 (August 1974), 63–74, to the version that appeared in *Conan the Barbarian* #16 (July 1972).
57. Brett Martin, "Using the Imagination: Consumer Evoking and Thematizing of the Fantastic Imaginary," *Journal of Consumer Research* 34 (June 2004): 136–49, 140.
58. Kurt Lancaster, *Warlocks and Warpdrive: Contemporary Fantasy Entertainments with Interactive and Virtual Environments* (Jefferson, NC: McFarland and Company, 1999), 46.
59. Michael Tresca, *The Evolution of Fantasy Role-Playing Games* (Jefferson, NC: McFarland and Company, 2011).
60. Gary Gygax and Jeff Perren, *Chainmail* (Evansville, IN: Guidon Games, 1971).
61. Gary Gygax and Dave Arneson, *Dungeons and Dragons* (Lake Geneva, WI: TSR, 1974).
62. Lancaster, *Warlocks and Warpdrive*, 34.
63. Ken St. Andre, *Tunnels and Trolls* (Scottsdale, AZ: Flying Buffalo, 1975); Edward Simbalist and Wilf Backhaus, *Chivalry and Sorcery* (New York: Fantasy Games Unlimited, 1977); Steve Perrin, *Runequest* (Hayward, CA: Chaosium, 1978).
64. Sammon, *Conan the Phenomenon*, 98.
65. Kenneth Turan, "The Barbarian in Babylon," *Savage Sword of Conan* #48 (January 1980), 56–66.
66. James Riordan, *Stone: The Controversies, Excesses, and Exploits of a Radical Filmmaker* (New York: Hyperion Books, 1994), 102.
67. Tony Shaw, *The Empire Strikes Back: Hollywood's Cold War* (Edinburgh: Edinburgh University Press, 2007), 48–49 and 267–69.

CHAPTER 5

1. But see Jill Lepore, *The Secret History of Wonder Woman* (New York: Knopf, 2014).
2. Robert E. Howard, "The Shadow of the Vulture," *Magic Carpet Magazine* 4, no. 1 (January 1934): 39–65, 51.

3. Howard Andrew Jones, "Howard's Journey: Historical Influences to Historical Triumphs," *Sword Woman and Other Historical Adventures*, ed. Robert E. Howard (New York: Del Rey, 2011), 515–36, 527.
4. Eric Leif Davin, *Partners in Wonder: Women and the Birth of Science Fiction, 1926–1965* (Lanham, MD: Lexington Books, 2006), 111–12.
5. Herodotus 4.110–17, Hippocrates *De Aere* XVII.
6. David Anthony, *The Horse, the Wheel, and Language: How Bronze-Age Riders from the Eurasian Steppes Shaped the Modern World* (Princeton, NJ: Princeton University Press, 2007), 329.
7. Further discussion of this brief list can be found in James M. Blythe, "Women in the Military: Scholastic Arguments and Medieval Images of Female Warriors," *History of Political Thought* 22, no. 2 (Summer 2001): 242–69.
8. Niketas Choniates, *O City of Byzantium, Annals of Niketas Choniates*, trans. Harry J. Magoulias (Detroit: Wayne State University Press, 1994), 2.1.60, 35.
9. Steven Runciman, *A History of the Crusades, Volume I* (Cambridge: Cambridge University Press, 1954), 469; and Philippe Contamine, *War in the Middle Ages*, trans. Michael Jones (London: Wiley-Blackwell, 1985), 241.
10. Orderic Vitalis, *The Ecclesiastical History of Orderic Vitalis*, ed. Marjorie Chibnall (Oxford: Oxford University Press, 1973), 4.8.14, 212–15.
11. Vergil, *Aeneid*, 11, especially lines 597–915; see Vergil, *Aeneid*, ed. and trans. H. R. Fairclough, revised by G. P. Goold (Cambridge, MA: Harvard University Press, 2000).
12. Raymond B. Waddington, "Elizabeth I and the Order of the Garter," *Sixteenth-Century Journal* 24, no. 1 (Spring 1993): 97–113, 99.
13. Elias Ashmole, *The institution, laws & ceremonies of the most noble Order of the Garter collected and digested into one body by Elias Ashmole* (London: Nathanael Brooke, 1672), ch. 3, sec. 3, 125–26; citing Joseph Micheli Márquez, *Tesoro Militar de Cavallería* (Madrid: Pedro Coello, 1642).
14. Amboise, *The Crusade of Richard Lion-Heart*, trans. Merton Jerome Hubert (New York: Octagon, 1976), 152.
15. *Royal Armouries MS I.33* (British Museum No. 14 E.iii, No. 20, D.vi), 32 recto and verso.
16. Hans Talhoffer, *Medieval Combat*, ed. and trans. Mark Rector (London: Greenhill, 2000), plates 242–50.
17. Jean Froissart, *Chronicles of England, France, Spain and the Adjoining Countries*, trans. Thomas Johnes (London: Longman, Hurst, Rees and Orme, 1808), 1.80.
18. Blythe, "Women in the Military," 248.
19. Chris Bishop, "Civilizing the Savage Ancestor: Representations of the Anglo-Saxons in the Art of Nineteenth-Century Britain," *Studies in Medievalism* 15 (2007): 55–76; "The Pear of Anguish: Torture, Truth and Dark Medievalism," *International Journal of Cultural Studies* 17 (2014): 591–602; "Stretching the Truth: The Rack in Anglo-Saxon England," *Journal of the Australian Early Medieval Association* 9 (2013): 89–112; but see also Albrecht Classen, *The Medieval Chastity Belt: A Myth-Making Process* (New York: Palgrave Macmillan, 2007), and Carolyn Dinshaw, *Getting Medieval: Sexualities and Communities, Pre- and Postmodern* (Durham, NC: Duke University Press, 1999).

20. Astrid Henry, *Not My Mother's Sister: Generational Conflict and Third-Wave Feminism* (Bloomington: Indiana University Press, 2004), 5.
21. Doris Weatherford, *American Women during World War II: An Encyclopedia* (Abingdon: Routledge, 2010), 255.
22. Weatherford, *American Women during World War II*, 146.
23. Betty Friedan, *The Feminine Mystique* (New York: W. W. Norton, 1963).
24. For criticism of *The Feminine Mystique*, see Joanne Meyerowitz, "Beyond the Feminine Mystique: A Reassessment of Postwar Mass Culture, 1946–1958," *Journal of American History* 79, no. 4 (March 1993): 1455–82; and Daniel Horowitz, "Rethinking Betty Friedan and *The Feminine Mystique*: Labor Union Radicalism and Feminism in Cold War America," *American Quarterly* 48, no. 1 (March 1996): 1–42.
25. Fred R. Shapiro, "Historical Notes on the Vocabulary of the Women's Movement," *American Speech* 60, no. 1 (Spring 1985): 3–16.
26. "The Anthem and the Angst," *The Sunday Magazine, Melbourne Sunday Herald Sun/Sydney Sunday Telegraph* (June 15, 2003), 16.
27. "Women of the Year: Great Changes, New Chances, Tough Choices," *Time* (January 5, 1976).
28. Lisa Duggan, *Sex Wars: Sexual Dissent and Political Culture* (Abingdon: Routledge, 1995), 6.
29. P. Le Boutillier, "The Amazons are Coming," *The Woman* (July 1943), 66.
30. Trina Robbins, *From Girls to Grrrlz: A History of Women's Comics from Teens to Zines* (San Francisco: Chronicle Books, 1999), 7–8.
31. Hadju, *The Ten-Cent Plague*, 157.
32. Trina Robbins, *The Great Women Superheroes* (Princeton, NJ: Kitchen Sink Press, 1996), 86.
33. Michael Uslan, "Introduction," in Bob Kane, *Batman in the Fifties* (Burbank: DC, 2002), 5.
34. Michelle Nolan, *Love on the Racks: A History of American Romance* (Jefferson, NC: McFarland and Company, 2008), 30.
35. Wright, *Comic Book Nation*, 250.
36. Whose superheroic alter egos have been, variously: Ant-Man; Goliath; Yellowjacket; Giant-Man; and Ultron.
37. Peter Brett and Walter Geovani, *Red Sonja: Blue* (Mt. Laurel, NJ: Dynamite Entertainment, 2011).
38. Gail Simone, *Women in Refrigerators* (April 28, 1999) http://www.lby3.com/wir/r-4_2899.html.
39. Carol A. Strickland, "The Rape of Ms. Marvel," in *LOC* 1 (January 1980).
40. John Bartol, "Dead Men Defrosting," *Women in Refrigerators* (March 1999).
41. Jeffrey A. Brown, *Dangerous Curves: Action Heroines, Gender, Fetishism, and Popular Culture* (Jackson: University Press of Mississippi, 2011), 175.

CHAPTER 6

1. Elements of this chapter were published previously as "Beowulf: The Monsters and the Comics," *Journal of the Australian Early Medieval Association* 7 (2011): 73–93.
2. Jason Tondro, "Hwaet If? Beowulf in Comics," in *Drawn from the Classics: Essays on Graphic Adaptations of Literary Works*, ed. Stephen E. Tabachnick and Esther Bendit Saltzman (Jefferson, NC: McFarland and Company, 2015), 33–45, 36–37.
3. Catherine Clarke, "Re-placing Masculinity: The DC Comics Beowulf Series and Its Context, 1975–6," in *Anglo-Saxon Culture and the Modern Imagination*, ed. David Clark and Nicholas Perkins (Cambridge: D. S. Brewer, 2010), 165–82.
4. *Comics as culture? Holy textbook, Batman!* Indiana University media release (September 8, 2005).
5. Michael Uslan, "Confessions of a Comic Book Professor," *The Amazing World of DC Comics* 3 (1974): 26–29.
6. Allen Asherman, "Beowulf: An Epic Comes Home," in *Beowulf: Dragon Slayer* #1 (May 1975), opposite p. 18.
7. Michael Uslan, "The Source of the Saga," in *Beowulf: Dragon Slayer* #2 (July 1975), opposite p. 18.
8. John Gardner, *Grendel* (New York: Alfred A. Knopf, 1971), 167–74.
9. *Beowulf: Dragon Slayer* #1 (May 1975), 2.
10. For more on this, see Colin Chase, ed., *The Dating of Beowulf* (Toronto: University of Toronto Press, 1997); for my own opinion, see "The *Lost* Literature of England: Text and Transmission in Tenth-Century Wessex," in *Text and Transmission in Medieval Europe*, ed. Chris Bishop (Newcastle: Cambridge Scholars Publishing, 2007), 76–126.
11. Grebnel is presumably a typographic error or else the implied name of Grendel's mother; see *Beowulf: Dragon Slayer* #2 (July 1975), 3.
12. *Beowulf: Dragon Slayer* #6 (March 1976), 9.
13. *Beowulf: Dragon Slayer* #1 (May 1975), 16.
14. All excerpts from *Beowulf* used in this chapter are taken from Frederick Klaeber, ed., *Beowulf and the Fight at Finnsburg* (Boston: D. C. Heath and Co., 1922). All other Anglo-Saxon poetry quoted in this chapter is taken from George P. Krapp and Elliot Van Kirk Dobbie, eds., *The Anglo-Saxon Poetic Records* (New York: Columbia University Press, 1931–42).
15. *Beowulf*, ll. 144–46.
16. See Donald Scragg's comments in D. G. Scragg, "Source Study," in *Reading Old English Texts*, ed. K. O'Brien O'Keeffe (Cambridge: Cambridge University Press, 1997), 39–58, particularly 44.
17. *Beowulf: Dragon Slayer* #1 (May 1975), 4.
18. *Beowulf: Dragon Slayer* #1 (May 1975), 7.
19. *Beowulf: Dragon Slayer* #6 (March 1976), 5–7.
20. Michael Uslan, "The Source of the Saga," in *Beowulf: Dragon Slayer* #2 (July 1975), opposite p. 18.
21. *Beowulf: Dragon Slayer* #3 (September 1975), 6.

22. Paul C. Bauschatz, *The Well and the Tree: World and Time in Early Germanic Culture* (Amherst: University of Massachusetts Press, 1982), 13. The terminology "Old Indian" is used by Bauschatz.
23. The *Epinal Glossary* provides the Latin *terrigina* [born of the earth] for the term *gigans* [giant] implying, perhaps, that the early Anglo-Saxons possessed no native cognates for these concepts. See Henry Sweet, ed., *The Epinal Glossary* (London: Early English Text Society, 1936), 10. For the sociolinguistic significance of this fact, see my article "Þyrs, ent, eoten, gigans—Anglo-Saxon ontologies of *giant*," *Neuphilologische Mitteilungen* 3, no. 107 (2006): 259–70.
24. Sweet, *The Epinal Glossary*, 25.
25. Sweet, *The Epinal Glossary*, 18.
26. Boethius, *Philosophiae Consolationis*, II met. 8, in *Boethius*, ed. and trans. H. F. Stewart, E. K. Rand, and S. J. Tester (London: William Heinemann, 1973).
27. Boethius, *De Consolatione Philosophiae*, XXI, in *King Alfred's Old English Version of Boethius' De Consolatione Philosophiae*, ed. W. J. Sedgefield (Darmstadt: Wissenschaftliche Buchgesellschaft, 1899).
28. Boethius, *De Consolatione Philosophiae*, XXXIX.
29. Dorothy Whitelock, *The Beginnings of English Society* (Harmondsworth: Penguin, 1952), 27–28.
30. B. J. Timmer, "Wyrd in Anglo-Saxon Prose and Poetry," *Neophilologus* 26 (1940–1): 24–33; and "Heathen and Christian Elements in Old English Poetry," *Neophilologus* 29 (1944): 180–85.
31. Ida L. Gordon, "Traditional Themes in *The Wanderer* and *The Seafarer*," *Review of English Studies* 5 (1954): 1–13, at 4.
32. Morton W. Bloomfield, "Patristics and Old English Literature: Notes on Some Poems," in Stanley B. Greenfield, ed., *Studies in Old English Literature in Honor of Arthur G. Brodeur* (Eugene: University of Oregon Press, 1963), 37, n. 1.
33. Joseph B. Trahern Jr., "Fatalism and the Millennium," in *The Cambridge Companion to Old English Literature*, ed. Malcolm Godden and Michael Lapidge (Cambridge: Cambridge University Press, 1991), 160–71, at 162.
34. Trahern, "Fatalism and the Millennium," 163.
35. Trahern, "Fatalism and the Millennium," 160 and 163.
36. Chris Bishop, "Fate, Virtue and the Metaphysical Winter in the Poetry of Wessex," *Journal of the Australian Early Medieval Association* 8 (2008): 33–52.
37. See Kevin J. Wanner, "Warriors, *Wyrms*, and *Wyrd*: The Paradoxical Fate of the Germanic Hero/King in *Beowulf*," in *Essays in Medieval Studies* 16 (1999): 1–15.
38. Wanner, "Warriors, *Wyrms*, and *Wyrd*," 5.
39. Ælfric, "Epiphania Domini," in *The Homilies of the Anglo-Saxon Church. The First Part, Containing the Sermones Catholici or Homilies of Ælfric, Volume I*, ed. and trans. Benjamin Thorpe (London: Ælfric Society, 1844), at 114.
40. *Beowulf: Dragon Slayer* #2 (July 1975), 6.
41. *Quid enim Hinieldus cum Christo*—see Bruce Mitchell and Fred Robinson, *Beowulf: An Edition with Relevant Shorter Texts* (Oxford: Blackwell, 1998), 225.

CHAPTER 7

1. Richard Bauckham and Trevor Hart, "The Shape of Time," in *The Future as God's Gift: Explorations in Christian Eschatology*, ed. David Fergusson and Marcel Sarot (Edinburgh: T&T Clark, 2000), 41–72, 48.
2. Brian Wood, "On the Ledge," *Northlanders* #1 (December 2007).
3. Andy Khouri, "Y1K Paranoia: Brian Wood Talks Northlanders," *Comic Book Resources News* (October 16, 2007).
4. Brian Wood, "On the Ledge," *Northlanders* #1.
5. Khouri, "Y1K Paranoia: Brian Wood Talks Northlanders."
6. Chris Arrant, "Viking Clash Pits Old Against New in Northlanders," *PW Comics Week* (November 13, 2007).
7. Brian Wood, *Northlanders* #7 (August 2008).
8. *The Cross and the Hammer* possibly also references *The Hammer and the Cross*, the 1993 book that began a Norse trilogy for Harry Harrison and John Holm. It is now known that John Holm is also a pseudonym for the Tolkien scholar Tom Shippey.
9. Shane McLeod, "Warriors and Women: The Sex Ratio of Norse Migrants to Eastern England up to 900 AD," *Early Medieval Europe* 19, no. 3 (2011): 332–53.
10. Brian Wood, *Northlanders* #39 (June 2011).
11. Arrant, "Viking Clash Pits Old Against New in Northlanders."
12. Kathleen S. Berry, *The Dramatic Arts and Cultural Studies: Educating Against the Grain* (New York: Falmer Press, 2000), 127.
13. Brian Wood and Becky Cloonan, *Demo* (San Francisco: AiT/Planet Lar, November 2003–September 2010).
14. Brian Wood and Riccardo Burchiello, *DMZ* (Vertigo, November 2005–February 2012).
15. Timothy Callahan, "Brian Wood Talks Northlanders," *Comic Book Resources News* (January 27, 2009).
16. Gerry Conway and Dick Dillin, *Justice League of America* #159–60 (DC Comics, October–November 1978).
17. Roy Thomas and Jan Duursema, *Arak, Son of Thunder* #8–11 (DC Comics, April–July 1982).
18. Bo Hampton, *Legends of the Dark Knight* #35 (DC Comics, August 1992).
19. *Birds of Prey*, Vol. 1 #29 (DC Comics, July 2001).
20. Darwyn Cooke, *DC: The New Frontier* (DC Comics, 2004), and Bruce Jones, *The War That Time Forgot* (DC Comics, 2008).
21. Callahan, "Brian Wood Talks Northlanders."
22. Chris Desjardins, *Outlaw Masters of Japanese Film* (London: Tauris, 2005), 9; and Phil Hardy, ed., *The BFI Companion to Crime* (Berkeley: University of California Press, 1997), 186.
23. Brian Wood, *Northlanders* #1–7 (Vertigo, December 2007–July 2008).
24. Quoted in Emily Leach, "Cool Japan: Why Japanese Remakes Are So Popular on American TV, and Where We're Getting It Wrong," in *Asianweek* (September 13, 2008). Lisa Katayama is a commentator on Japanese popular culture; see Lisa Katayama,

Urawaza: Secret Everyday Tips and Tricks from Japan (San Francisco: Chronicle Books, 2008).
25. W. David Marx, "Gross National Cool: A Japanese Response," *Neojaponisme* (June 4, 2005).
26. Douglas McGray, "Japan's Gross National Cool," *Foreign Policy* 130 (May/June 2002): 44–54, 46.

CONCLUSION

1. Thomas Carlyle, *The French Revolution: A History* (London: Chapman and Hall, 1837), 1.6.II.
2. ... *des invitations impérieuses hâtent les députés qui balancent : un sentiment de haine, un désir aveugle de vengeance, et non l'amour du bien, semblent animer les esprits*—Marquis de Ferrières, *Mémoires* (Paris: Baudouin Frères, 1821), Bk. 1, 186.
3. *'Assemblée offre l'aspect d'une troupe de gens ivres, placés dans un magasin de meubles précieux, qui cassent et brisent, à l'envi, tout ce qui se trouve sous leurs mains*—Marquis de Ferrières, *Mémoires*, Bk. 1, 186.
4. Mirabeau, Dumont, and Rivarol quoted in Charles Warwick, *Mirabeau and the French Revolution* (Philadelphia: George Jacobs & Co., 1905), 289.
5. Peter Kropotkin, "4 August and Its Consequences," in *The Great French Revolution, 1789–1793*, trans. N. F. Dryhurst (New York: Vanguard Printings, 1927).
6. Georges Lefebvre, *The French Revolution from Its Origins to 1793*, trans. E. M. Evanson (London: Routledge & Keegan Paul, 1965), 130.
7. Timothy Tackett, *Becoming a Revolutionary: The Deputies of the French National Assembly and the Emergence of a Revolutionary Culture, 1789–1790* (University Park: Pennsylvania State University Press, 1996), 173–74.
8. Michael Fitzsimmons, *The Remaking of France: The National Assembly and the Constitution of 1791* (Cambridge: Cambridge University Press, 1994), 53.
9. Alfred Cobban, *The Social Interpretation of the French Revolution* (Cambridge: Cambridge University Press, 1964), 35.
10. Cobban, *The Social Interpretation of the French Revolution*, 53.
11. John Markoff, *The Abolition of Feudalism: Peasants, Lords and Legislators in the French Revolution* (University Park: Pennsylvania State University Press, 1996), 519.
12. Jon Elster, "The Night of August 4, 1789. A Study of Social Interaction in Collective Decision-Making," in *Revue européenne des sciences sociales* 45, no. 136 (2007): 71–94, 92.
13. William Doyle, *The Oxford History of the French Revolution* (Oxford: Oxford University Press, 2002), 117.
14. Paul Hanson, *Contesting the French Revolution* (Chichester: Wiley-Blackwell, 2009), 63.
15. Markoff, *The Abolition of Feudalism*, 518.
16. Markoff, *The Abolition of Feudalism*, 517–19.
17. Cobban, *The Social Interpretation of the French Revolution*, 45.
18. See also Pierre de Saint-Jacob, *Les Paysans de la Bourgogne du Nord au dernier siècle de l'ancien régime* (Paris: Les Belles-Lettres, 1960).

19. *L'Assemblée nationale détruit entièrement le régime féodal. Elle décrète que, dans les droits et devoirs, tant féodaux que censuels, ceux qui tiennent à la mainmorte réelle ou personnelle, et à la servitude personnelle, et ceux qui les représentent, sont abolis sans indemnité, et tous les autres sont déclarés rachetables, et que le prix et le mode du rachat seront fixés par l'Assemblée nationale. Ceux desdits droits qui ne sont point supprimés par ce décret, continueront néanmoins à être perçus jusqu'au remboursement—Collection Complète des Lois, Décrets, Ordonnances, Réglemens, avis du Conseil-d'État, 1788—1830* (Paris: A. Guyot and Scribe, 1834), 33.
20. Markoff, *The Abolition of Feudalism*, 145.
21. Markoff, *The Abolition of Feudalism*, 518.
22. Gilbert Shapiro, "What Were the Grievances of France in 1789? The Most Common Demands in the *Cahiers de Doléances*," in *Revolutionary Demands: A Content Analysis of the* Cahiers de Doléances *of 1789*, ed. Gilbert Shapira and John Markoff (Stanford: Stanford University Press, 1998), 253–79, 271.
23. Markoff, *The Abolition of Feudalism*, 160.
24. *Des Lettres de Cachet et des Prisons d'Etat* (Hamburg, 1778), reviewed in *The Monthly Review or Literary Journal* (London: T. Beckett, July–December 1782), 537.
25. Marc Bloch, *La Société Féodale* (Paris: Albin Michel, 1939).
26. François-Louis Ganshof, *Qu'est-ce que la féodalité?* (Brussels: Office de Publicité, 1947), 11. The first edition was published in 1944.
27. Frederic Cheyette, "Some Notations on Mr. Hollister's Irony," *Journal of British Studies* 5, no. 1 (1965): 1–14, quotes taken from 1–2.
28. Elizabeth Brown, "The Tyranny of a Construct: Feudalism and Historians of Medieval Europe," *American Historical Review* 79 (1974): 1063–68.
29. Bernard Bachrach, "Neo-Roman vs Feudal: The Heuristic Value of a Construct for the Reign of Fulk Nerra, Count of the Angevins (987–1040)," *Cithara* 30 (1990): 3–32.
30. Susan Reynolds, *Fiefs and Vassals: The Medieval Evidence Reinterpreted* (Oxford: Oxford University Press, 1994).
31. For a more detailed discussion, see Alain Boureau, *The Lord's First Night: The Myth of the Droit de Cuissage*, trans. Lydia G. Cochrane (Chicago: University of Chicago, 1998).
32. George Orwell, *Nineteen Eighty-Four* (London: Penguin, 1954), 61.
33. Orwell, *Nineteen Eighty-Four*, 62.
34. "Milosevic Accused of 'Medieval Savagery,'" *BBC News* (February 12, 2002).
35. Stop the medieval cruelty in Iran, http://www.causes.com/causes/111694-stop-the-medieval-cruelty-in-iran (accessed March 1, 2015).
36. Matt Kennard, "Richard Dawkins interview on religion, evolution, and Iraq," on *The Comment Factory* (March 21, 2010), http://www.thecommentfactory.com/richard-dawkins-interview-on-religion-evolution-and-iraq-2777 (accessed February 3, 2015).
37. Brett Loguriato, "John Kerry: ISIS' Beheading of Steven Sotloff Was an 'Act of Medieval Savagery,'" *Business Insider Australia* (September 4, 2014).
38. Walter Sellar and Robert Yeatman, *1066 and All That: A Memorable History of England, comprising all the parts you can remember, including 103 Good Things, 5 Bad Kings and 2 Genuine Dates* (London: Methuen & Co., 1930), ch. 28.

39. . . . *nondum uerus sol iustitiae illuxerat . . . Elucebant tamen inter errors ingenia, neque ideo minus uiuaces erant oculi quamuis tenebris et densa caligine circumsepti, ut eis non errant odium, sed indignae sortis miseratio deberetur*—Petrarch, "Apologia contra cuiusdam anonymi Galli calumnias," *Opera Omnia* (Basel, 1554), 1195.
40. For a more detailed discussion, see Theodore Mommsen, "Petrarch's Conception of the Dark Ages," *Speculum* 17, no. 2 (April 1942): 226–42.
41. Leonardo Bruni, *History of the Florentine People*, ed. and trans. James Hankins (Cambridge, MA: Harvard University Press, 2001), xvii–xviii.
42. Augustine, "On the Catechizing of the Uninstructed," ch. 22 in Philip Schaff, *A Select Library of the Nicene and Post-Nicene Fathers of the Christian Church* (Edinburgh: T&T Clark, 2005).
43. Daniel 2: 31–45.
44. Gleason Archer, trans., *Jerome's Commentary on Daniel* (Grand Rapids: Baker Book House, 1958), 32.
45. Hugh Trevor-Roper, *Renaissance Essays* (Chicago: University of Chicago Press, 1989), 137.
46. Thomas McCoog, *The Society of Jesus in Ireland, Scotland, and England 1541–1588* (Leiden: Brill Publishing, 1996), 156.
47. Mark Greengrass, "Nicolas Pithou: Experience, Conscience and History in the French Civil Wars," in *Religion, Culture and Society in Early Modern Britain: Essays in Honour of Patrick Collinson*, ed. Anthony Fletcher and Peter Roberts (Cambridge: Cambridge University Press, 1994), 1–28.
48. John Arnold, *What Is Medieval History?* (Cambridge: Polity Press, 2008), 8.

BIBLIOGRAPHY

Ælfric. "Epiph ania Domini." In *The Homilies of the Anglo-Saxon Church. The First Part, Containing the Sermones Catholici or Homilies of Ælfric, Volume I.* Edited and translated by Benjamin Thorpe. London: Ælfric Society, 1844.
Allgemeine Deutsche Lehrerzeitung 18 (October 15, 1952).
Amboise. *The Crusade of Richard Lion-Heart.* Translated by Merton Jerome Hubert. New York: Octagon, 1976.
American Book Company. *Books by James Baldwin.* New York: American Book Company, 1920.
Anderson, Rasmus, and Albert Barton. *Life Story of Rasmus B. Anderson.* Madison, Wisconsin, 1915.
Andrae, Thomas. *Carl Barks and the Disney Comic Book: Unmasking the Myth of Modernity.* Jackson: University Press of Mississippi, 2006.
"The Anthem and the Angst." *Sunday Magazine, Melbourne Sunday Herald Sun/Sydney Sunday Telegraph* (June 15, 2003).
Anthony, David. *The Horse, the Wheel, and Language: How Bronze-Age Riders from the Eurasian Steppes Shaped the Modern World.* Princeton, NJ: Princeton University Press, 2007.
Archer, Gleason, trans. *Jerome's Commentary on Daniel.* Grand Rapids: Baker Book House, 1958.
Arnold, John. *What Is Medieval History?* Cambridge: Polity Press, 2008.
Arnold, Martin. *Thor: Myth to Marvel.* London: Continuum International, 2011.
Arrant, Chris. "Viking Clash Pits Old Against New in Northlanders." *PW Comics Week* (November 13, 2007).
Asherman, Allen. "Beowulf: An Epic Comes Home." *Beowulf: Dragon Slayer* #1 (May 1975).
Ashmole, Elias. *The institution, laws & ceremonies of the most noble Order of the Garter collected and digested into one body by Elias Ashmole.* London: Nathanael Brooke, 1672.
Auden, W. H. "At the End of the Quest, Victory." *New York Times* (January 22, 1956).
Auden, W. H., and Paul B. Taylor, trans. *The Elder Edda: A Selection.* London: Faber and Faber, 1969.
Augustine. "On the Catechizing of the Uninstructed." In *A Select Library of the Nicene and Post-Nicene Fathers of the Christian Church.* Edited by Philip Schaff. Edinburgh: T&T Clark, 2005.

Bachrach, Bernard. "Neo-Roman vs. Feudal: The Heuristic Value of a Construct for the Reign of Fulk Nerra, Count of the Angevins (987–1040)." *Cithara* 30 (1990): 3–32.

Baldwin, James. *The Story of Siegfried*. New York: Charles Scribner's Sons, 1882.

———. *In my youth: From the posthumous papers of Robert Dudley*. Indianapolis: Bobbs-Merrill, 1914.

Barczewski, Stephanie. *Myth and National Identity in Nineteenth-Century Britain: The Legends of King Arthur and Robin Hood*. London: Oxford University Press, 2000.

Bartol, John. "Dead Men Defrosting." *Women in Refrigerators* (March 1999).

Bauckham, Richard, and Trevor Hart. "The Shape of Time." In *The Future as God's Gift: Explorations in Christian Eschatology*. Edited David Fergusson and Marcel Sarot, 41–72. Edinburgh: T&T Clark, 2000.

Bauschatz, Paul C. *The Well and the Tree: World and Time in Early Germanic Culture*. Amherst: University of Massachusetts Press, 1982.

Berlin, Isaiah. *The Hedgehog and the Fox: An Essay on Tolstoy's View of History*. London: Weidenfeld & Nicolson, 1953.

Berry, Kathleen S. *The Dramatic Arts and Cultural Studies: Educating against the Grain*. New York: Falmer Press, 2000.

Bevan, Nathan. "Lydia Hearst Is Queen of the Castle." *Wales on Sunday* (August 3, 2008).

Bible of Stephen Harding. Dijon BM MS.14, Bibliothèque Municipale, Dijon.

Bishop, Chris. "Þyrs, *ent, eoten, gigans*—Anglo-Saxon ontologies of *giant*." *Neuphilologische Mitteilungen* 3, no. 107 (2006): 259–70.

———. "Civilizing the Savage Ancestor: Representations of the Anglo-Saxons in the Art of Nineteenth-Century Britain." *Studies in Medievalism* 15 (2007): 55–76.

———. "The *Lost* Literature of England: Text and Transmission in Tenth-Century Wessex." In *Text and Transmission in Medieval Europe*. Edited by Chris Bishop, 76–126. Newcastle: Cambridge Scholars Publishing, 2007.

———. "Fate, Virtue and the Metaphysical Winter in the Poetry of Wessex." *Journal of the Australian Early Medieval Association* 8 (2008): 33–52.

———. "Beowulf: The Monsters and the Comics." *Journal of the Australian Early Medieval Association* 7 (2011): 73–93.

———. "Stretching the Truth?: The 'Rack' in Anglo-Saxon England." *Journal of the Australian Early Medieval Association* 9 (2013): 89–111.

———. "The Pear of Anguish: Torture, Truth and Dark Medievalism." *International Journal of Cultural Studies* 17 (2014): 591–602.

Björnsson, Árni. *Wagner and the Volsungs: Icelandic Sources of Der Ring des Nibelungen*. Exeter: Short Run Press, 2003.

Blackbeard, Bill, ed. *R. F. Outcault's The Yellow Kid: A Centennial Celebration of the Kid Who Started the Comics*. Northampton: Kitchen Sink Press, 1995.

Bloch, Marc. *La Société Féodale*. Paris: Albin Michel, 1939.

Bloomfield, Morton W. "Patristics and Old English Literature: Notes on Some Poems." In *Studies in Old English Literature in Honor of Arthur G. Brodeur*. Edited by Stanley B. Greenfield. Eugene: University of Oregon Press, 1963.

Blythe, James M. "Women in the Military: Scholastic Arguments and Medieval Images of Female Warriors." *History of Political Thought* 22, no. 2 (Summer 2001): 242–69.

Boethius. *Philosophiae Consolationis*. Edited and translated by H. F. Stewart, E. K. Rand, and S. J. Tester. London: William Heinemann, 1973.

Boswell, James. *The Life of Samuel Johnson, Volume I*. New York: Sturgis & Walton, 1909.

Boureau, Alain. *The Lord's First Night: The Myth of the Droit de Cuissage*. Translated by Lydia G. Cochrane. Chicago: University of Chicago, 1998.

British Churchman (August 1844).

Brown, Elizabeth. "The Tyranny of a Construct: Feudalism and Historians of Medieval Europe." *American Historical Review* 79 (1974): 1063–68.

Brown, Jeffrey A. *Dangerous Curves: Action Heroines, Gender, Fetishism, and Popular Culture*. Jackson: University Press of Mississippi, 2011.

Brown, Mary Ellen. *Child's Unfinished Masterpiece: The English and Scottish Popular Ballads*. Urbana: University of Illinois Press, 2011.

Bruni, Leonardo. *History of the Florentine People*. Edited and translated by James Hankins. Cambridge, MA: Harvard University Press, 2001.

Bull, Hedley. *The Anarchical Society: A Study of Order in World Politics*. New York: Columbia University Press, 1977.

Bunn, Geoffrey. *The Truth Machine: A Social History of the Lie Detector*. Baltimore: Johns Hopkins University Press, 2012.

Callahan, Timothy. "Brian Wood Talks Northlanders." *Comic Book Resources News* (January 27, 2009).

Campbell, W. Joseph. *Yellow Journalism: Puncturing the Myths, Defining the Legacies*. Westport, CT: Praeger, 2001.

Carlson, Oliver, and Ernest Sutherland Bates. *Hearst: Lord of San Simeon*. Westport, CT: Greenwood Press, 1936.

Carlyle, Thomas. *The French Revolution: A History*. London: Chapman and Hall, 1837.

Carpenter, Humphrey. *Tolkien: A Biography*. New York: Ballantine Books, 1977.

Carter, Lin. "Chronicles of the Sword." *Savage Sword of Conan* #2 (October 1974), 42–45.

Cerasini, Marc, and Charles Hoffman. *Robert E. Howard: Starmont Reader's Guide #35*. Mercer Island: Starmont House, 1987.

Chandler, Alice. "Sir Walter Scott and the Medieval Revival." *Nineteenth-Century Fiction* 19, no. 4 (March 1965): 315–32.

Chase, Colin, ed. *The Dating of Beowulf*. Toronto: University of Toronto Press, 1997.

Cheesman, Tom, and Sigrid Rieuwerts. "Introduction: Child Who?" In *Ballads into Books: The Legacies of Francis James Child*. Edited by Tom Cheesman and Sigrid Rieuwerts, 9–18. Bern: Peter Lang, 1997.

Cheyette, Frederic. "Some Notations on Mr. Hollister's Irony." *Journal of British Studies* 5, no. 1 (1965): 1–14.

Child, Francis James. *Four Old Plays*. Cambridge, MA: G. Nichols, 1848.

———. "Robin Hood." *Atlantic Monthly* 1, no. 2 (December 1857): 156–66.

———. *English and Scottish Ballads*. Boston: Little, Brown and Company, 1858.

Choniates, Niketas. *O City of Byzantium, Annals of Niketas Choniates*. Translated by Harry J. Magoulias. Detroit: Wayne State University Press, 1994.
Churchill, Irving L. "William Shenstone's Share in the Preparation of Percy's *Reliques*." *PMLA* 51, no. 4 (December 1936): 960–74.
———. "Shenstone's Billets." *PMLA* 52, no. 1 (March 1937): 114–21.
Clarke, Catherine. "Re-placing Masculinity: The DC Comics Beowulf Series and Its Context, 1975–6." In *Anglo-Saxon Culture and the Modern Imagination*. Edited by David Clark and Nicholas Perkins, 165–82. Cambridge: D. S. Brewer, 2010.
Classen, Albrecht. *The Medieval Chastity Belt: A Myth-Making Process*. New York: Palgrave Macmillan, 2007.
Classified Catalogue of the Public Library of Fitchburg, Massachusetts. Fitchburg: Blanchard and Brown, 1886.
Clements, William M. "Schoolcraft as Textmaker." *Journal of American Folklore* 103 (1990): 177–90.
Clover, Carol, and John Lindow. *Old Norse-Icelandic Literature: A Critical Guide*. Toronto: University of Toronto Press, 2005.
Clunies Ross, Margaret. *A History of Old Norse Poetry and Poetics*. Cambridge: D. S. Brewer, 2005.
Cobban, Alfred. *The Social Interpretation of the French Revolution*. Cambridge: Cambridge University Press, 1964.
Collection Complète des Lois, Décrets, Ordonnances, Réglemens, avis du Conseil-d'État, 1788–1830. Paris: Chez A. Guyot and Scribe, 1834.
Comics as culture? Holy textbook, Batman! Indiana University media release (September 8, 2005).
Contamine, Philippe. *War in the Middle Ages*. Translated by Michael Jones. London: Wiley-Blackwell, 1985.
Coogan, Peter. *Superhero: The Secret Origin of a Genre*. Austin: MonkeyBrain Books, 2006.
Cottle, Amos Simon, trans. *Icelandic Poetry or the Edda of Saemund*. Bristol: N. Biggs, 1797.
"The Cowboy." *Daily Times* (Deadwood, South Dakota) (July 6, 1884).
Cramer, Michael. *Medieval Fantasy as Performance: The Society for Creative Anachronism and the Current Middle Ages*. Lanham, MD: Scarecrow Press, 2010.
Croucher, Martin. "Latter-Day Knights Battle for Imaginary Kingdoms." *Epoch Times* (March 17, 2008).
Davidson, Roberta. "The 'Reel' Arthur: Politics and Truth Claims in 'Camelot, Excalibur, and King Arthur.'" *Arthuriana* 17, no. 2 (2007): 62–84.
Davin, Eric Leif. *Partners in Wonder: Women and the Birth of Science Fiction, 1926–1965*. Lanham, MD: Lexington Books, 2006.
Delaware Art Museum. *Howard Pyle: The Artist and His Legacy*. Wilmington: Delaware Art Museum, 1987.
Desjardins, Chris. *Outlaw Masters of Japanese Film*. London: Tauris, 2005.
Diner, Hasia. *Erin's Daughters in America: Irish Immigrant Women in the Nineteenth Century*. Baltimore: Johns Hopkins University Press, 1983.

Dinshaw, Carolyn. *Getting Medieval: Sexualities and Communities, Pre- and Postmodern.* Durham, NC: Duke University Press, 1999.
Doyle, William. *The Oxford History of the French Revolution.* Oxford: Oxford University Press, 2002.
Dublin, Louis. "Look at the Bright Side of Marriage: Some Facts and Figures Concerning American Family Life." *Parents' Magazine* 23 (December 1948): 11, 68–70.
Duff, James H., ed. *An American Vision: Three Generations of Wyeth Art.* Boston: Little, Brown and Company, 1987.
Duggan, Lisa. *Sex Wars: Sexual Dissent and Political Culture.* Abingdon: Routledge, 1995.
Durant, Will. *The Age of Faith.* New York: Simon and Schuster, 1950.
Eco, Umberto. "Dreaming the Middle Ages." In *Travels in Hyperreality.* Translated by W. Weaver, 61–72. New York: Harcourt Brace, 1986.
Egan, Pierce. *Robin Hood and Little John, or the merry men of Sherwood forest.* London: Forster and Hextall, 1840.
Eliot, Thomas Stearns. *The Waste Land.* New York: Horace Liveright, 1922.
Elster, Jon. "The Night of August 4, 1789. A Study of Social Interaction in Collective Decision-making." *Revue européenne des sciences sociales* 45, no. 136 (2007): 71–94.
Faulkner, William. *Absalom, Absalom!* New York: Random House, 1936.
Faust, Albert Bernhardt. *The German Element in the United States.* Boston: Houghton Mifflin Company, 1909.
Ferrières, Marquis de. *Mémoires.* Paris: Baudouin Brothers, 1821.
Finn, Mark. *Blood & Thunder: The Life and Art of Robert E. Howard.* Austin: MonkeyBrain Books, 2006.
Fisher, Peter J. L., and Sheila Shapiro. "James Baldwin (1841–1925): A Man Who Loved Stories." *History of Reading News* 27, no. 1 (Fall 1993).
Fitzsimmons, Michael. *The Remaking of France: The National Assembly and the Constitution of 1791.* Cambridge: Cambridge University Press, 1994.
Frank, Robert. "The Invention of the Viking Horned Helmet." In *International Scandinavian and Medieval Studies in Memory of Gerd Wolfgang Weber.* Edited by Michael Dallapiazza, Olaf Hansen, Preden Sørensen, and Yvonne Bonnetain, 199–208. Trieste: Edizioni Parnaso, 2000.
Friedan, Betty. *The Feminine Mystique.* New York: W. W. Norton, 1963.
Froissart, Jean. *Chronicles of England, France, Spain and the Adjoining Countries.* Translated by Thomas Johnes. London: Longman, Hurst, Rees and Orme, 1808.
Fugelso, Karl, ed. *Studies in Medievalism XVII: Defining Medievalism(s).* Woodbridge: D. S. Brewer, 2009.
———. *Studies in Medievalism XVIII: Defining Medievalism(s) II.* Woodbridge: D. S. Brewer, 2009.
———. *Studies in Medievalism XIX: Defining Neomedievalism(s).* Woodbridge: D. S. Brewer, 2010.
———. *Studies in Medievalism XX; Defining Neomedievalism(s) II.* Woodbridge: D. S. Brewer, 2011.

Gaiman, Neil. *American Gods*. New York: William Morrow, 2001.
Ganshof, François-Louis. *Qu'est-ce que la féodalité?* Brussels: Office de Publicité, 1947.
Gardner, John. *Grendel*. New York: Alfred A. Knopf, 1971.
Gordon, Ida L. "Traditional Themes in *The Wanderer* and *The Seafarer*." *Review of English Studies* 5 (1954): 1–13.
Grafton, Richard. *Grafton's Chronicle, Volume I*. London: G. Woodfall, 1809.
Greengrass, Mark. "Nicolas Pithou: Experience, Conscience and History in the French Civil Wars." In *Religion, Culture and Society in Early Modern Britain: Essays in Honour of Patrick Collinson*. Edited by Anthony Fletcher and Peter Roberts, 1–28. Cambridge: Cambridge University Press, 1994.
Groom, Nick. *The Making of Percy's Reliques*. Clarendon: Oxford University Press, 1999.
Groth, Gary. "Jack Kirby." *Comics Journal* 134 (February 1990): 57–89, 91–99.
———. "Joe Kubert Interview." *Comics Journal* 172 (November 1994): 58–105.
———. "John Severin." *Comics Journal* 215 (August 1999): 46–93.
———. "Look out Batman! It's the Jerry Robinson Interview." *Comics Journal* 271 (October 2005): 73–112.
Gygax, Gary, and Dave Arneson. *Dungeons and Dragons*. Lake Geneva, WI: TSR, 1974.
Gygax, Gary, and Jeff Perren. *Chainmail*. Evansville, IN: Guidon Games, 1971.
Hadju, David. *The Ten-Cent Plague: The Great Comic Book Scare and How It Changed America* New York: Picador, 2008.
Hanson, Paul. *Contesting the French Revolution*. Chichester, West Sussex: Wiley-Blackwell, 2009.
Hardy, Phil, ed. *The BFI Companion to Crime*. Berkeley: University of California Press, 1997.
Harold R. (Hal) Foster Papers. Special Collections Research Center, Syracuse University Library.
Henry, Astrid. *Not My Mother's Sister: Generational Conflict and Third-Wave Feminism*. Bloomington: Indiana University Press, 2004.
Herodotus. *The Persian Wars*. Translated by A. D. Godley. London: Heinemann, 1921.
Herriman, George. *Krazy Kat*. New York: Madison Square Press, 1969.
Hippocrates. *De Aere Aquis et Locis*. In *Hippocrates, Collected Works*. Translated by W. H. S. Jones. Cambridge, MA: Harvard University Press, 1868.
Horowitz, Daniel. "Rethinking Betty Friedan and *The Feminine Mystique*: Labor Union Radicalism and Feminism in Cold War America." *American Quarterly* 48, no. 1 (March 1996): 1–42.
Howard, Robert E. "A Touch of Trivia." In *The Last Celt: A Bio-Bibliography of Robert Ervin Howard*. Edited by Glenn Lord, 31–36. West Kingston: Donald M. Grant, 1976.
———. "On Reading—And Writing." In Lord, *The Last Celt* 41–60.
———. "The Shadow of the Vulture." In Farnsworth Wright, ed., *Magic Carpet Magazine* 4, no. 1 (January 1934): 39–65.
Howe, Sean. *Marvel Comics: The Untold Story*. New York: Harper, 2012.
Indick, Ben. "The Western Fiction of Robert E. Howard." In *The Dark Barbarian: The Writings of Robert E. Howard, A Critical Anthology*. Edited by Don Herron, 99–116. Westport, CT: Greenwood Press, 1984.

Ito, Kinko. "Growing up Japanese Reading Manga." *International Journal of Comic Art* 6 (2004): 392–401.
Jackson, Rosemary. *Fantasy: The Literature of Subversion*. London: Methuen and Company, 1981.
John F. Kennedy Presidential Library and Museum. *Papers of John F. Kennedy. Presidential Papers, President's Office Files, 2 May 1945–13 December 1957* (Digital Identifier JFKPOF-129-003).
"Jonathan Ingersoll Bowditch." *Proceedings of the American Academy of Arts and Sciences*. 24 (May 1888–May 1889): 435–37.
Jones, Howard Andrew. "Howard's Journey: Historical Influences to Historical Triumphs." In Robert E. Howard, *Sword Woman and Other Historical Adventures*. New York: Del Rey, 2011. 515–36.
Kamen, Henry. *The Spanish Inquisition: A Historical Revision*. New Haven, CT: Yale University Press, 1998.
Kane, Brian. *Hal Foster: Prince of Illustrators—Father of the Adventure Strip*. Lebanon, NJ: Vanguard Productions, 2001.
Kaplan, Justin. *Mr. Clemens and Mark Twain: A Biography*. New York: Simon and Schuster, 1966.
Katayama, Lisa. *Urawaza: Secret Everyday Tips and Tricks from Japan*. San Francisco: Chronicle Books, 2008.
Kennard, Matt. "Richard Dawkins interview on religion, evolution, and Iraq." *The Comment Factory* (March 21, 2010), http://www.thecommentfactory.com/richard-dawkins-interview-on-religion-evolution-and-iraq-2777 (accessed February 3, 2015).
Kennedy, Rose Fitzgerald. *Times to Remember*. New York: Doubleday, 1974.
Kern, Adam. *Manga from the Floating World: Comicbook Culture and the Kibyoshi of Edo Japan*. Cambridge, MA: Harvard University Press, 2006.
Khouri, Andy. "Y1K Paranoia: Brian Wood talks Northlanders." *Comic Book Resources News* (October 16, 2007).
Klaeber, Frederick, ed. *Beowulf and the Fight at Finnsburg*. Boston: D. C. Heath and Company, 1922.
Knight, Stephen. *Robin Hood: A Complete Study of the English Outlaw*. Oxford: Blackwell, 1994.
"Knights of the Lariat." *North Adams Evening Transcript* (August 25, 1899).
Kobrin, Stephen. "Back to the Future: Neomedievalism and the Postmodern Digital World Economy." *Journal of International Affairs* 51, no. 2 (1998): 362–86.
Koshy, Nithin D. "The Cowboy of Ancient Times Comes Alive." *New Indian Express* (January 24, 2009).
Krapp, George P., and Elliot Van Kirk Dobbie, eds. *The Anglo-Saxon Poetic Records*. New York: Columbia University Press, 1931–42.
Kropotkin, Peter. "4 August and Its Consequences." In *The Great French Revolution, 1789–1793*. Translated by N. F. Dryhurst. New York: Vanguard Printings, 1927.
Lancaster, Kurt. *Warlocks and Warpdrive: Contemporary Fantasy Entertainments with Interactive and Virtual Environments*. Jefferson, NC: McFarland and Company, 1999.

Laughlin, Charlotte. "Howard, Robert Ervin." *Handbook of Texas Online*. Texas State Historical Association, 2013. https://tshaonline.org/handbook.
Lawrence, David Herbert. *Studies in Classic American Literature*. Edited by Ezra Greenspan, Lindeth Vasey, and John Worthen. Cambridge: Cambridge University Press, 2003.
Le Boutillier, P. "The Amazons Are Coming." *The Woman* (July 1943).
Le Guin, Ursula. *A Wizard of Earthsea*. Julian: Parnassus, 1968.
Leach, Emily. "Cool Japan: Why Japanese Remakes Are So Popular on American TV, and Where We're Getting It Wrong." *Asianweek* (September 13, 2008).
Lee, Stan, and George Mair. *Excelsior! The Amazing Life of Stan Lee*. New York: Boxtree, 2002.
Lefebvre, Georges. *The French Revolution from Its Origins to 1793*. Translated by E. M. Evanson. London: Routledge & Keegan Paul, 1965.
Leiber, Fritz. *Swords in the Mist*. New York: Ace Books, 1968.
Lenehan, Cary. *Post-Modern Medievalism: A Sociological Study of the Society for Creative Anachronism*. Unpublished Bachelor's Thesis, University of Tasmania, 1994.
Lepore, Jill. *The Secret History of Wonder Woman*. New York: Knopf, 2014.
Levkoff, Mary. *Hearst the Collector*. New York: Abrams, 2008.
Lewis, Clive Staples. "Tolkien's 'The Lord of the Rings.'" Reprinted in the *Chesterton Review* 28, no. 1/2 (February/May 2002): 73–77.
Liljegren, Sten Bodvar. *The Revolt against Romanticism in American Literature as Evidenced in the Works of S. L. Clemens*. New York: Haskell House, 1970.
Loguriato, Brett. "John Kerry: ISIS' Beheading of Steven Sotloff Was an 'Act of Medieval Savagery.'" *Business Insider Australia* (September 4, 2014).
Luce, Henry. "The American Century." Reprinted in *The Ambiguous Legacy: U.S. Foreign Relations in the "American Century."* Edited by Michael J. Hogan 11–29. Cambridge: Cambridge University Press, 1999.
Lupack, Alan, and Barbara Tepa Lupack. *King Arthur in America*. Cambridge: D. S. Brewer, 1999.
Lupack, Barbara Tepa. *Illustrating Camelot*. Cambridge: D. S. Brewer, 2008.
Lynch, Andrew. "*Le Morte Darthur* for Children: Malory's Third Tradition." In *Adapting the Arthurian Legends for Children: Essays on Arthurian Juvenilia*. Edited by Barbara Tepa Lupack, 1–49. New York: Palgrave Macmillan, 2004.
Major, John. *Historia Maioris Britanniae*. Translated by Archibald Constable. Edinburgh: Edinburgh University Press, 1892.
Manning, Shaun. "C2E2: Roy Thomas Reunited with Conan." *Comic Book Resources* (April 17, 2010).
Markoff, John. *The Abolition of Feudalism: Peasants, Lords and Legislators in the French Revolution*. University Park: Pennsylvania State University Press, 1996.
Márquez, Joseph Micheli. *Tesoro Militar de Cavallería*. Madrid: Pedro Coello, 1642.
Martin, Brett. "Using the Imagination: Consumer Evoking and Thematizing of the Fantastic Imaginary." *Journal of Consumer Research* 34 (June 2004): 136–49.
Marx, W. David. "Gross National Cool: A Japanese Response." *Neojaponisme* (June 4, 2005).
Matthews, David. *Medievalism: A Critical History*. Woodbridge: D. S. Brewer, 2015.

Matthews, John. "The Games of Robin Hood." In *Robin Hood: An Anthology of Scholarship and Criticism*. Edited by Stephen Knight, 393–410. Cambridge: D. S. Brewer, 1999.
Matthews, Tom Dewe. "The Outlaws." *Guardian* (October 7, 2006).
May, Jill, and Robert May. *Howard Pyle: Imagining an American School of Art*. Urbana: University of Illinois Press, 2011.
McAvennie, Michael. "1970s." In *DC Comics Year by Year: A Visual Chronicle*. Edited by Michael McAvennie and Hannah Dolan. London: Dorling Kindersley, 2010.
McCoog, Thomas. *The Society of Jesus in Ireland, Scotland, and England 1541–1588*. Leiden: Brill Publishing, 1996.
McDonnell, Patrick, Karen O'Connell, and Georgia Riley de Havenon. *Krazy Kat: The Comic Art of George Herriman*. New York: Harry N. Abrams, 1986.
McGray, Douglas. "Japan's Gross National Cool." *Foreign Policy* 130 (May/June 2002): 44–54.
McLeod, Shane. "Warriors and Women: The Sex Ratio of Norse Migrants to Eastern England up to 900 AD." *Early Medieval Europe* 19, no. 3 (2011): 332–53.
McParland, Robert. *Mark Twain's Audience: A Critical Analysis of Reader Responses to the Writings of Mark Twain*. Lanham, MD: Lexington Books, 2014.
Meyerowitz, Joanne. "Beyond the Feminine Mystique: A Reassessment of Postwar Mass Culture, 1946–1958." *Journal of American History* 79, no. 4 (March 1993): 1455–82.
"Milosevic Accused of 'Medieval Savagery.'" *BBC News* (February 12, 2002).
Mitchell, Bruce, and Fred Robinson. *Beowulf: An Edition with Relevant Shorter Texts*. Oxford: Blackwell, 1998.
Moffett, Marian, Michael Fazio, and Lawrence Wodehouse. *A World History of Architecture*. London: Laurence King, 2003.
Mommsen, Theodore. "Petrarch's Conception of the Dark Ages." *Speculum* 17, no. 2 (April 1942): 226–42.
Monthly Review or Literary Journal. London: T. Beckett, July–December 1782.
Moorcock, Michael. *Stormbringer*. London: Herbert Jenkins, 1965.
Moreland, Kim. *The Medievalist Impulse in American Literature: Twain, Adams, Fitzgerald, and Hemingway*. Charlottesville: University Press of Virginia, 1996.
Moskowitz, Jennifer. "The Cultural Myth of the Cowboy, or, How the West Was Won." *Americana: The Journal of American Popular Culture (1900–present)* 5, no. 1 (Spring 2006).
Moyne, Ernest John. *Hiawatha and Kalevala: A Study of the Relationship between Longfellow's 'Indian Edda' and the Finnish Epic*. Helsinki: Suomen Tiedeakatemia, 1963.
Nasaw, David. *The Patriarch: The Remarkable Life and Turbulent Times of Joseph P. Kennedy*. New York: Penguin, 2012.
Nielsen, Leon. *Robert E. Howard: A Collector's Descriptive Bibliography of American and British Hardcover, Paperback, Magazine, Special and Amateur Editions, with a Bibliography*. Jefferson, NC: McFarland and Company, 2007.
Nolan, Michelle. *Love on the Racks: A History of American Romance*. Jefferson, NC: McFarland and Company, 2008.
Norton, Charles Eliot. "Francis James Child." *Proceedings of the American Academy of Arts and Sciences* 32, no. 17 (July 1897): 333–39.

O'Brien, Michael. *John F. Kennedy: A Biography.* New York: St. Martin's Press, 2005.
O'Neil, Dennis. "Green Thoughts." *Green Lantern/Green Arrow: Hard Travelling Heroes.* New York: DC Comics, 1992. i–ii.
Obituary: "J.R.R. Tolkien Dead at 81; Wrote 'The Lord of the Rings.'" *New York Times* (September 3, 1973).
Orderic Vitalis. *The Ecclesiastical History of Orderic Vitalis.* Edited by Marjorie Chibnall. Oxford: Oxford University Press, 1973.
Orwell, George. *Nineteen Eighty-Four.* London: Penguin, 1954.
Osborn, Chase S., and Stellanova Osborn. *Schoolcraft—Longfellow—Hiawatha.* Lancaster, PA: Jaques Cattell Press, 1942.
Overvold, Lieselotte. "Wagner's American Centennial March: Genesis and Reception." *Monatshefte* 68, no. 2 (Summer 1976): 179–87.
Perrin, Steve. *Runequest.* Hayward, CA: Chaosium, 1978.
Petrarch. "Apologia contra cuiusdam anonymi Galli calumnias." *Opera Omnia.* Basel, 1554.
Price, E. Hoffmann. "Introduction." In *The Last Celt: A Bio-Bibliography of Robert Ervin Howard.* Edited by Glenn Lord, 9–16. West Kingston: Donald M. Grant, 1976.
Procter, Ben. *William Randolph Hearst: The Early Years, 1863–1910.* New York: Oxford University Press, 1998. 84–87.
Quattro, Ken. *The New Ages: Rethinking Comic Book History* (2004). http://www.comicartville.com/newages.htm.
Regalado, Aldo. "Modernity, Race and the American Superhero." In *Comics as Philosophy.* Edited by Jeff McLaughlin, 84–99. Jackson: University Press of Mississippi, 2005.
———. *Bending Steel: Modernity and the American Superhero.* Jackson: University Press of Mississippi, 2015.
Rennger, N. J. "European Communities in a Neo-medieval Global Polity: The Dilemmas of Fairyland?" In *International Relations Theory and the Politics of European Integration: Power, Security and Community.* Edited by Morten Kelstrup and Michael Williams, 50–63. London: Routledge, 2000.
Reynolds, Pat. *The Lord of the Rings: The Tale of a Text.* Online: The Tolkien Society, 2003.
Reynolds, Susan. *Fiefs and Vassals: The Medieval Evidence Reinterpreted.* Oxford: Oxford University Press, 1994.
Riordan, James. *Stone: The Controversies, Excesses, and Exploits of a Radical Filmmaker.* New York: Hyperion Books, 1994.
Ripp, Joseph. *Middle America Meets Middle-Earth: American Publication and Discussion of J. R. R. Tolkien's Lord of the Rings, 1954–1969.* Master's thesis, University of North Carolina, Chapel Hill, 2003.
Rippley, La Verne. *The German Americans.* Lanham, MD: University Press of America, 1984.
Ritson, Joseph, ed. *Robin Hood: A Collection of all the Ancient Poems, Songs and Ballads, now extant, relative to that celebrated Outlaw.* Whitehall: T. Egerton, 1795.
Robbins, Trina. *From Girls to Grrrlz: A History of Women's Comics from Teens to Zines.* San Francisco: Chronicle Books, 1999.
———. *The Great Women Superheroes.* Princeton, NJ: Kitchen Sink Press, 1996.

Rosenberg, John D. *The Darkening Glass: A Portrait of Ruskin's Genius*. New York: Columbia University Press, 1980.
Rossetti, Dante Gabriel. *Letters, Volume I*. London: Oxford University Press, 1965.
Royal Armouries MS I.33. British Museum No. 14 E.iii, No. 20, D.vi.
Runciman, Steven. *A History of the Crusades, Volume I*. Cambridge: Cambridge University Press, 1954.
Ruskin, John. *Lectures on Architecture and Painting, Volume IV*. London: Smith Elder, 1854.
———. *The Seven Lamps of Architecture*. New York: Dover Publications, 1880.
Saba, Arn. "Hal Foster: Drawing Upon History." *Comics Journal* 102 (September 1985): 61–84.
St. Andre, Ken. *Tunnels and Trolls*. Scottsdale, AZ: Flying Buffalo, 1975.
Saint-Jacob, Pierre de. *Les Paysans de la Bourgogne du Nord au dernier siècle de l'ancien régime*. Paris: Les Belles-Lettres, 1960.
Sammon, Paul. *Conan the Phenomenon: The Legacy of Robert E. Howard's Fantasy Icon*. Milwaukee: Dark Horse Books, 2007.
Schodt, Frederik. *Dreamland Japan: Writings on Modern Manga*. Berkeley: Stone Bridge Press, 1996.
———. *The Four Immigrants Manga: A Japanese Experience in San Francisco, 1904–1924*. Berkeley: Stone Bridge Press, 1998.
Schröter, Hans Rudolf von. *Finnische Runen*. Upsala: Palmblad & Co., 1819.
Scott-Elliot, George. *Romance of Early British Life: From the Earliest Times to the Coming of the Danes*. London: Seeley and Company, 1909.
Scragg, Donald. "Source Study." In *Reading Old English Texts*. Edited by Katherine O'Brien O'Keeffe, 39–58. Cambridge: Cambridge University Press, 1997.
Sedgefield, W. J., ed. *King Alfred's Old English Version of Boethius' De Consolatione Philosophiae*. Darmstadt: Wissenschaftliche Buchgesellschaft, 1899.
Seldes, Gilbert. "The Krazy Kat That Walks by Himself." *The Seven Lively Arts*. New York: Harper and Brothers, 1924.
Sellar, Walter, and Robert Yeatman. *1066 and All That: A Memorable History of England, comprising all the parts you can remember, including 103 Good Things, 5 Bad Kings and 2 Genuine Dates*. London: Methuen & Co., 1930.
Selling, Kim. "Fantastic Neomedievalism: The Image of the Middle Ages in Popular Fantasy." In *Flashes of the Fantastic*. Edited by David Ketterer, 211–18. Westport, CT: Praeger, 2004.
Shapiro, Fred R. "Historical Notes on the Vocabulary of the Women's Movement." *American Speech* 60, no. 1 (Spring 1985): 3–16.
Shapiro, Gilbert. "What Were the Grievances of France in 1789? The Most Common Demands in the *Cahiers de Doléances*." In *Revolutionary Demands: A Content Analysis of the Cahiers de Doléances of 1789*. Edited by Gilbert Shapiro and John Markoff, 253–79. Stanford: Stanford University Press, 1998.
Shaw, Tony. *The Empire Strikes Back: Hollywood's Cold War*. Edinburgh: Edinburgh University Press, 2007. 48–49 and 267–69.
Simbalist, Edward, and Wilf Backhaus. *Chivalry and Sorcery*. New York: Fantasy Games Unlimited, 1977.

Simone, Gail. *Women in Refrigerators* (April 28, 1999). http://www.lby3.com/wir/r-4_2899.html.
Skeat, Walter William, ed. *Piers Plowman*. Clarendon: Oxford University Press, 1886.
Slatta, Richard W. *Cowboys of the Americas*. New Haven, CT: Yale University Press, 1990.
Snyder, Thomas D., ed. *120 Years of American Education: A Statistical Portrait*. Washington, DC: National Center for Education Statistics, 1993.
Southern Literary Messenger, Vol. 15. Richmond: White, 1849.
Stocqueler, Joachim Hayward. *Maid Marian: The Forest Queen*. London: George Peirce, 1849.
"Stop the Medieval Cruelty in Iran." http://www.causes.com/causes/111694-stop-the-medieval-cruelty-in-iran (accessed March 1, 2015).
Strickland, Carol A. "The Rape of Ms. Marvel." *LOC* 1 (January 1980).
Swedenborg, Emanuel. *True Christian Religion*. Translated by John C. Ager. New York: Swedenborg Foundation, 1853.
Sweet, Henry, ed. *The Epinal Glossary*. London: Early English Text Society, 1936.
Tackett, Timothy. *Becoming a Revolutionary: The Deputies of the French National Assembly and the Emergence of a Revolutionary Culture 1789–1790*. University Park: Pennsylvania State University Press, 1996.
Talhoffer, Hans. *Medieval Combat*. Edited and translated by Mark Rector. London: Greenhill, 2000.
Thomas, Roy. "The Hyborian Page." *Conan the Barbarian* #6 (June 1971).
———. "The Hyborian Page." *Conan the Barbarian* #8 (August 1971).
Thompson, Stith. "The Indian Legend of Hiawatha." *Periodical of the Modern Languages Association of America* 37 (1922): 128–40.
Thoms, William John. *Early English Prose Romances with Bibliographical and Historical Introductions*. London: Nattali and Bond, 1858.
Timmer, B. J. "Wyrd in Anglo-Saxon Prose and Poetry." *Neophilologus* 26 (1940–41): 24–33.
———. "Heathen and Christian Elements in Old English Poetry." *Neophilologus* 29 (1944): 180–85.
Todorov, Tzvetan. *The Fantastic: A Structural Approach to a Literary Genre*. Ithaca, NY: Cornell University Press, 1975.
Tolkien, John Ronald Reuel. *The Monsters and the Critics*. London: HarperCollins, 1997.
Tondro, Jason. "Hwaet If? Beowulf in Comics." In *Drawn from the Classics: Essays on Graphic Adaptations of Literary Works*. Edited by Stephen E. Tabachnick and Esther Bendit, 33–45. Jefferson, NC: McFarland and Company, 2015.
Trahern, Joseph B., Jr. "Fatalism and the Millennium." In *The Cambridge Companion to Old English Literature*. Edited by Malcolm Godden and Michael Lapidge, 160–71. Cambridge: Cambridge University Press, 1991.
Tresca, Michael. *The Evolution of Fantasy Role-Playing Games*. Jefferson, NC: McFarland and Company, 2011.
Trevor-Roper, Hugh. *Renaissance Essays*. Chicago: University of Chicago Press, 1989.
Turan, Kenneth. "The Barbarian in Babylon." *Savage Sword of Conan* #48 (January 1980): 56–66.

Turner, James C. *The Liberal Education of Charles Eliot Norton*. Baltimore: Johns Hopkins University Press, 2002.
Twain, Mark. *Life on the Mississippi*. New York: P. F. Collier, 1917.
Uslan, Michael. "Confessions of a Comic Book Professor." *The Amazing World of DC Comics* 3 (1974): 26–29.
———. "The Source of the Saga." *Beowulf: Dragon Slayer* #2 (July 1975).
———. "Introduction." In Bob Kane, *Batman in the Fifties*. Burbank: DC, 2002.
Vergil. *Aeneid*. Edited and translated by H. R. Fairclough, revised by G. P. Goold. Cambridge, MA: Harvard University Press, 2000.
Volo, James, and Dorothy Volo. *The Antebellum Period*. Westport, CT: Greenwood Press, 2004.
Waddington, Raymond B. "Elizabeth I and the Order of the Garter." *Sixteenth Century Journal* 24, no. 1 (Spring 1993): 97–113.
Wæver, Ole. "After Neo-Medievalism: Imperial Metaphors for European Security." In *Cultural Politics and Political Culture in Postmodern Europe*. Edited by J. Peter Burge, 321–64. Amsterdam: Postmodern Studies Volume 24, 1997.
Wanner, Kevin J. "Warriors, *Wyrms*, and *Wyrd*: The Paradoxical Fate of the Germanic Hero/King in *Beowulf*." *Essays in Medieval Studies* 16 (1999): 1–15.
Warwick, Charles. *Mirabeau and the French Revolution*. Philadelphia: George Jacobs & Co., 1905.
Wawn, Andrew. *Northern Antiquity: The Post-Medieval Reception of Edda and Saga*. Enfield Lock: Hisarlik Press, 1994.
Weatherford, Doris. *American Women during World War II: An Encyclopedia*. Abingdon: Routledge, 2010.
Wertham, Fredric. *Seduction of the Innocent*. New York: Rinehart & Company, 1954.
Whitelock, Dorothy. *The Beginnings of English Society*. Harmondsworth: Penguin, 1952.
Whyte, Kenneth. *The Uncrowned King: The Sensational Rise of William Randolph Hearst*. Berkeley: Counterpoint, 2009.
Williams, Mentor L., ed. *Schoolcraft's Indian Legends*. East Lansing: Michigan State University Press, 1956.
"Women of the Year: Great Changes, New Chances, Tough Choices." *Time* (January 5, 1976).
Wong, Wendy Siuyi. *Hong Kong Comics: A History of Manhua*. New York: Princeton Architectural Press, 2001.
Wood, Brian. "On the Ledge." *Northlanders* #1. Vertigo. December 2007.
Wright, Bradford. *Comic Book Nation*. Baltimore: Johns Hopkins University Press, 2001.
Yates, Nigel. *Liturgical Space: Christian Worship and Church Buildings in Western Europe 1500-2000*. Aldershot: Ashgate Publishing, 2008.

INDEX

Ace Books, 103, 106–7, 109, 138
Action Comics, 15
Adventure Comics, 15, 49, 66–68, 88, 135
All Star Comics, 132
All-American Comics, 132
Amazing Spider-Man, The, 70, 85
American Century, 3, 5, 20, 33, 48, 72, 96, 102, 119, 128, 144, 161–62, 174, 192
Anderson, Rasmus Bjørn, 23, 80–85, 99
Arak, Son of Thunder, 170
Arthur, King, 3, 11, 21–22, 38, 48, 55, 68, 97, 159, 162; Arthuriana/Arthurianism, 21–22, 29, 33–34, 37–45, 61–62, 72, 74, 96, 98, 108, 119, 161–63
Association of Comics Magazine Publishers (ACMP), 16
Atlantic Monthly, 59
Atlas Comics. See Timely Comics
Atlas/Seaboard Comics, 112
Auden, Wystan Hugh (W. H.), 105
Avengers, The, 19, 94
Avengers, The, 136

Bakin Kyokutei, 13
Balder the Brave, 93–95
Baldwin, James, 23, 33, 83–84, 91
Barks, Carl, 45, 89
Bat Girl, 46
Batgirl, 135, 141
Batman, 46, 90, 142
Batman, 15–16, 18–19, 46, 66–67, 69, 90–91, 93, 98, 135, 142, 151, 170

Batman: Gotham by Gaslight, 46
Beowulf (Anglo-Saxon poem), 10, 24, 145–55, 158–60
Beowulf: Dragon Slayer, 25, 145–62
Bewick, Thomas, 52
Bilder Bücher, 31
Birds of Prey, 170
Black Cat, 134
Black Pirate, 46
Blade, 19
Blondie, 32, 44
Blue Beetle, 88
Brandywine School, 32–34
Brave and the Bold, 65, 69, 89–91, 135, 169–70
Broderick, Pat, 139
Brodeur, Arthur Gilchrist, 23, 82–83, 107
Bull, Hedley, 12
Bulletproof Monk, 19
Burroughs, Edgar Rice, 28, 110
Buscema, John, 139
Buscema, Stephanie, 143

Camelot (musical), 37–38, 40
Camelot 3000, 162–63
Captain America, 88
Captain Marvel Adventures, 88
Carlyle, Robert, 54, 60, 177–78
censorship, 16, 18–19, 134
Centsprenten, 13
Channel Zero, 169
Child, Francis James, 22, 55–62, 72, 158

Chōjū-jinbutsugiga, 13
Claw the Unconquered, 112
Comics Code Authority (CCA), 16–19, 70, 111, 113, 116, 140, 163–64
Conan the Barbarian, 23–24, 46, 97–120, 136–39, 157, 164, 168
Conan the Barbarian, 23–24, 46, 97–104, 107–14, 116–24, 136–40, 144–46, 157–58, 161–62, 164, 168; in comics, 23–24, 46, 97–120, 136–39, 157, 164, 168; in movies, 116–19; television series, 118–19
Constantine, 19
Cowboy Love, 134
cowboys, 101–2
Creepy, 111
Crisis on Infinite Earths, 71, 142

Dagar the Invincible, 112
Daring New Adventures of Supergirl, 135
Dark Knight Returns, The, 18
DC: The New Frontier, 170
DC Comics. *See* National/DC/Detective Comics
DC Implosion, 18, 146, 156
Demo, 169
Detective Comics, 15, 66, 135
Detective Comics. *See* National/DC/Detective Comics
Dick Tracy, 19
Dingbat Family, 31
DMZ, 169
Dodsley, Robert, 51
Donenfeld, Harry, 15
Donjon, 163
Doyle, Sir Arthur Conan, 33, 99
Dracula, 18
Dungeons and Dragons (D&D), 115, 163. *See also* fantasy role-playing games; live action role-playing

EC, 16
Eco, Umberto, 11–12

Edda: Edda Sæmundar Hinns Froða: The Edda Of Sæmund The Learned, 78, 81; poetic, 74–75, 78, 82–83, 93–95, 152, 158; prose, 24, 74–75, 78, 81–82, 93–95, 158
Educational Comics. *See* EC
Edward, Duke of Windsor (King Edward VIII), 47
Eerie, 111
Elfquest, 112, 137
Eliot, Thomas Stearns, 39

Fantastic Four, 18, 86, 135
fantasy role-playing games (FRPGs/RPGs), 23, 114–16, 163; *Dungeons and Dragons*, 115, 163
Faulkner, William, 22, 39
Fawcett Publications, 64, 89, 106, 110
Feminism, 124, 128–32, 135–36, 144
Feudalism, 6, 25, 54, 177–86
Fight Comics, 134
Fitzgerald, Francis Scott (F. Scott), 3–4, 22, 29, 33, 39, 119; *The Great Gatsby*, 3, 29, 39, 119
Flash, 46
Flash Gordon, 46
Foster, Harold (Hal), ix, 14, 22, 25, 27–28, 30, 32, 34–35, 38, 41–48, 96, 98, 109, 140, 158
Four Students Manga, 14–15
Fox Comics, 87–88
French Revolution, 7, 9, 52, 76, 177–84
From Hell, 19

Gaiman, Neil, 88–89, 161
Gaines, Max (Charlie), 15, 132
Gaines, William (Bill), 15–16
Ghost World, 19
Ghostrider, 18
Giordano, Dick, 69, 134, 139
Grainger, James, 51
Green Arrow, 21–24, 49–72, 120, 162
Green Arrow, 16, 21–24, 46, 49–73, 97–98, 119–21, 144, 146–47, 162, 164, 170
Green Lantern, 46, 69–70, 141

Grimm, Jacob, 22, 53, 57–58, 62, 77–78
Grimm, Wilhelm, 53, 58, 62, 77
Guðbrandur Vigfússon, 78

Harper & Brothers publishing, 32–33, 83; *Harper's Monthly*, 32; *Harper's Weekly*, 33
Hawkman, 46
Hearst, William Randolph, 14, 22, 27–32, 34–37, 47, 68, 99
Hellboy, 46
Hemingway, Ernest, 4, 22, 39, 119
Herriman, George, 14, 31–32
Hippies (1960s counter-culture), 108
History of Violence, A, 19
Hogan's Alley, 29
Hogarth, William, 14
Hokusai Katsushika, 13
Hollander, Lee Milton, 23, 82, 107
Hollywood Production Code, 17
House Un-American Activities Committee (HUAC), 64
Howard, Robert Ervin (Robert E.), 23–24, 97–104, 108–14, 116–20, 122–25, 136, 139–41, 143, 146, 158
Hugo, Victor, 11

Ibis the Invincible, 89
immigration into the United States, 21, 36, 74, 79–80, 121; from Germany, 21, 79–80; from Ireland, 36, 80; from Scandinavia, 74, 80
Incredible Hulk, The, 85
Infantino, Carmine, 46
Iron Man, 19
Ironjaw, 112

Johnson, Samuel, 22, 50–51
Joker, 46
Journey into Mystery, 86, 90–95
Judge Dredd, 19
Jungle Comics, 133–34
Justice League of America, 66, 69, 135, 170
juvenile delinquency. *See* Senate Subcommittee on Juvenile Delinquency

Kane, Gil (Eli Katz), 111, 117
Kane, Robert (Bob), 46
Katzenjammer Kids, The, 14, 31
Keats, John, 53
Kennedy family, 36–38, 40, 47, 69–70; Jacqueline (nee Bouvier), 37–38, 40, 47; John Fitzgerald (John F.), 22, 36–37, 40, 47; Joseph, 36; Robert, 69–70
Kick-Ass, 19
King Conan, 104, 114
King Features, 28–29, 43
King Kull, 46
Kirby, Jack, 45, 85–91, 96
Kiyama Yoshitaka, 14, 174
Kobrin, Stephen, 12
Krazy Kat, 14, 31
Kubert, Joseph (Joe), 46
Kull the Conqueror, 111

Lanier, Sidney, 33–34, 39, 84
Lawrence, David Herbert (D. H.), 102
Le Guin, Ursula, 109
League of Extraordinary Gentlemen, The, 19
Lee, Stan (Stanley Martin Lieber), 18, 85–86, 89
Legends of the Dark Knight, 170
Leiber, Fritz, 109, 112, 114–15
Lewis, Clive Staples (C. S.), 105
Liebowitz, Jack, 15
Life magazine, 5, 37
live action role-playing (LARP), 116
Longfellow, Henry Wadsworth, 22, 33, 56, 58–59, 73, 77, 84, 95
Lönnrot, Elias, 58
Losers, The, 19
Lovecraft, Howard Phillips (H. P.), 23, 99, 103, 122, 138
Luce, Henry, 5, 102, 119, 165

Macpherson, James, 10, 22, 49–51, 99
Mad Magazine, 46
Malory, Thomas, 11, 22, 39
Man-Thing, 18

Manzoni, Alessandro, 10
Marston, William Moulton, 15–16, 132–33
Marvel Comics. *See* Timely Comics
Marvel Family, 89
Marvel Super-Heroes, 88
McCay, Winsor, 14
Medievalism, 4–7, 9–15, 20, 22–25, 34, 36–39, 44, 48, 53–54, 61, 96–99, 108, 120–21, 128, 132, 144, 163–64, 168, 175–77, 183, 192–93
Merimeé, Prosper, 8
Middle Ages, 6–7, 184–86, 187–92
Mighty Thor, The, 21–25, 73–98, 119–21, 162, 164
Mignola, Michael (Mike), 46
Mills, June Tarpé, 133
Milner, John, 8
Miss Fury, 133
Modernism/modernity, 3, 5–6, 22, 24, 41, 62, 97, 132, 149, 151, 164–65, 168, 170, 175, 185–87, 191
Moldoff, Sheldon (Shelly), 46, 90
More Fun Comics, 66–68
Morris, William, 9, 159
movies, 19, 25, 39–40, 65, 67, 72, 84–85, 116–19, 131, 161, 171–72; fantasy, 116–19; medieval, 39–40; pornographic, 131; Robin Hood in, 65, 67, 72; Vikings in, 84–85; Yakuza in, 25, 171–72
My Life, 134
Mystery Men, 19

National/DC/Detective Comics (National Allied Publications/National Comics), 15–16, 18, 24, 46, 64–71, 86–87, 89–91, 94–95, 109–10, 112, 132, 134–35, 137, 142, 146–47, 156–58, 161–63, 169–70
New Adventure Comics, 64
New Comics, 15
New Fun, 15
New York Journal, 14, 29, 31, 35
New York Times, 107, 128
New York World, 14, 29

newspaper comic strips, 14–15, 25–26, 29, 41, 48, 113
Northlanders, 24–25, 90, 162–75
Norton, Charles Eliot (Charlie), 22, 56–57, 60

Oeming, Michael, 138, 140–41
O'Neil, Dennis, 49, 69–71, 96, 147
Orwell, George (Eric Blair), 184
Our Army at War, 90, 169
Out of This World, 90, 110
Outcault, Richard, 14, 29, 31

paperbacks, advent of, 106–9
Peanuts, 26
Percy, Thomas, 22, 49–52, 58, 60, 62
Pini, Wendy and Richard, 112, 137
Plunkett, Edward (Baron Dunsany), 99
Postmodernism, 12, 164, 168, 170, 175
Post–Second World War "baby-boom" in US, 44, 107, 129
Pre-Raphaelite Brotherhood, 9–10
Prévost, Auguste le, 8
Prince Valiant, 14, 21–49, 72–73, 84, 97–98, 119–21, 140, 144, 146, 158, 162, 164, 168
Project Girl Wonder, 142
Pugin, Augustus Welby, 8–10, 54
Pulitzer, Joseph, 14, 29–31, 47
Pyle, Howard, 22, 27, 33–34, 39–42, 45, 48, 61–64, 67–69, 72, 74, 83–84, 91, 96, 158

Range Romances, 134
Rask, Rasmus Christian, 22, 77–78
Raymond, Alex, 46
Red, 19
Red Raven, 88
Red Sonja, 21, 24, 121–44, 164
Red Sonya of Rogatino, 112, 122–25, 136, 140, 143
Remington, Frederic, 30
Rickman, Thomas, 8
Rip Hunter, Time Master, 66
Ritson, Joseph, 52–53, 58–59, 61–62

Road to Perdition, 19
Robbins, Trina, 133
Robin, 46
Robin Hood, 21–24, 33, 40, 49–55, 58–66, 72, 74, 84, 96–97, 144, 158–59, 161; in comic books, 64–66; in movies, 65, 67, 72; television series, 64–66; in US popular culture, 61–63
Robin Hood Tales, 64–65
Rocketeer, 19
Romantic Adventures, 134
Ruskin, John, 6, 8–10, 54, 60

Saga of the Swamp Thing, 18
Sandman, 88, 161
Sarmatian warrior-women, 124–25
Savage Sword of Conan, The, 112–13, 116–18, 124, 137–40
Savage Tales, 111–13, 117
Scott, Sir Walter, 10, 53–54, 61, 65, 75, 99, 101
Scott Pilgrim vs. the World, 19
Second World War, 15, 35, 46, 89, 103, 129, 133
Secret Origins, 71
Senate Subcommittee on Juvenile Delinquency (1954), 16, 67–68, 134
Severin, John, 46
Sgt. Rock, 46
Shenstone, William, 50–51, 60
Shining Knight, 46, 109
Shuster, Joe, 87
Siegel, Jerry, 46, 87
Silver Surfer, 18
Simon, Joe, 88
Simone, Gail, 121, 138, 141, 143–44
Simonson, Louise, 140
Sin City, 19, 166
Snorri Sturluson, 24, 74, 167
Society for Creative Anachronism (SCA), 108, 113, 116
Son of Satan, 18
Song of the Nibelungs, 74
Spirit Section, 133

Stalker, 112
Star-Studded Comics, 110
Steinbeck, John, 4, 22, 39
Stieglitz, Christian Ludwig, 9
Supergirl, 135
Supergirl, 135, 142
Superman, 4, 84, 87, 135
Superman, 15–16, 46, 64, 98
Superman's Girl Friend, Lois Lane, 66
Swamp Thing, 18
Sword of Sorcery, 112

Tales from the Crypt, 16
Tales of Asgard, 93, 95
Tales of the Unexpected, 90–91
Tarzan, 28, 32
Tarzan, 28, 32
television, 16, 64–65, 72, 85, 118, 137, 147, 158–59, 161–62, 175; *Adventures of Robin Hood*, 64–65, 72; Conan, 118; Green Arrow, 72; "school for violence" (Wertham), 16; Vikings, 85
Tennyson, Alfred Lord, 11, 22, 27, 34, 61, 63, 99
30 Days of Night, 19
Thor. See *Mighty Thor, The*
Thor (comic book character), 73–96, 121, 144, 146, 162
Thor (Norse god), 24, 42, 73, 86, 97, 161
Thoreau, Henry David, 33
Thorpe, Benjamin, 78, 81
Thrilling Comics, 133
Timely Comics, 17–18, 45, 70, 73, 86–89, 91–95, 110–12, 114, 117, 119, 135–40, 142, 146, 157–58, 162–63
Tolkien, John Ronald Reuel (J. R. R.), 23, 93, 98–99, 104–10, 113, 120, 145, 158, 160; *Fellowship of the Ring*, 105–6; *Hobbit*, 104–5; *Lord of the Rings*, 93, 104–9; paperback editions, 106–7; *Silmarillion*, 105; *Two Towers*, 105–6
Töpffer, Rodolphe, 14
Transformers, 19

True War Romances, 134
Twain, Mark (Samuel Langhorne Clemens), 11, 41, 54, 68, 98–99, 101

Uncanny X-Men, 136
Unearthly Spectaculars, 110
United Features Syndicate, 28
US Comics in postwar Germany, 47
Uslan, Michael, 24, 134, 147–52, 155, 157, 159–60

V for Vendetta, 19
Vampirella, 111
Vault of Horror, 16
Venus, 89
Viking Prince, 46
Vikings, 13, 24, 77–78, 81, 87, 99, 125, 158, 165, 187; in the Americas, 81, 99, 187; depiction with horned helmets, 87
Viollet-le-Duc, Eugène-Emmanuel, 8, 10
Voltaire (François-Marie Arouet), 184

Wagner, Richard, 22, 77, 79, 87, 160
War That Time Forgot, The, 170
Warlord, The, 112
Warriors Three, 95
Watchmen, 18–19
Weird Comics, 87–88
Weird Science, 19
Werewolf by Night, 18
Wertham, Fredric (Wertheimer), 16–17; *Seduction of the Innocent*, 16
Wham Comics, 88
Wheeler-Nicholson, Malcolm, 15
White, Terence Hanbury (T. H.), 22, 37–40, 63, 98
Whiz Comics, 89
Wild West, 98, 101
Wilshire, Mary, 139–40
Windsor-Smith, Barry, 111, 113, 117, 139
Wings, 134
women, 15–16, 107, 123, 125–29, 134–35, 138, 141–44; as authors of "pulp fiction," 123; in college, 107; in comic book industry, 133–34, 138, 143–44; as readers of comic books, 15–16, 134–35; violence against in comic books, 141–43; as warriors in the European middle ages, 125–28; in workforce during WWII, 128–29. *See also* Feminism; *Women in Refrigerators*
Women in Refrigerators (website), 121, 141–43
Wonder Woman, 66, 121, 133, 135
Wonder Woman, 15–16, 66, 121, 131–33, 135, 142
Wood, Wallace (Wally), 46, 109
World War II. *See* Second World War
World's Finest Comics, 49, 66, 68, 90, 135
Wulf the Barbarian, 112
Wyeth, Newell Convers, 22, 32–34, 41, 45, 48, 63, 66, 74, 83, 96, 158

X-Men, 135–36

Yakuza, in movies, 25, 171–72
Yakuza Papers, The, 170–75
Yellow Journalism, 29, 197n12
Yellow Kid, 14
Young Romance, 134

www.ingramcontent.com/pod-product-compliance
Lightning Source LLC
Chambersburg PA
CBHW030620230426
43661CB00053B/2074